As The Waters Cover The Sea

Millennial Expectations in the Rise of Anglo-American Missions 1640-1810

James A. De Jong

AUDUBON PRESS

2601 Audubon Drive / P.O. Box 8055
Laurel, MS 39441-8000   USA

Orders: 800-405-3788
Inquiries: 601-649-8572
Voice: 601-649-8570 / Fax: 601-649-8571
E-mail: buybooks@audubonpress.com
Web Page: www.audubonpress.com

Original Publication:

J.H. Kok N.V. Kampen, Netherlands, 1970

To
LOIS
and to
my PARENTS

Propositions

1. Without further qualification the terms "premillennialism" and "post-millennialism" are inadequate and misleading as categories for seventeenth and eighteenth century Anglo-American millennial views.

2. Political developments in the years after 1640 must be regarded as a major stimulus of the Anglo-American missionary movement.

3. Apocalyptic expectations played a central role in the summoning of the "Reforming Synod," which met in Boston in 1680.

4. The eschatology of Daniel Whitby had English antecedents which render inaccurate the widely held conclusion that he is the father of postmillennialism.

> *Contra,* among others, C. C. Goen, "Jonathan Edwards: a New Departure in Eschatology," *Church History,* XXVIII, 1959, 37.

5. The missionary thrust of Jonathan Edwards' eschatology was made explicit and credible by his edition of David Brainerd's diary.

6. William Carey's usage of the Great Commission in *An Enquiry into the Obligations of Christians to Use Means for the Conversion of the Heathens* can only be properly understood in terms of his expectation of the universal spread of the gospel.

7. Martin Schmidt's conclusion that Puritanism was "im Kern keine kirchenpolitische, sondern eine Predigtbewegung" is predicated on an invalid abstraction of the one factor from the other.

> "Eigenart und Bedeutung der Eschatologie im englischen Puritanismus," *Theologia Viatorum,* IV, 1952, 225.

8. Geoffrey Thomas correctly judges that Eifion Evans' failure to take account of Charles G. Finney's influence on the Welsh revival of 1904 impairs Evans' evaluation of that movement.

> "The Welsh Revival of 1904," *The Banner of Truth,* no. 74, Nov. 1969, 16-21.

9. The N.E.B.'s translation of בְּגִיא צַלְמָוֶת in Psalm 23 : 4 as "in a valley dark as death" has less semantic support than the rendering "in the valley of the shadow of death."

10. The current archeological excavations at the Heshbon site in Jordan should enhance our understanding of the conquest of Canaan by the Israelites.

11. The translation of the derivatives of ἀρσενοκοίτης by the N.E.B. as "homosexual perversion" (I Cor. 6 : 9) and "perverts" (I Tim. 1 : 10) is a blurring of the pointed force of that word.

12. Although the letter to the Philippians gives evidence of previous correspondence between Paul and the Philippians, the conclusion of J. Hugh Michael that 4 : 10-20 "is intelligible only on the supposition that he [i.e., Paul] is expanding in self-defence some previous statement which his readers had misconstrued" is unacceptable.

> The Epistle of Paul to the Philippians (London: 1948), 210-211.

13. Although the underground church gives evidence of being part of the true body of Jesus Christ, its appearance must be lamented as a regression in the movement towards visible Christian unity.

14. When Perry Miller states, "I have been compelled to insist that the mind of man is the basic factor in human history," he represents an idealism which clashes with a Reformed understanding of God and Providence.

> Errand into the Wilderness (Cambridge, Mass.: 1956), ix.

15. The Christian Church should regard Islam both more critically and more sympathetically than she does religions less directly influenced by Christianity.

16. In the present world situation substantial unilateral disarmament by either of the two super powers would be a morally questionable policy.

17. Ordained women should not be granted the right to preach in a sister church solely on the basis of the official, sister church relationship.

18. There is good Biblical-theological warrant for maintaining the concept "foreign mission(s)."

19. Understood as the writer intended it, the line "the brightest glories earth can yield" in Timothy Dwight's hymn found in the Christian Reformed denomination's official *Psalter Hymnal* (no. 479, stanza 5) is incompatible with the a-millennial position generally accepted in that church.

20. The practice of locating the baptismal font permanently and prominently just inside a main entrance of the church sanctuary is pedagogically desirable and liturgically justifiable.

21. In 1688 Johannes Leusden thought it important that the Reformed minister in Scheveningen be informed of contemporary mission work among the American Indians.

These propositions belong to the dissertation of J. A. de Jong,
As the waters cover the sea (1970).

Acknowledgments

It is with a deep sense of indebtedness and gratitude that I reflect on my formal academic training, which is rapidly drawing to a close. To mention all those who have helped to bring me to this point in my life is obviously impossible. Yet, as I write these lines I think of them all, from my elementary school teachers in the Christian school system in the United States to the theologians of the Free University of Amsterdam whose lectures I have followed with so much interest and profit.

This dissertation is the product of converging influences in my theological studies. At Calvin Theological Seminary Dr. John H. Kromminga stimulated my interest in American church history, and Professor Harold Dekker guided me to important literature in the history of missions. It is the careful and exhaustive scholarship of my promotor, Professor Johannes van den Berg, which has given me inspiration and insight for my work of the last several years, however. His patient helpfulness, his courteous indication of infelicities and weaknesses in the origial draft of this study, and his kind interest in myself and my family have made my work under him a cherished experience. Any worth which this book may have is in large measure attributable to him.

The members of the Christian Reformed Church awarded me the Centennial Missions Scholarship through their mission boards. This grant enabled me to begin my studies in Amsterdam. Those studies were enriched by lectures which I was graciously permitted to attend at the missions seminaries in Baarn and Oegstgeest. The Netherlands Organization for the Advancement of Pure Research financed a three-month stay in London which enabled me to do the necessary reading in many of the primary sources used in this dissertation. Discussions and correspondence with Rev. Charles L. Chaney of Chicago, Rev. Iain Murray and Dr. Geoffrey F. Nuttall of London, Dr. Stephen Orchard of Abercarn, and Dr. Peter Toon of Ormskirk were of invaluable assistance in my research. Mr. Dale Cooper, Rev. Iain Murray, and my father read drafts of the early chapters of this study and offered many valuable suggestions. Without the co-operation of the staffs and the use of the facilities of a number of libraries this study never could have been completed. The major share of my work was done through the Royal Library in The Hague and in the library of the British Museum. I have also made occasional use of Dr. Williams's Library in

London and of the libraries of the missions seminary in Oegstgeest, the Free University of Amsterdam, and the municipal universities of Amsterdam, Leiden, and Utrecht. For the aid rendered by all the people, organizations, and institutions mentioned in this paragraph I am deeply grateful.

What I owe to my parents and to my wife can never be repayed or expressed in mere words. They have been the three most important influences in my life. My earliest memories are of my mother kindly and gently leading me into the way of truth, the way of loving and obedient service to our Lord. She has taught me more profoundly than any theologian the essence of the Christian life. My father has been a living example of selfless service to Christ and to His church. I count myself highly fortunate to have known him not only as a devoted parent but also as my pastor who has instructed me in the rudiments of the Christian faith, as a counsellor always available with sound advice, and a theological professor for whom I have the highest respect and esteem. My wife, Lois, has for almost seven years shouldered the responsibilities of wife, mother, and teacher. She has done so with admirable love and devotion and in spite of her apprehensions regarding life in a foreign culture. Her resolve to see this project through to its completion has given me the necessary certainty and incentive to continue. At all times she has been a source of strength and a confidante. To her I owe more than to any other person for the completion of this project. In gratitude to God for his unmistakable and gracious leading in my life, therefore, I dedicate this book to my wife and to my parents.

Table of Contents

Considered in historical perspective, the Protestant branch of the Christian church is an astounding phenomenon. Less than two centuries ago Protestantism was nothing more than an Occidental reality with only the most precariously held beachheads beyond Europe and North America. Today, after the great, nineteenth century in world missions, we can speak of the church on six continents. Anglo-American — as we shall refer to British and American efforts collectively throughout our study — contributions to the growth of world-wide Protestantism were significant. These contributions were in part the realization of a seventeenth and eighteenth century vision of the global spread of Christian knowledge. It is this early vision, or stated more accurately, this Biblically based expectation, which is the subject to be investigated in this monograph.

The expectation of an era when knowledge of and faith in Christ would be universal took historical form in the millennial categories of the seventeenth and eighteenth centuries. Already in those centuries various millennial expectations, all some form of hope for ecumenical or world-wide Christianity, elicited repeated, earnest, and sometimes highly successful missionary enterprises. The present study attempts to investigate the role which millennial expectations played in the rise of the Anglo-American missionary movement during the seventeenth and eighteenth centuries. It is presented in the conviction that Anglo-American missions of this period cannot be fully understood apart from the Christian hopes and ideals that enlivened and sustained them and that the nineteenth century surge in missions from Britain and America was partially the result of this earlier vision.

In dealing with millennial expectations in the rise of Anglo-American missions we are obliged to investigate several issues. First of all, do the thought and work of such missionary figures as John Eliot, David Brainerd, and William Carey bear the accent of millennial expectancy? By looking once more at their writings we shall attempt to establish the fact that they do. Furthermore, when did millennial expectations become current in the Anglo-American religious tradition and when did they begin to affect missions? We believe that they can be traced to the late sixteenth and early seventeenth centuries and that they stimulated missionary interest and work from the time Englishmen planted their first colonies in America, a full century earlier than is conceded by many scholars. Were millennial views consistently maintained throughout seventeenth and eighteenth century Anglo-American missionary efforts? Although these expectations underwent modifications, we shall try to show that they were an essential part of missionary theology and missionary motivation throughout the period covered by our study. It would appear, therefore, that the discussions on eschatology which have resumed in missionary circles since the Willingen conference of the International Missionary Council in 1952 [1] have an historical precedent in the seventeenth and eighteenth century Anglo-American missionary movement.

But before we launch into the subject of this study, it is necessary that we clarify the terms used in the subtitle, indicate the sources employed, explain our approach to our subject matter, and mention several technical points.

Perhaps the most vexing problem we face at the outset of our study is that of finding a term which adequately covers the hopes or expectations with which we shall be dealing. To say that we shall be dealing with "millennialism" or "chiliasm" is to ignore the fact that many of the staunchest supporters of missions, especially in the seventeenth century, loathed the utopian premillennialism which these terms connoted in their day. Yet these mission enthusiasts held many of the eschatological expectations which were part of systematic millennial positions. Furthermore, their expectations were crucial to the rise of Anglo-American missions. To disqualify them from our study for the lack of an adequate, standard theological rubric to cover their positions would be to impair our work, therefore. On the other hand such terms as "eschatological expectations," "prophetic hopes," and "hopes for the kingdom" embrace anticipations with a much broader focus than those days at the end of history to which the hopes which we shall be studying refer. Consequently we have chosen to use the term "millennial expectations," by which we understand Scripturally-based hopes regarding the latter days or the times near the end of world history. These expectations include such anticipations as the conversion of the Gentile nations, the conversion of the Jews, the destruction of the Roman Catholic establishment, and an era of glory for the church when the gospel will triumph among all nations. There were endless variations of these themes throughout the period of our survey. Some men accepted only one or two of these expectations, and then in only a very mild version. Others accepted them all and integrated them in a carefully developed millennial system. But wherever these expectations, in whatever form, contributed to the rise of Anglo-American missions, they qualify for inclusion in our study.

Under the preposition "in" in the subtitle we include any influence that millennial expectations had on missions. Often a strong desire to realize the promised age of glory for the church motivated mission work. Chronological

1 R. Pierce Beaver, "Eschatology in American Missions," *Basileia*, Jan Hermelink and Hans J. Margull (eds.) (Stuttgart: 1959), 61.

2

theories and signs of the times sometimes established a timetable for missions. Speculation on the character of that period often defined the objectives of the mission program. But basically it was the belief in the approach of an era when the gospel would be universally proclaimed which motivated the formation of missionary societies and revitalized existing missions.

This study is deliberately a study in the history of "Anglo-American missions," for neither side of the Atlantic Ocean can be understood apart from the other. Thinking on the millennium and work in missions were carried on during the period of our survey in a spirit of English, Scottish, and American co-operation. The linguistic, cultural, and theological ties were intimate. Except for the last thirty-five years with which we deal Britain and the American colonies were under one government. It becomes impossible, therefore, to treat the one area in isolation from the other. On the other hand, little or no attention will be given to the mission work of the non-Anglo-Saxon colonies in America, since they were products of other cultural and theological traditions. Ecclesiastically we find that within the Anglo-American tradition those denominations within the Calvinistic family were the most consistent and most articulate proponents of missions on the basis of millennial expectations. It is their missionary propaganda which will engage the bulk of our attention, therefore. The views of other groups will be considered to the extent that they also manifest a relationship of millennial expectations and missions.

The year 1640 marks not only the inception of a new era in English history but also the beginning of the decade in which Anglo-American missions were given a secure and relatively permanent basis. For the subsequent one hundred seventy years the American Indians were the primary objects of Anglo-American missionary work. Out of these efforts and the millennial hopes which kept them alive throughout this period the modern missionary movement from Britain and America began. Although the leading British societies were founded in the 1790's, we carry our survey to 1810, when the American Board of Commissioners for Foreign Missions was born. After that date we can no longer speak of "the rise" of Anglo-American missions.

Our primary sources are the published reports, sermons, periodical accounts, and letters of the missionary movement. We have tried to examine as many missionary sources as possible to gain an exact impression of the scope of millennial expectations in the missionary movement. Where secondary sources are nonexistent or weak we have also used primary sources for our chapter-by-chapter surveys of millennial expectations. These sources consist mainly of commentaries on the prophetic and apocalyptic books of the Bible. Since the purpose of these surveys is to provide background information, however, and since the purpose of our study is to examine millennial ideas in the missionary movement, no claim of a complete or even thorough investigation of primary sources on Anglo-American millennial expectations as such is made. Our research has concentrated on the Eliot tracts,[2] sermons preached before the annual gatherings of the missionary societies, and leading missionary figures' writings on the millennium. The secondary sources include surveys and studies of British and American church history, eschatology, and missions.

Since our purpose is to demonstrate the impact of millennial expectations on the concrete mission efforts in Britain and America, it seems best to employ an historical rather than a more analytical approach in this study. Therefore, the chapters are arranged chronologically. Chapters V and VI of necessity parallel one another, since both the bulk of material and the effects of the American Revolutionary War require independent treatment of the British and American scenes between 1776 and 1810. All of the chapters begin and terminate with prominent events in Anglo-American history which are generally of great significance for missions: the resummoning of Parliament (1640), King Philip's War (1675), early events in the Great Awakening and the Evangelical Awakening (1735), and the Revolutionary War (1776). While the first of these four events has more bearing on English history and the second on American history, neither is without significance for the other area.

The internal chapter development is logical. Each chapter except the first is divided into four sections. Section one relates the general background of the period covered in that chapter. This enables us to place our subject in its historical setting for the reader and to highlight events of particular significance for missions. Section two broadly surveys the millennial discussions of the period. Section three does the same for the main developments in missions. The bulk of the discussion occurs in section four, where the effect of millennial expectations on missions is demonstrated. Since Chapter I is completely background material, it does not contain the usual fourth section.

In closing, a few remarks of a technical nature are in order. In the case of double quotations in which our source employs the old procedure of italicizing his quotation, we use double quotation marks. The orthography of the sources — including their shorthand — has been honored with the exceptions of the modernization of the letter "s" and when this has been altered in quotations from secondary sources. Where deemed necessary, elucidation of spelling or shorthand has been provided in brackets. Extensive foreign language citations are relegated to the notes. Except in the bibliography dates have been adjusted to coincide with the modern calendar year. There publications which appeared between January 1 and March 25 under the Julian system of reckoning are dated both according to the old style and the new style.

2 A series of eleven missionary tracts issued between 1643 and 1671 chiefly to gain support for missions, they were edited by and contained contributions from leading ministers and missionaries including John Eliot, after whom they were popularly called.

Chapter I

Millennial views and missions prior to 1640

A. General Background

The ecclesiastical scene in mid-sixteenth century England was as unsettled as the political. With the restoration of Protestantism at Elizabeth's accession England was again faced with the question of reformation. Marian exiles, enamored of the Reformed religion of Switzerland and the Rhine valley, agitated for the abolition of all liturgical practices resembling those of Rome. Clerical vestments, kneeling for the administration of the sacrament, the sign of the cross at baptism, and the sacramental status of marriage [1] were based on theological notions incompatible with their Reformed convictions. In 1570 Thomas Cartwright was relieved of his Cambridge professorship for defending a Presbyterian form of church government as the logical consequence of Scriptural teaching and England's regained Protestant course. In discussions which were to continue for generations John Jewel, John Whitgift, Hadrian Saravia, and Richard Hooker defended episcopacy. Echoes of the radical reformers were heard in Robert Browne's espousal of separatistic principles. The Prayer Book was increasingly deprecated after Puritans [2] in Northampton began their "prophesyings" in 1571. These weekday meetings of clergy and laity for "Bible study, discussion and prayer" were condemned by the queen as "disloyal and subversive" in a circular letter of 1577. [3] On the Roman Catholic side there

1 Williston Walker, *A History of the Christian Church* (New York: 1949), 403.
2 Basil Hall, "Puritanism: the Problem of Definition," in *Studies in Church History*, II, G. J. Cuming (ed.) (London: 1965), 283-296, argues for restricting the term "Puritan" to those members of the Church of England before 1640 who agitated for greater reform in their communion. Although Hall's plea for giving the term a carefully circumscribed or restricted and therefore a clear historical content is to be commended, his ecclesiastical limitation is unnatural. The New England colonists of Massachusetts Bay can rightly only be called Puritans even though they established their Congregational churches. They continued to think of the Anglican communion as their "mother church" and hoped for reform in her. That spirit flickered among those who are known as Separatists as well. Our usage of "Puritan," therefore, also covers early New England colonists who harbored hope for reform in the Anglican communion and extends to the Restoration in 1660.
3 John R. H. Moorman, *A History of the Church in England* (London: 1953), 210. For an extended treatment of prophesyings see Geoffrey Nuttall, *The Holy Spirit in Puritan Faith and Experience* (Oxford: 1946), Chapter V.

were rumors of intrigues to return England to Roman ecclesiastical jurisdiction. The year 1570 saw Mary Stuart plotting to overthrow her cousin, while in Rome the pope had officially excommunicated Elizabeth.[4] The queen determined to walk a middle course in an effort to maintain a united, national church. Like her father and brother she promulgated acts of supremacy and uniformity. Her resolve to control ecclesiastical issues was equalled, however, by her discretion. She gave the various factions as much freedom as was feasible within a unified church. Only skillful diplomacy made the Elizabethan settlement workable for forty-five years.

Both Catholic and Puritan expectations were disappointed in 1603 when Mary Stuart's son from Presbyterian Scotland, James I, indicated that he would follow his predecessor's policies. Although he authorized a new translation of the Bible, he denied the mild Puritan requests of the Millenary Petition. His opposition to Scottish Presbyterianism as it had received its consistent form under Andrew Melville's influence should have given English Puritans a strong premonition of James I's position: "No bishop, no king!" Throughout his reign he strengthened episcopacy in Scotland. The Gunpowder Plot and negotiations to marry his son to a Spanish princess enlivened fears of Catholicism. Separatist and Puritan unrest grew under his son, Charles I, and under the bishop of London, William Laud, who in 1633 was appointed archbishop. In 1629 Charles dissolved Parliament, which contained a considerable Puritan faction. Laud implemented anti-Puritan and anti-Separatist policies. As conditions for them worsened, many of the oppressed sought refuge in Holland and New England. After the defeat of the Spanish Armada in 1588 vigorous Elizabethan sea power, explorations, and commercial endeavors had secured the latter area as a British sphere of influence. Commercialism and religious discontent attracted colonists to present-day Virginia, Maryland, and New England. In Britain unrest and extremism grew.[5] Although unfounded when seen in the light of Laud's refusal, fear of a revived "Romanism" under a churchman who had twice been "offered a cardinalate"[6] increased. When Charles was compelled in 1640 to reconvene Parliament, requesting that it appropriate the funds necessary to suppress his rebellious Presbyterian subjects in Scotland, the Puritan majority gained the political leverage which so dramatically shifted the course of events in English history.

B. Millennial Expectations

The dimension of Protestant, and particularly Puritan, eschatology which

4 William Haller, *Foxe's Book of Martyrs and the Elect Nation* (London: 1963), 98-99.
5 William Haller, *The Rise of Puritanism* (New York: 1938), 269.
6 Walker, 411

emphasized the individual Christian's life-long pilgrimage through an evil world in aspiration for the eternal city of God is well known. Homiletically and devotionally it was expressed in countless sermons on evil, the judgment, and deliverance. The many editions of Arthur Dent's *The Plaine Mans Pathway to Heaven*, Lewis Bayly's *Practice of Piety*, and John Bunyan's *Pilgrim's Progress* led Puritan piety in this ascetic, world-denying direction.[7] Complete deliverance would come only with death and the final judgment.

However important this individualistic emphasis was in Puritan eschatology, it was not the total picture. Rooted deeply in the Reformation tradition were expectations of greater, more glorious days for the church on earth. Undoubtedly the spread of the Reformation itself enlivened such corporate, historical hopes. Later reformers evaluated it as "a hastening of the great day of paradisiac bliss."[8] While most Protestants concurred with Calvin's condemnation of the extreme chiliasm of some of the church fathers and Anabaptists,[9] they were nevertheless optimistic about the course of history in the sixteenth century. This optimism took several forms: anticipation of the approaching fall of the Roman Catholic and Turkish Antichrists; hope for the conversion of the Jews and many heathen to the Reformed faith; predictions of an age of peace, unity among Christians, and a great decline in the power of Satan and evil; the belief in the destined wealth and prestige of the Protestant powers. These hopes were found both on the Continent and in Britain, although the last one was especially strong in England. In the early seventeenth century several writers, while condemning the excesses of the Anabaptists, combined and arranged many of these hopes in various versions of millennialism. By no means all Englishmen adopted a synthesis or systematization of these expectations, though they often continued to hold to various elements included in it.

In this section we shall survey these widespread millennial expectations and give a synopsis of the most influential millennial systems in England prior to 1640.

7 Martin Schmidt, "Eigenart und Bedeutung der Eschatologie im englischen Puritanismus," *Theologia Viatorum*, IV, 1952, 205-266. Regarding all three pieces Schmidt concludes, "Übrig bleibt eine ausschlieszlich eschatologische Haltung, die die positive Beziehung zum irdischen Leben und seiner konkreten Verantwortung verloren hat. Die Frage nach dem Seelenheil hat alle anderen Wirklichkeiten und Möglichkeiten aufgesogen, unter denen die ethische die gewichtigste ist." (264) Later he says, "Jedoch war sie kein angemessener Ausdruck für die weltbewegende Kunde vom neuen Himmel und von der neuen Erde." (266) Dent's work first appeared in 1601 and Bunyan's in 1678. The date of the first edition of Bayly's work is unknown, though a subsequent edition appeared in 1636. (*R.G.G.*, I, 948) All three went through many editions in the seventeenth century.

8 Charles L. Sanford, *The Quest for Paradise* (Urbana, Ill.: 1961), 79.

9 Ioannes Calvinus, *Institutio Christianae Religionis*, C.R., XXX, 734-735.

1. *Continental sources*

English theologians were indebted to Continental thinkers for guidance in formulating the millennial expectations in their eschatology. This is true of the various hopes of the Elizabethan age and the more systematized millennial ideas of the seventeenth century.

In 1520 Martin Luther, who believed that the judgment day and the end of history were near, identified the pope as Antichrist and Rome as apocalyptic Babylon in a number of his early writings.[10] His comments on Revelation written in 1545 explain it as a prophecy of the progressive downfall of the papal Antichrist.[11] Not only were Luther's conclusions on these matters "extremely influential among Protestant reformers,"[12] but they provided the basis for further speculation on the time and means by which Antichrist would fall.

John Calvin's commentaries give some scholars cause for concluding that he anticipated the spread of the gospel and true religion to the ends of the earth.[13] He did not include a national conversion of Israel in this vision, however, as his exegesis of Romans 9-11 shows.[14]

Ulrich Zwingli's successor as a lecturer in theology at the University of Zurich, Theodor Bibliander, demonstrated interest in the Moslems by publishing a Latin translation of the Koran and by advocating missions to Moslems in the Arabic tongue. He foresaw an age when humanity would be united as one flock under one Shepherd. Significantly for us, Bibliander believed that this age of true faith, love, knowledge, and holiness would dawn through the preaching of the evangelical faith of the Reformation. Justice, peace, humanity, wisdom, and the spread of science would characterize this era.[15] The even more prominent Zwinglian theologian and pastor

10 *P.F.F.*, II, 253-255, 257. Notice, for example, *De captivitate Babylonica ecclesiae praeludium* (*W.A.*, VI, 484f.); *Adversus execrabilem Antichristi bullam* (*W.A.*, VI, 595f.). Both of these works appeared in 1520.

11 *P.F.F.*, II, 273.

12 Sanford, 79.

13 Donald Maclean, "Scottish Calvinism and Foreign Missions," *Records of the Scottish Church History Society* (Glasgow: 1938), VI, 4; Samuel Zwemer, "Calvinism and the Missionary Enterprise," *Theology Today*, VII, 1950, 209 *et passim*; H. Bergema, "De Betekenis van Calvijn voor de Zending en de Missiologie," *Vox Theologica*, XXIX, 1958-1959, 49f.

14 On Calvin's exegesis of this passage see A. J. Visser, *Calvijn en de Joden* ('s-Gravenhage: [n.d.]), 7f. J. van den Berg, *Joden en Christenen in Nederland gedurende de Zeventiende Eeuw* (Kampen: 1969), 25f., while showing that Calvin's understanding of the "Israel of God" included both Jews and non-Jews, indicates that for the reformer the concept of the conversion of the Jews did not function as an eschatological motif with its own weight and significance. ("...met eigen gewicht en eigen betekenis." 25.)

15 Walter Holsten, "Reformation und Mission," *Archiv für Reformationsgeschichte*, XLIV, 1953, 29-30.

Heinrich Bullinger had personal contact with Henry VIII, Edward VI, and Elizabeth I and enjoyed the esteem of many Marian exiles as being "something of an oracle." [16] He preached a series of one hundred sermons on the book of Revelation. "Published with a dedication to the refugees" from England, Italy, and France who had found refuge in Zurich, these sermons developed a sense of apocalyptic hope in hearers such as John Jewel, who carried these hopes to the English scene upon returning to his homeland after Mary's death.[17] Bullinger's sermons later went through both an English and a Latin edition in London.

A very early form of Reformation optimism regarding the church's future is Martin Bucer's belief that in Romans 11 : 25f. Paul guarantees the future conversion of the Jewish people.[18] It was perhaps from Bucer that Peter Martyr, his fellow reformer at Strassburg, accepted these ideas. In his influential *Most learned and fruitfull Commentaries ... upon ... the Romanes*, first published in 1568 in England as a translation of the Latin edition issued ten years before, Martyr argued convincingly for a literal rather than a figurative understanding of "Israel" in this passage. Bucer's and Martyr's influence in England was sustained. After Martyr's appointment as professor of Hebrew at Zurich in 1556, he maintained "a long correspondence on English affairs" with Jewel and other English leaders.[19] The long history of this interpretation of Romans 11 in England can undoubtedly be traced to Archbishop Cranmer's 1548 appointments of Bucer and Martyr as professors at Cambridge and Oxford respectively. David Paraeus, the Heidelberg expositor, adopted their position rather than Melanchthon's and Calvin's exegesis of Romans 11.[20] Early in the seventeenth century Thomas Brightman cited Theodore Beza as propounding a time when the world would " 'be restored from death to life againe, at the time when the Iews should also come, and be called to the profession of the Gospel.' " [21]

When the German theologian Johann Heinrich Alsted wrote his influential *Diatribe de mille annis Apocalypticis* in 1627, he relied on a number of Continental theologians. This commentary on Revelation 20 predicted a future, literal millennium. Translated into English in 1643 as *The Beloved City or, The Saints Reign on Earth a Thousand Yeares*, this study did much to establish the credibility of this doctrine in England and to acquaint Englishmen with Alsted's sources. He quoted Alfonsus Conradus of Mantua's

16   *O.D.C.C.*, 206.
17   Haller, *Foxe's Book of Martyrs ...*, 90.
18   Holsten, 17-18.
19   *O.D.C.C.*, 1055.
20   Thomas Sutton, *Lectures upon the Eleventh Chapter to the Romans* (London: 1632), 238-239.
21   Thomas Brightman, *The Workes of that Famous, Reverend, and Learned Divine, Mr. Tho. Brightman* (London: 1644), 834.

commentary on Revelation, published in Basel in 1574, which defended the millennial position. "From hence it appears, That our opinion concerning these 1000 years is not new, and unheard of," concluded Alsted.[22] He then cited Lucas Osiander, son of reformer Andreas Osiander of Nuremberg, who indicated in his commentary on Daniel that a period when the Roman papacy would be overturned was forthcoming. Mattheus Cotterius, Reformed minister of Tours, and Joannes Piscator, prominent Reformed theologian who succeeded Caspar Olevianus at Herborn, anticipated the millennium, as their commentaries on Revelation show.

> Many Writers of the former aud [sic] this present Age, have published many things concerning *Elias the Artist*, who is to come; Of the *Lion of the North*, who is neer at hand; Of a *fourth Northern Monarchy*; Of a great *Reformation*; Of the *Conversion* of the Jews; and the like. See Theophrastus Paracelsus, Michael Sendivogius *in his Treatise of Sulphur*, Stephanus Pannonius *Of the circle of the Works and Judgments of God;* . . . John Dobricius also in the year 1612. did set forth a notable book entitled χρονομηνύτωρ, that is, *The Interpreter of times.*[23]

Alsted concluded with a reference to the French Reformed theologian, Pierre du Moulin, who argued in his *Du Combat Christien* that Christians could expect an era free from persecution of the church and rich in peace and blessing.[24] In the appendix, compiled by another hand than that of Alsted, the Danish astronomer Tycho Brahe's *Tome Astronomicorum Progymnasmatum* is referred to as mentioning a golden era before the destruction of the world.[25] Also mentioned there is Carolus Gallus, professor of divinity at Leiden from 1587 to 1591 who published *Clavis prophetica nova Apocalypseos Johannis Apostoli & Evangeliographi* in 1592, a work advocating a mild millennialism.[26]

Because Alsted himself represents the "conservative millenarianism"[27]

---

22 Johann Heinrich Alsted, *The Beloved City or, The Saints Reign on Earth a Thousand Yeares* (London: 1643), 59. Alsted's widespread influence in England was felt mainly through the writings of Joseph Mede and through this translation of his commentary, from which our citations are taken. On Conradus, whose reformed sympathies forced him to flee from Italy, see *Allgemeine Encyclopaedie der Wissenschaften und Kunste,* J. S. Ersch and J. G. Gruber (eds.) (Leipzig: 1829), IX, 106-107.

23 Alsted, 60.

24 *Ibid.,* 61-62.

25 *Ibid.,* "Appendix," xxi.

26 *Ibid.,* xxiii.

27 Peter Toon, "Puritan Eschatology: 1600 to 1648" in *The Manifold Grace of God,* papers read at the Puritan and Reformed Studies Conference, 1968 ([London: 1969]), 54f. By this term Toon correctly distinguishes Alsted from the politically and materialistically oriented hopes of the Anabaptists and later fanatical, or as he calls them, "extreme" millennialists in England. Alsted's expectations manifest the

which had become respectable among Protestant theologians and because he had an unusually great following in England in the crucial second quarter of the seventeenth century, his views are worthy of extended treatment here.

Alsted was a Reformed theologian and philosopher in Herborn, Germany, who served as a delegate to the famous Synod of Dort, 1618-1619. Written during the devastation of the Thirty Years' War, his commentary had as its chief aim the comfort of the church in Germany.[28] The overriding emphasis in Revelation 20 is "the singular happiness of the Church, both under its *Warfare*, and *Triumph*," he asserted.[29] Due to begin before the end of the century, the millennium will be the last period of history before Christ's return. It will follow the period from 51 A.D. until the millennium, during which "the Church spread over the whole world" and "the calling and conversion of most nations" occurred.[30] Alsted called this the first or former calling of the Gentiles. Since 1517 the popes have witnessed a decline in their power and kingdom. What is yet to transpire prior to the dawn of the millennium, said Alsted, "we cannot in particular determine."[31] In general the church must be purified by its present sufferings, which are preparing it for "that great *Reformation*"[32] which the millennium will bring.

Alsted listed the charasteristics of the millennium:

> ... it consisteth of these Parts;
> 1. Of the *Resurrection of the Martyrs*, and of rheir [sic] Reign here upon Earth.
> 2. Of the *encrease of the Church*, and multitude thereof, through the *conversion* of the *Gentiles* and *Jews*.
> 3. Of the setting of the Church at *liberty from the persecution* of Enemies thereof, by the finall destruction of them.
> 4. Of the continuall and lasting *peace* thereof.
> 5. Of the *Reformation* of the same both in *doctrine* and *life*.
> 6. Of the *Majesty*, and great *glory* thereof.
> 7. Of its true and sincere *Joy*.[33]

The resurrection of the martyrs must be taken literally, contended Alsted. They will reign on earth in Christ's stead, since Christ will "reign visibly in heaven, invisibly upon earth."[34] These martyrs will rise from the dead at the inception of the millennium. Alsted emphatically rejected the notion

classic Reformed emphasis on the church and the kingdom, and he placed as much distance as possible between himself and the "carnal chiliasts."
28 Alsted, 1.
29 *Ibid.*, 4.
30 *Ibid.*, 7.
31 *Ibid.*
32 *Ibid.*
33 *Ibid.*, 10.
34 *Ibid.*, 17.

that the first resurrection would be spiritual, that is figurative of a renewal of life in the church.

There is a "double *Conversion* or calling of the Gentiles." [35] The former applies to the ministry of the apostles and has been carried on all through the present age, the Herborn theologian explained. The latter is future, to be realized "a little before the Conversion of the *Jews.*" [36] Thus the conversion of Gentiles and Jews "are joyned together" as Isaiah 11 : 12 and Zachariah 2 : 10 show and as Justus Heurnius and Johannes Kepler have advocated in more modern times. The conversion of the Jews has been clearly predicted throughout both Old and New Testaments. Alsted listed numerous texts from the Pentateuch, Psalms, and especially the prophets which contain this prediction. Matthew, Luke, and Paul are New Testament witnesses to this event. The fall of Antichrist will be "an occasion of their conversion" [37] rather than a consequence of it. The fall of Antichrist, resurrection of the martyrs, and conversion of Gentiles and Jews will be followed by the other blessed characteristics of this era.

Having set forth his basic position, Alsted exegeted sixty-five texts which he felt supported what he had said. This section was followed by thirty-six possible objections to his views and his answers to them. Throughout his work he made liberal use of predecessors who had defended one or another of the positions which he took.

Alsted's anticipation of the beginning of the millennium within a matter of decades and his emphasis on the conversion of the Gentiles and the Jews early in that era contributed significantly to millennial incentives for missions among Puritans and Separatists in the 1630's and 1640's.

It is obvious from the Continental sources considered in this section, therefore, that after the initial days of the Reformation many heirs of that movement — both Lutheran and Reformed, theologians as well as scientists — expressed in one form or another their optimism regarding the dawn of an era of growth, purity, and unity for the church. From Scripture they calculated that it was imminent. Their views departed from the notions of Luther and Calvin. Yet they were equally as careful as their mentors to distinguish themselves from fanatical chiliasm, whose excesses they consistently condemned. Gallus had been a particularly strong opponent of the Anabaptists.[38] Alsted concluded his elaboration of the similarities of and differences between his position and that of the "*Chiliasts, or Millenaries*" [39] by saying, " . . . he is not straightway a *Chiliast,* who defends the truth of

35 *Ibid.,* 8.
36 *Ibid.*
37 *Ibid.,* 9.
38 *Biographisch Woordenboek van Protestantsche Godgeleerden in Nederland* ('s-Gravenhage: [n.d.]), III, 173-177.
39 Alsted, 70.

any thing which the *Chiliasts* also do rightly maintain out of Scripture. For this they do not hold, and teach, as *Chiliasts*." [40] The extensive acceptance of a conservative millennialism among Continental Protestants and the care with which they distinguished their position from questionable forms of this doctrine prepared Englishmen for a reconsideration of a more complete and systematized version of the expectations which many of them already held. It is impossible to speak of an English millennialism until the reigns of the first Stuart kings, however. But before we consider that story we must retrace our footsteps to the hopes that were current during the reign of Elizabeth.

2. *Elizabethan expectations*

Alsted's distinction between an acceptable and an unacceptable millennialism was unknown in Tudor England. Millennialists were associated with Anabaptists. Anabaptists advocated a free church, the body of saints governed by the Spirit rather than by sinful human rulers. Such colonies of heaven on earth not only jeopardized the political fabric, reasoned Englishmen, but their utopian dreams corrupted the moral order. All Anabaptists were painted in shades of Munster. Their millennial views were anathema. Henry VIII burned "thirteen Dutch Anabaptists in one year" and Elizabeth condemned two others to the same fate as late as 1575.[41] The 1552 edition of the Thirty-nine Articles contained a stinging rejection of the doctrine of the millennium.[42] Bishop John Jewel's boast to the Continent in 1567, "Your Anabaptists . . . we know not," [43] was true with only infrequent exceptions until well into the seventeenth century.

Rather, from the time Henry VIII had arrogated so much ecclesiastical jurisdiction, in England hope for the church's future was identified with the sovereign and the course set by that person for the nation as a whole. During Edward VI's reign Martin Bucer's thoughts which were later published in *De Regno Christi* stimulated hopes that God's kingdom would be established in England.[44] Protestant hopes which had risen during his reign

---

40   *Ibid.*, 72.
41   Owen Chadwick, *The Reformation* (Grand Rapids: 1965), 203. See also A. G. Dickens, *The English Reformation* (London: 1964), 237.
42   *V.R.G.*, IV, 228, n. 24.
43   Chadwick, 203.
44   Wilhelm Pauck, *Das Reich Gottes auf Erden* (Berlin and Leipzig: 1928), 4. While Bucer's ideal was not realized under Elizabeth or the Stuarts, it persisted among Englishmen: "Zweifellos blieb das von Butzer vertretene Ideal lebendig in der Gruppe der englischen Protestanten, welche die Reformation im ganzen Umfange in ihrem Lande zur Durchführung bringen wollten, in den Puritanern. In diesen Kreisen leben anders gewendet und von Calvin herkommend, die von Butzer in seinem Werke

fell when Mary ascended the throne, however. For exiles like John Bale the reversion to Catholicism under Mary meant that the Antichristian forces of the false church were triumphing. His *The Image of Both Churches,* published in London in 1550, was an exposition of "Revelation as the key to the understanding of the past, present and future course of the Church." [45] His position was essentially that of Eusebius and Augustine. History is a continuous struggle between the true and false church, Christ and Antichrist, good and evil. Although the Marian exiles in general shared Bale's and John Foxe's interpretation of Revelation 20 as referring to the millennium beginning with Constantine's reign, they waited "to be called back to England to resume the building of the New Jerusalem" [46] begun under Henry VIII and his son. To people who were accustomed to explaining their plight in Biblical imagery, Mary's death was seen as an act of deliverance.

As the intellectuals returned to assume positions of leadership under the new monarch, they felt a new day of God's favor had dawned in England.[47] Jewel believed that God had given Elizabeth to England "to be an instrument of His glory in the sight of the world." [48] In a reference to the Reformation Jewel showed his elation over England's participation in it.

> This is the day which the Lord hath wrought: to thee, O Lord, the praise hereof is due: thou hast turned our mourning into joy: thou hast put to silence the spirit of error: thou hast inflamed the hearts of thy people: thou hast brought princes and kings to the obedience of thy Son Jesus Christ: thou hast opened the eyes of the world to espy out and to cry for the comfort of the gospel.[49]

The writings of John Aylmer and Foxe spread the same vision of England's place in God's plan. In his Good Friday sermon in 1570 Foxe described Elizabethan England as the bastion of the church. "The Turk has been driving the Church back and back into a 'little angle of the west', while the Bishop of Rome has been everywhere 'stirring up his bishops to burn us, his confederates to conspire our destruction...'" [50] Although Archbishop Matthew Parker walked the middle road between Romanists and Puritans, "he shared the apocalyptical expectations" [51] regarding England under Elizabeth propounded by Jewel and Foxe.

---

ausgesprochenen Ideen fort und das Ideal, einen christlichen Staat zu schaffen, ist das Programm der Zeit Cromwells." (113) Also *D.N.B.,* VII, 177.

45   Haller, *Foxe's Book of Martyrs* . . . , 61.

46   *Ibid.,* 85.

47   Pauck says, "Man sah nun die besondere Gnade Gottes wieder über England, und die Erwartungen, die man vorher mit Eduard verbunden hatte, stellte man nun an die neue Königin." (182)

48   As quoted by Haller, *Foxe's Book of Martyrs* . . . , 94.

49   John Jewel, *The Works of John Jewel,* 4 vols. (Cambridge: 1847), II, 1032.

50   Haller, *Foxe's Book of Martyrs* . . . , 102.

51   *Ibid.,* 105.

With the defeat of Spain's Armada and the rise of English sea power the horizons of England's national anticipations and aspirations became global. Englishmen shared Richard Hakluyt's justification for raiding the Spanish galleons which poured gold into Antichristian coffers.[52] Hakluyt advocated planting colonies in the New World to offset Catholic power there and to fulfill England's divine mandate to spread true religion. The basic premise of his influential writings was that England must "propagate the true gospel."[53] Piracy and colonization were means to that end. Many Elizabethans and later Englishmen understood their colonization efforts as that which "prolonged and perfected a Sacred History begun at the outset of the Reformation."[54] Their expectations and efforts to realize them had profound implications for missions.[55]

No other book with the exception of the Bible did as much as Foxe's *Actes and Monuments* to keep alive in Englishmen the belief that they were God's "elect nation." From the appearance of its definitive edition in 1570, it went through eight major editions by 1684.[56] Indebted to Bale for his interpretation of history based on Revelation, Foxe saw the martyrs, and particularly those of Mary's reign, as the victims of the struggle between the two churches. This struggle would one day reach its culmination, however. According to Foxe's calculations the millennium had ended approximately in 1300, when Satan's forces in the form of a degenerate church and the Turkish onslaught had been unleashed. Wycliffe and the Marian martyrs had been their victims. Yet he anticipated better days. The Reformation had restored the pristine church of the apostles, "pointing forward to a day of perfect restoration and triumph, after which time would be no more."[57] His account of the Marian persecutions, the climax of his *Book of Martyrs* as it came to be known, was concluded with "a prayer for the shortening of the days of the kingdom of Satan and the early coming of the kingdom of Christ on earth."[58] How long this last act in the drama of history was yet to play Foxe could not say; "the Lord and Governor of all times, he only knoweth."[59]

Other Englishmen were not content to wait in ignorance, however, especially not when they felt that the "Governor of all times" had given a much more definite timetable for history in Revelation and other prophetic sections of Scripture than Foxe had ever imagined. In the first quarter of

52 Sanford, 88.
53 *Ibid.*, 89.
54 Mircea Eliade, "Paradise and Utopia," *Utopias and Utopian Thought,* Frank E. Manuel (ed.) (Boston: 1966), 263.
55 *vide infra,* 31f.
56 Haller, *Foxe's Book of Martyrs . . . ,* 9.
57 *Ibid.,* 136.
58 *Ibid.,* 220.
59 *Ibid.,* 137. As quoted by Haller.

the seventeenth century they elaborated their views. Although their millennialism was a Continentally-derived departure in English eschatology, it breathed the spirit of Elizabethan optimism and found Elizabethan precedents for its preoccupation with the prophetic and apocalyptic portions of the Bible.

3. *Thomas Brightman and Joseph Mede*

The interest in eschatology of the Tudor era persisted and assumed a note of Continental chiliasm under the Stuarts. Commentaries on prophetic and apocalyptic books of Scripture continued to appear. Ernst Staehelin speaks of the numerous Anglican theologians, both Puritan and non-Puritan, who wrote expositions of Revelation.[60] These studies were not all of the same caliber. The Scottish mathematician Napier and James Durham are judged by one historian as having "made distinguished contributions to the confusion" [61] surrounding the understanding of that book. In the dedication to James I of *An Exquisite Commentarie upon the Revelation of Saint John* Patrick Forbes complained about an age in which so much excellent literature was produced on the subject, but "yet infinitely more paper miserably spoiled." [62] Not all of it came to immediate light. Durham's works did not appear until after his death in 1658. The renowned Puritan who fled to Holland in 1607 to avoid prosecution by the High Commission, Robert Parker, had written two expositions on Revelation before his death in 1614. These appeared in print in 1650 and 1651 as *An Exposition of the fourth Vial mentioned in the 16th of Revelation* and *The Mystery of the Vialls opened.*[63]

Along with their expositions of other books, the commentaries of Thomas Brightman and Joseph Mede on Revelation "were among the most noted works" [64] articulating the doctrine of an era of triumph for the church. Their fame rests on their definition of this optimism in millennial categories. This was a new element in English expositions of Revelation which was to gain widespread acceptance by the 1640's and which was to markedly affect English and New England political, social, and religious history.

While Brightman and Mede agreed on the fact of a future millennium of a thousand years, their works showed notable differences. Brightman stressed the conversion of the Jews and the downfall of the papacy as the main

60   *V.R.G.*, IV, 312.
61   G. D. Henderson, *The Burning Bush: Studies in Scottish Church History* (Edinburgh: 1957), 80.
62   *Ibid.*, as quoted by Henderson.
63   *D.N.B.*, XLIII, 269-271.
64   Haller, *The Rise of Puritanism*, 269.

characteristics of the millennium, which had begun, he believed, three hundred years previously. Mede was interested in chronology and corresponded with Archbishop James Ussher, whose interest in this subject is well-known. He was concerned to establish the credibility of the concept of a literal millennium among Englishmen. Writing at a time when millennial opinions were rampant in England, Thomas Hayne opposed such views. His subtitle singled out Brightman, Alsted, Mede, and Henry Archer, whose writings post-date those of the other three by a generation, as the four men chiefly responsible for the prevalence of that idea during the Civil Wars and Interregnum in England: "What Mr. *Th. Brightman,* Dr. *J. Alsted,* Mr. *I. Mede,* Mr. *H. Archer, The Glimpse of Sions Glory,* and such as concurre in opinion with them, hold concerning the thousand years of the Saints Reign with Christ, And of Satans binding: Herein also their arguments are answered." [65] This acknowledged influence warrants a closer look at the views of Brightman and Mede.

Thomas Brightman was a Puritan preacher and commentator whose "disaffection to church establishment was no secret." [66] He became a fellow of Queen's College, Cambridge in 1584, the same year in which he earned his M.A., and was later appointed rector of Hawness. His writings were printed subsequent to his death in 1607.

Apocalypsis Apocalypseos was published in a Latin edition in 1609 and in an English translation in 1616. In 1644 it appeared in an edition of his works. Dedicated to "the holy Reformed Churches of Britany, Germany, and France," Brightman's "new Interpretation of this Book of the Revelation" took its place among the "great variety of Interpretations old and new" already in existence.[67] His purpose for writing this commentary was dual. His first objective was to warn the true church of the hard days at hand and to urge her to stedfastness during them. Brightman felt that she could receive strength for these days by considering the course of history from the apostles' days until the end of the world as explained in Revelation. His second reason for writing pertained to the church of Rome. His pity for the many Catholics who, "ignorant of the sacred truth," worshiped Antichrist and his desire to refute the errors of Ribera's commentary on Revelation and Cardinal Bellarmine's denial of the Protestant identification of the pope as Antichrist moved him to publish his own commentary.[68]

In his explanation of the structure of the Apocalypse Brightman regarded all the seals, trumpets, and the angels with their vials of divine wrath as historically identifiable with past, present, or future events or persons. The

---

65 T. Hayne, *Christ's Kingdome on Earth, Opened according to the Scriptures* (London: 1645), title page.
66 *D.N.B.,* VI, 239.
67 Brightman, A2r.
68 *Ibid.,* B1r and 612-746.

seven seals refer to events prior to Constantine; the seven trumpets are applicable to events from Constantine until, roughly, the Reformation; the seven vials refer to Reformation and post-Reformation events. He estimated that three vials had already been emptied upon the Roman church. Under the four vials still to come the afflictions and joys pertaining to the last days will transpire. The events in store under the flowing of the last vials Brightman cited as a source of encouragement for the church of his day. He gave detailed attention to those events. Because his discussion of those days later encouraged Anglo-American mission work, it merits a fuller summary.

John clearly predicts the flood of miseries now inundating the church, said Brightman. The last act of the "long and dolefull Tragedy" has begun, complete with its "scourges, slaughters, destructions." [69] Eventually the Roman Catholic Antichrist will be overthrown, however. Hence, Brightman's commentary did not "bring only mournfull and weeping matter," but also brought the true church „matter of exceeding joy, and ... most glorious triumph." [70] Here he showed his debt to the tradition of Bale and Foxe, for the issues were drawn between the true and false church, between "the 'whore of Rome'" and the "Holy Reformed Churches." What can afford the true spouse of Christ more joy "than to see *this impudent harlot* at length slit in the nostrills, stript of her garments and tires, besmeared with dirt and rotten eggs, and at last burnt up and consumed with fire?" [71] The humbling of Rome is near, consoled Brightman. Christ, the true church's spouse, "is about to arise even now" [72] and avenge his wife's grief. Further joy may be derived from knowing that the "finall *destruction of the Turks*" [73] will follow hard on the fall of Rome. The subsequent "*calling of the Jewes* to be a Christian Nation" and "a most happy tranquillity from thence to the end of the world" round out "the full heap of joy" which the apostle offers to the church of Brightman's day. [74]

In addition to the fall of Antichrist the extensive conversions of the latter days engaged the expositor's attention. While there will be "some beginning" of the conversion of the Jews during the pouring out of the last four vials, "there shall not be an absolute perfecting of their calling, till they [*i.e.*, the vials] shall be wholly past." [75] Rome is restraining the entrance of the Jews into the church. But when all the vials against her have run out and she is "sunk and consumed, then shall the Jewes at last, and many of the Gentiles

69 *Ibid.*, A2v.
70 *Ibid.*
71 *Ibid.*
72 *Ibid.*
73 *Ibid.*
74 *Ibid.*
75 *Ibid.*, 518.

that remain, come to the Church flocking and striving who shall come first . . . ."[76] The present troubles do not restrain many elect Gentiles from entering the true church, however, "but the Jewes only, and the fulness of the Gentiles."[77] The fifth vial is designated specifically for the "City of Rome, the Throne of the beast,"[78] and will cripple her sinister restraint of the Jews' conversion. The sixth will cause the Euphrates to dry up, allowing "the kings of the east" or the many Jews living in the Orient to return to their homeland to establish the New Jerusalem. Here they "shal worship Christ purely, and sincerely, according to his wil & Commandement alone."[79] This news will astonish Gentiles everywhere. Yet this first conversion and return of the Jews will not yet be the complete conversion of that people, but only a "beginning." With the pouring out of the seventh vial will come Armageddon, the complete defeat of both the Roman and Turkish Antichrists, and the fulness of the Jews.

> Now shall the end of all prophets come, both when all the enemies shall be utterly and at once abolished, and when there shall be one sheepfold made upon earth, of all the Elect both Jewes and Gentiles under one shepheard Jesus Christ. It is certain, that this Kingdom of Christ that is thus begun, shall be eternall, and shall never be broken off againe, and discontinued, and that it shall be translated at length from earth into heaven; But I finde no mention in this Booke of the time, into which this translation shall fall, that shall be finished perfectly in Christs second coming.[80]

Brightman's position on the manner of the first and second callings of the Jews is significant. The first will be accomplished without human agency, he said. The voice coming from the throne recorded in Revelation 19 : 5 he interpreted as the voice of the Son at the time of the drying of the Euphrates. Here Christ is calling the Jews, argued Brightman. Their conversion will be "by his own power alone," and not "by any helpe of man" for these Jews beyond the Euphrates "are the furdest of[f] from hearing of the Gospell."[81] This voice "is the efficacie of the spirit" in the hearts of the elect. At the second or full calling of the Jews God will "marvellously restore unto life and saving knowledge of his Son, men that were past recovery in themselves, and seemed so to be both in their own eyes, and in the eyes of all the world . . . ."[82] Here Brightman left room for a calling by means of gospel proclamation, although he did not explicitly speak of evangelizing the Jews. During the unique events of the Interregnum Puritan

76 *Ibid.,* 519.
77 *Ibid.*
78 *Ibid.,* B2v.
79 *Ibid.,* 544.
80 *Ibid.,* 552-553.
81 *Ibid.,* 786.
82 *Ibid.,* 842.

and Separatist students of Brightman's writings assumed the role of divinely appointed instruments to proclaim the gospel to those whom they thought were the descendants of Israel.

The unity of Jews and Gentiles in the revitalized church during the millennium was a truth which Brightman found not only in the book of Revelation. He cited corroborating Biblical evidence and in so doing emphasized the basis which Anglo-American millennial views had in the entirety of Scripture. Romans 11 he regarded as crucial proof of the forthcoming unity of Jews and Gentiles. He stressed the harmony of Old Testament prophecy on this point:

> 'The Lord shall be King over all the earth, in that day there shall be one Lord, and his name shall be one,' Zach. 14.9. 'And the Lord shall destroy in this mountaine the covering that covereth all people, and the vaile that is spread upon all Nations, and the Lord God shall wipe avvay the Teares from all faces, and he will take avvay the rebuke of his people out of all the Earth,' Esay, Chap. 25.7,8. 'For then they that dvvell in the vvildernesse, shall bovv themselves dovvn before him, and his enemies shall licke the Dust; the Kings of Arabia and Saba shall bring gifts, yea all kings shal vvorship him, al nations shal serve him,' Ps. 72.9,10,11.[83]

On the new life which shall quicken the entire church in the millennial day Isaiah 26 : 19, Daniel 12 : 2-3, and Romans 11 agree, as Beza has shown. Ezekiel's vision of the dry bones "which were moved with a great and mighty noise..."[84] also depicts the beginning of this new life among the Jews. Brightman's concern with the calling of the Jews is apparent also from his exposition of Daniel 11 : 36-chapter 12, which he felt treats this theme. He interpreted the Song of Solomon as he did Revelation. He considered it to be a history of the church told allegorically and regarded its climax as its prophecy of the restoration of the Jews to full fellowship with men of all nations. John, Daniel, and Solomon all agree on God's "deliverance of his nation," therefore.[85]

Besides the doctrines of the fall of Antichrist and of the conversion of Jews and Gentiles, Brightman considered the millennium itself. He interpreted the two references to the millennium in Revelation 20 (verses 2f. and 5) as referring to two different millenniums. The first extended from 300-1300 and corresponded to the traditional Augustinian understanding. The second began in 1300 at the time of the first resurrection (Rev. 20 : 5), which he interpreted as the return of men like Wycliffe to Scriptural truth. According to Brightman the second millennium included the pouring out of the vials against Antichrist, the Reformation, the conversion of the Jews

---

83 *Ibid.,* 847.
84 *Ibid.,* 793. Ez. 37.
85 *Ibid.,* 893.

and the Gentiles, the increase of truth, and the latter-day glory of the church. He defined this age as "the Kingdom of Christ," for during it Christ in increasing measure would rule the nations "with the Scepter of his word."[86] By his calculation Brightman and his contemporaries were three hundred years into the second millennium, therefore, and he assured his readers that the condition of the church could only improve.

An analysis of the ideas contained in Brightman's exposition shows that he was indebted to past scholars and that in certain important respects he departed from their positions. He himself admitted as much.[87] His debt to Bale's, Jewel's, and Foxe's Augustinian construction of history as a struggle between good and evil forces is obvious. He shared with many other Englishmen the ideas which these leaders had popularized: Rome as Antichrist, a period of glory for the English church, interest in Revelation as the key to understanding history, the millennium as extending from Constantine to 1300. He differed from them in positing a future millennium, into which he felt the church had already entered. His position has aptly been labelled "revised Augustinianism" by a recent study.[88] His mediate position between various loosely held millennial expectations and more literalistic, premillennial systems was unique in his day. It is one of the earliest forms of English postmillennialism. He showed his indebtedness to Bucer, Martyr, and others who adopted the belief in a future conversion of Israel by the strong emphasis he placed on the conversion of the Jews. Fifty years after his death it was to aid the birth of Anglo-American missions under his Puritan successors.

A later contemporary of Brightman whose views corresponded closely to those of Alsted was Joseph Mede.[89] From 1613 until his death in 1638 Mede taught at Christ College, Cambridge, where he proved himself to be a loyal Anglican on such cardinal issues as church government and the Eucharist.[90] He has been accused of having excessively Calvinistic sympathies.[91] Although competent in several fields, his stature in "the minds of his contemporaries" was based on his exposition of Revelation.[92] His best known work, *Clavis Apocalyptica*, appeared in 1627, was translated in 1642, and recurred in subsequent editions of his works. Peter Toon suggests that between the first and second editions of the book Mede fell under Alsted's influence.[93]

---

86   *Ibid.,* 824.
87   *Ibid.,* A2v.
88   Toon, 51f.
89   Also spelled "Mead" and Latinized "Medius." We use "Mede."
90   *D.N.B.,* XXXVIII, 178-179.
91   James B. Mullinger, *The University of Cambridge,* 3 vols. (Cambridge: 1873, 1884, 1911), III, 17.
92   *Ibid.,* 21.
93   Toon, 56.

Like Brightman Mede interpreted Revelation as a prophetic history of the church culminating in the millennium.[94] Revelation's prophecies form two distinct sections, said Mede: the future of earthly governments and the future of the church. The prophecy of the seals (Rev. 6f.) constitutes the *Fata Imperii*,[95] and the prophecy of the open book (Rev. 10) the *Status Ecclesiae*.[96] Ultimately both sections converge in the prophecy of the seventh trumpet or that of the *Ecclesia regnans*.[97] Mede dated the first seal from the time of Christ, when the Roman empire was initially assaulted by the gospel. Identifying the subsequent seals with events from ancient Roman history, he associated the sixth with Constantine. The seventh, which embraces the prophecies of the trumpets (Rev. 8 : 7f.), marks the last stages in Rome's progressive downfall. Under the first four trumpets the civil power of the old Roman empire devolved upon "the Antichristian State of the Beast or Kingdom of the False Prophet."[98] The power of this Roman Catholic or Antichristian establishment has been undermined by the Saracens and Turks, the fifth and sixth trumpets. The seventh is future and will bring the complete downfall of Rome. Contemporaneous with the fulfillment of the prophecies of the seals and the first six trumpets are those of the open book. Thus the war between Michael and the dragon (Rev. 12 : 7) refers to the long battle between Christ's "undaunted Souldiers" and the persecuting Roman emperors. Constantine eliminated this beast. An era of apostacy in the church ensued, described as the trampling of the outer temple court by the Gentiles (Rev. 11 : 2). The few faithful "witnesses in sackcloth" (Rev. 11 : 7-9) and the hundred and forty-four thousand (Rev. 14 : 1) were spared during the sounding of the trumpets. This was not so with the false church or "*Antichristendom*," composed of the seven-headed, tenhorned beast (Roman Catholic Church) presided over by the two-horned, false prophet (pope) in Babylon (Rome).[99] This beast (Rev. 17) is the object of the seven vials of God's wrath (Rev. 16). It has already been considerably weakened by the pouring out of a number of these vials. Mede admitted that these vials correspond closely to the trumpets, since this beast has succeeded the old Roman empire or dragon, against which the trumpets sound. Both ecclesiastical and civil affairs have reached a point which makes the sounding of the seventh trumpet and the coming of Christ's kingdom imminent, indicated the Cambridge scholar.

94 For discussions of his work see *V.R.G.*, IV, 312-313; *P.F.F.*, II, 559, 567, 785; and Mullinger, III, 17-25 and 153-154.
95 Joseph Mede, *Works* (3rd. ed.: London: 1672), 917. All our subsequent references to Mede's writings are to this edition of his works, which contains unpublished theological fragments and Mede's correspondence as well as those works published before his death in 1638.
96 *Ibid.*, 918.
97 *Ibid.*
98 *Ibid.*, 919.
99 *Ibid.*, 921.

Regarding the kingdom of Christ Mede took a cautious position. Precisely what it is "posterity will better understand." [100] He showed this caution in all his writings. He was unwilling to speculate on the character of this millennial kingdom,[101] for it is "neither easie nor safe" [102] to discern what it will be. Similarly, he refused to commit himself on the dates suggested by Alsted,[103] and was careful to distinguish the respectable millennialism of the ancient church fathers from the "carnal and intolerable conceits" [104] of later millennialists. A frequent correspondent of Mede, Dr. Charles Potter, confided to a Mr. Mason that Mede "doth but modestly conjecture" on points about which Anabaptists and their ilk "are confident." [105] The writer of "The Author's Life" likewise proclaimed the *Pure* and *Peaceable* character of Mede's millennial views, which are "altogether free from the least suspicion of Luxury and Sensuality." [106] Mede did give the general traits of that kingdom throughout his writings, however, and we shall survey them in the ensuing paragraphs.

The simultaneous sounding of the seventh trumpet and coming of the millennium can be described as "*Magnus dies Domini,*" "*Magnus dies Judicii,*" and "*Dies magni Judicii,*" said Mede.[107] In a syllogism he proved that "... the whole thousand years is included in the *Day of Judgment.*" [108]

> The Kingdom of the Son of man and of the Saints of the Most High in *Daniel* begins when the Great Judgment sits.
> The Kingdom in the *Apocalyps,* wherein the Saints reign with Christ a thousand years, is the same with the Kingdom of the Son of man and Saints of the most High in *Daniel.*
> *Ergo,* It also begins at the Great Judgment.[109]

This reign will follow the fall of Antichrist, he said, and for its duration Satan will be bound.[110] After much study Mede reluctantly yielded that the first resurrection, namely that of the saints, will be physical and not " 'a rising of the Church from a dead estate.' " [111] In a study on the dates for the beginning and termination of the forty-two months (Revelation 11 : 2-3) he distinguished between the martyrs who, resuming their bodies at this resurrection, will reign with Christ in heaven and the faithful who will not

100 *Ibid.,* 923.
101 *Ibid.,* 771.
102 *Ibid.,* 603.
103 *Ibid.,* 600, *vide infra.* 24.
104 *Ibid.,* 602.
105 *Ibid.,* 770.
106 *Ibid.,* xi.
107 *Ibid.,* 603.
108 *Ibid.,* 763.
109 *Ibid.*
110 *Ibid.,* 603.
111 *Ibid.,* 770. The source of Mede's quotation is not given.

worship the beast and will still be alive at the dawn of the millennium. These latter will reign on earth.[112] In a later letter Mede spoke only of the raised saints who will reign in the New Jerusalem "in a state of beatitude and glory." [113] The Savior's reign will be one of "victory over his Enemies" [114] and one of security for the church and freedom from apostacy and error. Though "glorious and evident," Christ's presence in this kingdom will not be physical, for his is a *Regnum Caelorum*.[115] The New Jerusalem or "Metropolis" of the church and "of the New world" [116] will be distinct from other nations at this time and will not encompass the whole church. Hers is a position of special favor, for unlike the nations whose state will be "changeable," the New Jerusalem will be immutable and free from the power of the second death. At the close of the millennium Satan will be loosed and Gog and Magog will assault the saints and "the *Beloved City.*" [117] Then the universal resurrection of the dead and final judgment will take place.

Revelation 11 : 2-3 was crucial for millennialists in calculating the date when the millennium would begin. They interpreted the forty-two months during which the Gentiles would trample the outer court as the duration of Antichrist's reign. Believing that the millennium would commence with the fall of Antichrist, they needed only to determine the time when he had assumed his power and to add 1260 — the number of prophetic days in the forty-two months — to determine the blessed date. Alsted had reportedly given four possible sets of dates: 362-1622, 376-1636, 382-1642, and 433-1693. These were reviewed and weighed by Mede, who felt that the second "hath more probability" than the others.[118] Ultimately, however, Mede decided "against precise determination of Years in this business" [119] and placed the beginning of the twelve hundred sixty years between 365 and 455 and their termination between 1625 and 1715.[120]

Although Mede said relatively little regarding the Jews in the millennium, his position is significant. William Twisse, who was later to become prolocutor of the Westminster Assembly, broached the subject in his first of many letters to Mede. Writing in 1629, Twisse desired Mede's reaction to several questions concerning Romans 11. The provocation there mentioned, responded the millennialist, means only that salvation has been given to the Gentiles in an effort to provoke the Jews to jealousy and repentance.

---

112 *Ibid.,* 604.
113 *Ibid.,* 771-772.
114 *Ibid.,* 603.
115 *Ibid.*
116 *Ibid.,* 722.
117 *Ibid.,* 605.
118 *Ibid.,* 601. Mede was reacting to passages in a work identified only as Alsted's *Chronology.* (600)
119 *Ibid.,* 602.
120 *Ibid.,* 600.

Unmoved, the Jews can only be converted by a *"Vision* and *Voice from Heaven,* as S. Paul was. . . . They will never believe that Christ reigns at the right hand of God, until they see him." [121] Mede elaborated this position in an essay entitled "The Mystery of S. *Paul's* Conversion: *or,* The Type of the Calling of the Jews." The Jews will not be converted to Christ in the manner in which the other nations were, that is, by "the Ministerie of Preachers sent unto them." [122] Christ's miraculous appearance to them, which will go unnoticed by their Gentile neighbors, will bring them to zealous allegiance to the truths of the Reformed churches. Only then will the general conversion of Gentiles occur. Israel's conversion will be "the riches of the World," for then "the whole world shall come unto Christ." [123] In a second letter to Twisse Mede indicated that Christ's miraculous appearance to the Jews will precede his coming in judgment and the setting up of his millennial kingdom.[124] The potentially negative effect of this position on missions to the Jews is obvious.

Another point in Mede's millennial theory deserves emphasis, since it proved to be of later significance. Also raised by Twisse, it involved the American colonies. Although Twisse had for a time adopted current "odd conceits" that America would be the location of the New Jerusalem, he acknowledged that Mede's arguments for its being in "the land of *Jury* [*i.e.,* Jewry]" have "handsomely and fully clear'd" him of these notions.[125] This raised for Twisse, however, the problem of explaining the colonies and the relation of the colonists to the natives. Conversion of the Indians appeared hopeless. "Shall our *English* there degenerate and joyn themselves with *Gog* and *Magog?"* [126] On March 23, 1635 Mede answered negatively. While he disagreed with the motives for which the colonies were settled — indicating that he had New England in mind — and while conversion of the natives did appear to be hopeless, Mede admitted that God was undoubtedly using the settlements "to affront the Devil with the sound of the Gospel and Cross of Christ" in his own stronghold.[127] Mede calculated that when Europe became increasingly Christian, Satan seduced barbarians into America and established a haunt unmolested by the gospel. After some time Christ sent his Spanish "Mastives" to harass the devil by hunting and destroying many of his subjects. A better way to torment the devil is to save rather than destroy his subjects, continued Mede. Now perhaps Christ has begun "his *second affront* with better Christians," who as a bright light

---

121 *Ibid.,* 761. See also 603-604, where Mede links the Jews' conversion with the revelation to them of Christ in his *Regnum Caelorum.*

122 *Ibid.,* 891.

123 *Ibid.,* 892.

124 *Ibid.,* 766.

125 *Ibid.,* 799.

126 *Ibid.*

127 *Ibid.,* 800.

will "dazle and torment the Devil at his own home." [128] Many of the colonists, therefore, are Christ's faithful witnesses and will not degenerate into soldiers of the armies of Gog and Magog. Mede only hinted at the possibility of the natives being converted, however, and his views on the priority and manner of the conversion of the Jews led to later allegations of an anti-mission spirit among his New England students. [129]

It would be difficult to exaggerate the influence of Brightman and Mede on subsequent Anglo-American exegetes, scientists, politicians, and missionaries. Written at a time of unrest and therefore of expectancy in English life, their writings were the best known of a corpus "which captivated the imaginations of men of all classes and opened a particularly thrilling prospect to the most discontented, enthusiastic and uncritical." [130] The hardening of Laud's anti-Puritan and anti-Separatist policies in the late twenties and thirties fueled such burning expectations. During the Civil Wars and Interregnum the writings of these two men served as the basis for literally dozens of other works and hundreds of sermons. The leading Fifth Monarchist writer praised Brightman as "the brightest man of his age, that I have met with." [131] The prominent Independent divine Thomas Goodwin openly acknowledged his dependence on Brightman and Mede in his *An Exposition of the Revelation*. [132] Brightman's ideas were formative for Thomas Shepard's missionary propaganda. [133] Alsted and Mede were highly regarded by John Davenport and Increase Mather, as is evident from the latter's *The Mystery of Israel's Salvation, Explained and Applied*. [134] Samuel Sewall, prominent Boston judge and missionary leader, referred to Mede's study as "so beautiful, and well-born a Work." [135] Mede's position at Cambridge, the stronghold of Puritanism, guaranteed his direct influence on the majority of Puritan divines of the mid-seventeenth century. James Mullinger states that his *Clavis Apocalyptica* "won for its author the regard of Hartlib and the praise of nearly all learned Holland; it modified the religious belief of John Milton..." and as a theological classic deeply influenced theological thinking "for more than a century," including the calculations of Sir Isaac

128 *Ibid.*
129 Robert Baillie, *The Disswasive from the Errors of the Time, Vindicated from the Exceptions of Mr. Cotton and Mr. Tombes* (London: 1655), 42-43.
130 Haller, *The Rise of Puritanism*, 269.
131 John Rogers, *A Tabernacle for the Sun* (London: 1653), 19.
132 Thomas Goodwin, *An Exposition of the Revelation*, in *The Works of Thomas Goodwin* (Edinburgh: 1861), III, *passim*.
133 Thomas Shepard, *The Clear Sun-Shine of the Gospel Breaking Forth upon the Indians of New England* (London: 1648), 30.
134 Increase Mather, *The Mystery of Israel's Salvation, Explained and Applied* (London: 1669), A6r, C1v-C3r.
135 Samuel Sewall, *Phaenomena quaedam Apocalyptica* (2nd. ed.; Boston: 1727), 41.

Newton.[136] His writings assured a widespread defection from the long dominant Augustinian interpretation of the millennium as having begun with Constantine.

Both Brightman and Mede developed a complicated millennialism. Several of the ideas and themes which they popularized recur in the most important Anglo-American missionary sources until early in the eighteenth century. As late as the 1790's and early 1800's millennial and missionary writers consulted and praised the work of these two men. It must be emphasized, however, that the discussions which they provoked did not guarantee the acceptance of their complete systems. In many cases they merely reinforced the millennial expectations which had been current in England since Elizabethan days.

4. A widespread emphasis

Great as the influence of Brightman and Mede was, however, others also deserve acknowledgment for helping spread the millennial expectations in England and America which were to generate missionary interest and work in the 1640's. While not espousing the detailed, systematized millennialism of the two men just considered, many of the leading theologians of the period popularized individual millennial expectations.

William Perkins, the Elizabethan theologian and fellow of Christ's College who was to have enormous influence on New England Puritans, believed there would be a national conversion of the Jews. These views found expression in *A Commentarie upon the first five chapters of the Epistle to the Galatians*, which appeared posthumously in 1617.

Richard Sibbes and Thomas Goodwin followed Perkins in these views. Sibbes wrote,

> The Jews are not yet come in under Christ's banner; but God, that hath persuaded Japhet to come into the tents of Shem, will persuade Shem to come into the tents of Japhet, Gen. 9 : 27. The 'fulness of the Gentiles is not yet come in', Rom. 11 : 25, but Christ, that hath the 'utmost parts of the earth given him for his possession', Psa. 2 : 8, will gather all the sheep his Father hath given him into one fold, that there may be one sheepfold and one shepherd, John 10 : 16.[137]

136 Mullinger, III, 24-25. The influence of English millennial views on Dutch theological thought can be seen in Jacobus Koelman, *Sleutel ter opening van de donkerste Kapittelen in de Openbaaringe gedaan aan Johannis* (2nd. ed.; Amsterdam: [1768]). The first edition of Koelman's study appeared in 1689 with a slightly different title. Not only does Koelman show a broad knowledge of English chiliasm. deep dependence on English writers like Brightman and on some points Mede, and a critical use of these sources, but he gives what must rank as one of the clearest and most complete seventeenth century surveys of English millennialism.

137 Richard Sibbes, *The Bruised Reed*, in *The Complete Works of Richard Sibbes*, 6 vols. (Edinburgh: 1862-1863), I, 99.

Sibbes felt that he was living in "the latter end of the world" and that "blessed times" [138] were almost upon him. Soon Antichrist would be overthrown. The fulness of the Gentiles to be followed by the conversion of Israel would characterize those days. Sibbes' and Goodwin's views on these matters may well have been spread via their afternoon lectures in Cambridge. In succession John Preston, Sibbes, and Goodwin used "the afternoon lectureship at Trinity Church" as a platform for Puritan thought in the university and the community after 1624.[139]

The commentary of yet another Cambridge alumnus had widespread influence among Puritans and Separatists. After 1620 Elnathan Parr's commentary on Romans saw numerous editions. Parr's views were similar to Brightman's, though contact between the two men has not been proven. Parr regarded the fulness of the Gentiles in a dual sense. The first fulness precedes the Jews' conversion, the second fulness follows it in a bright new age for the world and the church, he said. "The end of this world shall not be till the Jews are called, and how long after that none yet can tell." [140] Whether or not this apparent relationship between Brightman and Parr did in fact exist does not detract from Parr's influence in spreading these ideas in the several editions of his commentary on Romans in the 1620's and 1630's.

A work which brought down the wrath of James I on its publisher, William Gouge, and on its author, Sir Henry Finch, was *The Worlds Restauration. Or the Calling of the Iewes, and (with them) of all the Nations and Kingdoms of the earth, to the faith of Christ.* It was suspected of treasonous sentiments because it depicted the "chiefe sway and soueraignty" of the Jews, the honor all nations would bring them, and the Jews' subjugation of all the enemies of the church.[141] Arrested after the appearance of the book in print, Gouge soon cleared himself by issuing a statement denying the charges alleged against himself and the book and by expressing his loyalty to the crown. In "To the Reader" Gouge noted Paul's promise in Romans 11 : 13f. regarding the grafting of the Jews into the true olive tree. Therefore, he asked, "ought not we in gratefull recompence to pray for the accomplishment of that promise? And if to pray for it, then to enquire and diligently to search after that fullnesse of time?" [142] Finch's inquiry, which Gouge found worthy of publication, consisted of forty-six propositions regarding the Jews' conversion and restoration to their homeland. These

138 As quoted by Sidney H. Rooy, *The Theology of Missions in the Puritan Tradition* (Delft: 1965), 59.

139 Mullinger, III, 99.

140 Elnathan Parr, *Commentary on Romans, The Works of Elnathan Parr* (3rd. ed.; London: 1633), 175.

141 [Henry Finch], *The Worlds Restauration*, William Gouge (ed.) (London: 1621), 5.

142 *Ibid.,* "To the Reader".

were Biblically explained and defended, largely on the basis of the Old Testament prophets. Finch singled out Isaiah 24-27, Daniel 9 : 24f., and the entire book of Hosea for more intense study. Gouge published the work because Finch had "dived deeper into that mysterie" than he was able to do.[143]

Eleven years later John Downame published a five hundred page collection of Thomas Sutton's sermons on Romans 11.[144] The writer followed Martyr and Paraeus in interpreting Romans 11 : 25-26 as referring to the Jews as a race rather than as a symbol of all believers. Our interest in this work stems from Downame rather than Sutton, however, for Downame's interest in the conversion of the Jews came to later expression in his support of the missionary literature which advocated the theory that the American Indians were descendants of the ten lost tribes of Israel.[145] He became an overt sponsor of Anglo-American missions.

In conclusion we note that through these and many other Anglo-American theological leaders before the Civil Wars there developed a widespread emphasis on the conversion of Jews and Gentiles in the latter days of history.

5. *New England*

Various elements of the Elizabethan expectations recur in the ideals for the new settlements in America. Hakluyt's notion of propagating the gospel through colonization, the association of the West with the success of the gospel and true Christianity, and a sense of national election and purpose all shaped the hopes on which the American colonies were founded. Massachusetts Bay is the best example of a colony founded on these expectations. Driven from their homeland by persecution, the New England Puritans hoped to found a city set on a hill, a light shining in the darkness, which would call England and their mother church back to true reformation. The fulfillment of this mission [146] by God's faithful, covenant people would serve as the basis for the full realization of the kingdom of God in America. It was believed that from America the kingdom would spread throughout the world. The seeds of this vision can be found in the 1628 "Proclamation for Volunteers" for colonizing New England as quoted by Edward Johnson:

143 *Ibid.*
144 [Thomas] Sutton, *Lectures upon the Eleventh Chapter to the Romans,* John Downame (ed.) (London: 1632).
145 *vide infra,* 48.
146 Much in the opening sentences of this paragraph is based on Gustav Blanke, "Die Anfange des amerikanischen Sendungsbewusztseins: Massachusetts-Bay 1629 bis 1659," *Archiv für Reformationsgeschichte,* LVIII, 1967, 171-211.

'All you the people of Christ that are here Oppressed, Imprisoned and scurrilously derided, gather your selves together, your Wifes and little ones, and answer to your severall Names as you shall be shipped for his service, in the Westerne World, and more especially for planting the united Collonies of new *England*; Where you are to attend the service of the King of Kings, upon the divulging of the Proclamation by his Herralds at Armes.'[147]

Paraphrasing the objection of many Puritans, Johnson noted that they felt they would be deserting the scene of Christ's battle and forsaking their fellow soldiers. Johnson's answer to that objection is given with the certainty and accuracy of historical hindsight: Christ has his purposes in causing his army to retreat, for in his own time he will recall to England

such instruments as he thinks meete to make use of in this place, from whence you are now to depart, but further that you may not delay the Voyage intended, for your full satisfaction, know this [New England] is the place where the Lord will create a new Heaven, and a new Earth in new Churches, and a new Common-wealth together.[148]

Preaching the farewell sermon to those about to embark for the New World aboard the *Arbella*, John Cotton, whose later writings developed millennial thought for New England settlers, demonstrated high expectations for the enterprise. This appears from the texts which are cited on the title page and which set the perspective for the entire sermon: 2 Sam. 7 : 10 and Ps. 22 : 27, 30, 31.

'Moreover I will appoint a place for my people *Israel*, and I will plant them, that they may dwell in a place of their owne, and move no more . . . .'
'All the ends of the world shall remember and turne unto the Lord, and all the kindreds of the Nations shall worship before thee. A seede shall serve him, it shall be accounted to the Lord for a generation.'
'They shall come, and shall declare his righteousness unto a people that shall be borne, that he hath done this.'[149]

The settlers were obviously "Israel," the "seeds" that would serve the Lord. Their faithfulness would be a witness to all nations of the world, which in the future would acknowledge the God of New England.

Citing from an unidentified document drafted by the original proposers of the Massachusetts Bay colony, Cotton Mather shares with us their sense of "service unto the Church" by carrying the Gospel to the New World

---

147 Edward Johnson, *The Wonderworking Providence of Sions Saviour* (London: 1654), 2.
148 *Ibid.*, 3.
149 John Cotton, *God's Promise to His Plantation* (London: 1630), title page.

30

and by erecting there "a *bulwark* against the kingdom of anti-christ." [150]

The mild millennial hopes attached to the founding of the Massachusetts Bay colony stressed the deliverance of God's oppressed people from the forces of Antichrist which had made gains in the English church under the Stuarts. The better day for God's faithful servants was guaranteed by Old Testament prophets and psalmists and would culminate in God's use of his people to call all men to worship him. In the 1640's and 1650's these low-keyed expectations gave way to full-blown millennial interpretations of New England's founding and place in God's plan of salvation. The historians, preachers, and politicians of that period, however, had the benefit of seeing the original "wonderworking providences" of God from the vantage point of his shakings of the old order in England and of her return to Reformed religion. Not the least of aids in developing these millennial systems were the numerous commentaries and sermons which appeared during the Interregnum and which convincingly applied prophetic and apocalyptic passages to the events of the previous generation. As we shall see in the following chapter, John Cotton, New England's leading theologian during his lifetime, developed a millennialism akin to that of Brightman in the unsettled 1640's.

C. *Mission Efforts*

The earliest English mission efforts were rooted in decades of theorizing regarding the heathen and England's responsibility toward them. With Elizabethan sea power came contact with the outside world. Englishmen were convinced that God had given them victory over the Catholic powers that they might enlighten the heathen. John Norden expressed it in a prayer written for the queen in 1596. Thanking God for this deliverance through his instrument, the queen, Norden said,

> And thy fame in her is spread from one nation to another people, yea, from one end of the earth to the other, and all nations of the world do see and consider that great is her God: for the wonders that thou hast done for her are marvellous even in the eyes of her enemies. . . .[151]

The many editions of Richard Hakluyt's writings on English maritime exploits depicted a more active role for England in Christianizing the world's heathen. Colonization would provide centers from which English trade and

---

150 Cotton Mather, *Magnalia Christi Americana*, 2 vols. (Hartford: 1855), I, 69.
151 As quoted by Pauck, 194. Pauck's thesis is that "Die Wurzeln für den religiösen britischen Imperialismus jedenfalls liegen in der elisabethanischen Zeit und im besonderen in der Staatskirche." (194)

customs and the gospel would penetrate all nations of the earth.[152] John Davis in *The Worldes Hydrographical Description* also linked English mercantile expansion and sea power with her destiny "...to give light to all the rest of the world."[153]

To impart the gospel to heathen was cited as a main objective for colonization in the royal charters of several American colonies: Virginia, Plymouth, Massachusetts Bay, and Connecticut. The colonial authorities of Massachusetts Bay were empowered by their charter, for example, to implement any legislation necessary for creating an orderly Christian society among the settlers. This would so impress the natives, it was theorized, that they would be won and incited "to the Knowledge and Obedience of the only true God and Sauior of Mankinde, and the Christian Fayth, which in our Intencon, and the Adventurers free Profession is the principall End of this Plantacion."[154] The colonial seal depicted an Indian uttering the Macedonian call, "Come over and help us."[155] Intense concern for the salvation of the American native, for offsetting Spanish expansion in the New World, and for realizing there a "New Canaan" as England's God-appointed destiny in the West mark the annual sermons delivered before the Virginia Company after 1609.[156] In his incomparable rhetoric John Donne in 1622 urged that body to engage in missions as a preliminary event to the consummation of history:

> Before the end of the world come, before this mortality shall put on immortality, before the creature shall be delivered of the bondage of corruption under which it groans, before the martyrs under the altar shall be silenced, before all things shall be subdued to Christ, his kingdom perfected, and the last enemy death destroyed; the Gospel must be preached to those men to whom ye send; to all men; further and hasten you this blessed, this joyful, this glorious consummation of all, and happy reunion of all bodies to their souls, by preaching the Gospel to those men.[157]

John White related latter-day conversions and the end of history to the New England colonies and the Indians. In words similar to those of Mede White declared that the New World had for centuries been the devil's domain. It was incumbent upon the colonists to rescue it for Christ before

---

152 See Pauck, 196-198 and William Kellaway, *The New England Company* (London: 1961), 2-3.

153 As quoted by Blanke, 199.

154 As cited by R. Pierce Beaver, *Pioneers in Mission* (Grand Rapids: 1966), 2.

155 Acts 16 : 9.

156 These sermons are analyzed by Lewis B. Wright, *Religion and Empire* (Chapel Hill: 1943), 90-114.

157 John Donne, *The Works of John Donne, D.D.*, Henry Alford (ed.), 6 vols. (London: 1899), 140-141. This passege is quoted by Perry Miller, *Errand into the Wilderness* (Cambridge, Mass.: 1956), 109.

the day of judgment could dawn, however. "The Indians must needs bee gathered in before that day; and any man may make the conclusion of our duty to endeavour the effecting of that which God hath determined." [158] John Cotton reinforced the stipulation of the Massachusetts Charter in his sermon to departing colonists. They had many responsibilities: to plant pure gospel ordinances, to be mindful of England, their fellow colonists, their children, and the natives, with whom they were urged to share their knowledge of the gospel. "Who knoweth whether God have reared this whole Plantation for such an end," queried Cotton.[159]

Theory was applied when Alexander Whitaker, the Apostle to Virginia, established contact with the Indians. Under his ministry Pocahontas was converted and elaborate plans for Christianizing, educating, and civilizing Virginia's natives were laid. These dreams were shattered by the 1622 massacre of dozens of white settlers. In spite of an absence of organized missions in New England, such contemporary sources as Roger Williams' writings, William Bradford's *History of Plymouth Plantation*, and *New Englands first fruits* mention Squanto, Hobomock, John Sagamore, and Wequash Cook as natives interested in the colonists' religion prior to 1640. Williams had particularly close contact with the Narragansett tribe. In both Plymouth and Massachusetts Bay individual natives, impressed with English culture and customs, showed interest in Christianity, though tribal leaders and the bulk of their constituency were chary of adopting English ways.[160] In 1637 Massachusetts Bay passed legislation calculated to promote the Christianization of the Indians.[161] But not until the following decade did missions to the Indians begin in earnest.

We note in conclusion that although there was little mission effort prior to 1640, there was a long English tradition which regarded England as God's chosen instrument for carrying Reformed Christianity to the corners of the world on English vessels and for establishing it there by means of English colonies. It was believed that better times, particularly in the West, lay just ahead. These ideas, refined in the crucible of revolution and Puritan ascendency in the 1640's and alloyed with the more exegetical anticipations of the theologians, gave birth to Anglo-American missions.

---

158   As quoted by Blanke, 199, n. 114.
159   Cotton, 19-20.
160   Alden T. Vaughan, *New England Frontier* (Boston and Toronto: 1965), 239-243.
161   Beaver, *Pioneers in Mission*, 12.

Chapter II

Dry bones and first fruits
(1640-1675)

A. General Background

Charles I's 1637 proclamation ordering adoption of the worship propounded by the Scottish Book of Common Prayer brought down a storm of protest in Scotland and began the well-known chain of events which ultimately culminated in rebellion and execution of the king. In St. Giles Cathedral in Edinburgh the reading of the service from the new book caused a riot. Early in the next year Scots, fearing a reversion to Romanism, rallied around the widely signed National Covenant.[1] When bishops were attacked and episcopal structure in Scotland was threatened by the General Assembly which the king had initially authorized as a step toward conciliation, Charles Stuart mustered an army to suppress what he regarded as the rebellion in the North. Raising the necessary revenues forced him to call the Short and Long Parliaments in 1640. Predominately Puritan in composition, Parliament demanded that their religious grievances against the Laudian establishment be settled. Parliament imprisoned Laud, dissolved those dreaded instruments for suppressing dissent, the Star Chamber and the High Commission, and banned bishops from the House of Lords.[2] In an effort to protect his threatened interests, the king considered the possibility of using Irish troops to squash opposition. That and rumors of other intrigues with Catholics, who had killed thousands of Protestants in the 1641 uprising in Ireland, further strained relations between Charles and his Parliament, who by 1642 were engaged in a political and religious power struggle. Civil war ensued, lifting Oliver Cromwell to fame on the merit of his New Model Army's brilliant victories over the royalist forces.

The Westminster Assembly was convened by Parliament to advise her on matters of ecclesiastical reform. Composed of one hundred twenty-one clergymen and thirty laymen, it included Episcopalians, a small but powerful group of Independents, Erastians, and Presbyterians, who "were much the

---

1 The course of these events in masterfully traced by J. H. S. Burleigh, *A Church History of Scotland* (London: 1960), 210f. For a discussion of the issues surrounding the signing of the National Covenant and of its consequences see Henderson, Chapter IV, "The Idea of Covenant in Scotland," 61-74.

2 Chadwick, 233.

largest group."[3] In return for Scottish aid against the royalist forces, Parliament conceded to Presbyterian desires and seated a Scottish delegation in the Assembly. Rather than rewrite the Thirty-nine Articles, Westminster drafted a new confession and catechisms along Calvinistic lines.

The Long Parliament, protected by the army under the council of generals, sought an acceptable alternative to Britain's old political and ecclesiastical order. The former was partial to Presbyterian and the latter to Independent interests. Scottish collusion with the king afforded Independents the pretext for ridding Parliament of her Presbyterian majority in what came to be known as "Pride's Purge." By 1653 Oliver Cromwell had achieved sufficient political power to personally dissolve the wrangling, inefficient Parliament. During his protectorate he attempted to instill a spirit of toleration in Englishmen, and listened, often with admirable patience, to the claims and charges of various sectarians. His partiality toward a moderate Independency represented by men like John Owen and Thomas Goodwin emboldened Independents to meet openly and draft the Savoy Declaration in 1658. Having failed to find a workable political or religious settlement, Cromwell passed control to a son who was not his equal. In 1660 strife-weary Englishmen restored Charles II to the throne. With him came the Anglican liturgy, episcopacy, and the legislated conformity of the several provisions of the Clarendon Code. Presbyterianism and Independentism in both its milder and more radically individualistic varieties were forced outside the establishment and into a stance of dissent. Not until the Toleration Act of 1689 did these groups enjoy freedom from persecution in England. And only then did murder and uprising cease in Scotland, where episcopacy had also been restored after Charles II had returned from his exile in Holland.

In North America the decade of colonial growth during the 1630's was followed by the return of many Puritans to Old England. Their hopes had been renewed "for getting on with that more perfect reformation which, they held, had been prevented since Elizabeth's passing by papists and prelates."[4] Nevertheless, there was internal colonial growth and continuing development of colonial institutions. The Congregational way was established by the Cambridge Synod of 1646, which asserted its agreement with the theology of Westminster. Harvard College produced the ministers necessary for New England pulpits. New England Congregationalists were reprimanded for their intolerance by "thirteen leading Independent divines" in England as early as 1645.[5] In spite of sustained efforts to keep them out, sectarians continued to infiltrate New England's borders and suffered harsh penalties inflicted upon them for their presumption. The internal threat to the New England way posed by indifferent, second generation

3   O.D.C.C., 1450.
4   Haller, *Foxe's Book of Martyrs...*, 228.
5   Miller, 13.

New Englanders was resolved by the adoption of the half-way covenant, a compromise designed to recognize the baptized but non-confessing member as an upstanding citizen with political privileges. As New and Old England increasingly went their own ways, however, contact was sustained by formal political and religious ties and by a common heritage. Missions to the Indians conducted by the New England Company constitute one such important religious link.

The turn of events in favor of the Puritans during the 1640's and 1650's gave rise to a virtual flood of Old and New World speculation on the times. Many concluded that the millennium had dawned or was about to dawn and that the Puritan was God's favored instrument for furthering it. In this climate theological and political attention to the Jews flourished.[6] It is to a sorting out of the main lines of millennial thought during this period that we now give our attention.

B. *Millennial Expectations*

With the political upheavals of the 1640's millennial views spread rapidly in England and America. Events in the early years of that decade were identified by many as those which would give birth to the millennium. The detailed work of the expositors ceased being abstract. Hope flooded the lives of English Puritans who a few short years before had despaired of seeing reform in the church, and that hope was exhilarating. As the saints gained more power throughout that decade and the next, hope was strengthened. Eager to participate in ecclesiastical renewal and the birth of the kingdom of Christ and his saints, the colonists who had fled to the New World and to the Continent returned to England. New England leaders and historians depicted in sharply defined terms her relevance as a divinely ordained model for the new kingdom.

The greatest proof of this wave of millennial thought is the high incidence of writing and preaching on the subject, which makes these important years for the student of Anglo-American millennial views. Alsted's commentary was translated in 1642, the same year in which Henry Archer's *The Personall Reign of Christ* appeared. Collections of Brightman's and Mede's works were published in 1644. *A Glimpse of Sions Glory,*[7] 1641, and the many

6   Geoffrey F. Nuttall, *Visible Saints* (Oxford: 1957), 143-146, surveys Puritan attitudes towards and dealings with the Jews during this period. See also Lucian Wolf, *Menasseh Ben Israel's Mission to Oliver Cromwell* (London: 1901).

7   This work has been attributed both to William Kiffin and to Hanserd Knollys. See Haller, *The Rise of Puritanism,* 271. A more recent study favors Thomas Goodwin or perhaps Jeremiah Burroughs as the author. See John F. Wilson, "A Glimpse of Syons Glory," *Church History,* XXXI, 1962, 66-73.

subsequent writings of millennialist extremists, especially during their initial disenchantment with Cromwell in the early 1650's, advocated a more radical utopianism. The famous Independents William Strong and Thomas Goodwin inclined in this direction, while in England John Owen and in America John Cotton produced numerous works of a more moderately millennial tone. Cotton alone published three such studies in 1642. These are only the more influential writings. Their ideas filtered into countless subsequent sermons and books. Taken as representative of the spirit of the times, they demonstrate that millennial expectations reached a peak in England and America during this period.[8] The 1640's and 1650's, therefore, were years of the keenest and most widespread millennial expectancy of any in England and America until perhaps the 1820's, when a millennialism of a more radical and literalistic tone prevailed. And then millennial views had little of the political prestige which they were given by Cromwell and Parliament.

Rigid classification of the millennial expectations of this period is impossible because of the individual nuances of each millennialist writer. Therefore, rather than rely solely on the nouns "premillennialism" and "postmillennialism," which by themselves awaken too many associations with nineteenth century issues and movements, we also use synonyms and a number of descriptive adjectives when speaking of seventeenth and eighteenth century millennial views. Given these qualifications, however, we can speak of three major types of millennial expectations which are capable of being characterized in a rather general fashion.

The majority of Independents and Presbyterians entertained a mild millennialism which, if placed on a continuum, would include hopes ranging from what we have described in our first chapter as unsystematized or individual expectations to Brightman's brand of postmillennialism. These people constitute the first group of Anglo-American millennialists. That they were the largest group is evident from several sources. First, the Westminster documents reflect these views. The section entitled "Of Publike Prayer before the Sermon," which was included in Westminster's *A Directory for the Publique Worship of God,* petitioned "for the Propagation of the Gospell and Kingdome of Christ to all Nations, for the conversion of the Jewes, the fulnesse of the Gentiles, the fall of Antichrist, and the hastening of the

---

8 Sanford summarizes Haller's survey of millennial views and writings *(The Rise of Puritanism,* 174-175 and 269-287) by noting that these "increased remarkably just prior to the settlement of America and during the Cromwellian revolution." (80) Eliade gives a loose version of Sanford's generalization. (264) While these have the merit and validity of synopses, it should be indicated, (1) that since Haller's *terminus* is 1643 (see *The Rise of Puritanism,* vii), he is not concerned with the veritable flood of millennial literature after that date; and (2) the literature and views prior to, say, 1640 were more theoretical, while those after that date were often a popularized version of the former and were applied to the events and issues of the day.

second comming of our Lord." [9] The *Larger Catechism,* in treating the second petition of the Lord's Prayer, gave virtually identical thoughts.[10] The *Westminster Confession of Faith* identified the pope as "the man of sin," a concept which had a definitely millennial dimension for Westminster divines.[11] Secondly, *The Savoy Declaration,* the creed drafted by the Independents in 1658 and officially recognized by American Congregationalists in 1680 and 1706 at the Synods of Boston and Sayville respectively, confessed in the article on the church that according to God's promise

> we expect that in the latter days, Antichrist being destroyed, the Jews called, and the adversaries of the kingdom of his dear Son broken, the churches of Christ being enlarged and edified through a free and plentiful communication of light and grace, shall enjoy in this world a more quiet, peaceful, and glorious condition than they have enjoyed.[12]

These mildly millennial statements show what in England and America both Presbyterians and Independents accepted as their confessional position regarding the latter-day age of glory for the church. Thirdly, the second generation New England theologian Increase Mather conceded that "most of our *Reforming Worthies* have been against the *Chiliad,*" by which he meant the complicated millennial systems developed by men like Alsted, Mede, and Twisse.[13] In a later work, however, he admitted that the leading New England theologians of the previous generation advocated a type of "'simple Chiliasm.'"[14]

---

9   Bard Thompson, *Liturgies of the Western Church* (Cleveland and New York: 1961), 360. See J. van den Berg, *Constrained by Jesus' Love* (Kampen: 1956), 24.

10   E. F. Karl Müller, *Die Bekenntnisschriften der reformierten Kirche* (Leipzig: 1903), 641. *vide infra,* 62-63.

11   Ibid., 599. See *P.F.F.,* II, 553. Froom's assertion that this document may be considered "the strongest premillennialist symbol of Protestantism" and that "woven into [its] historical interpretation of the Antichrist" is an "implicit ... premillennial expectation of the advent" (*P.F.F.,* II, 553.) is utterly without foundation in the confession itself or in the eschatology of the majority of divines at the Assembly. The document is silent on the physical return of Christ before or at the beginning of a literal, thousand-year millennium, on the time when the millennium will begin, on the physical resurrection of the saints at the inauguration of this extended period—in short, millennialism. Rather, in the context of the views current then, Westminster's formulation must be seen as a deliberate choice of mild, unsystematized, postmillennnial expectations.

12   Philip Schaff, *The Creeds of Christendom,* 3 vols. (3rd. revised ed.; New York: 1877), III, 723. See C. C. Goen, "Jonathan Edwards: A New Departure in Eschatology," *Church History,* XXVIII, 1959, 34.

13   Increase Mather, C2v.

14   Sanford, 82. Sanford's reference is to Mather's *A Discourse Concerning Faith and Fervency in Prayer* (Boston: 1710), i. In the remainder of our study we shall use "simple chiliasm" as a synonym for mild, unsystematized, postmillennial expec-

John Owen, leading Independent theologian and Cromwell's advisor, typifies the expectations of this first group. This is evident from the dominant thought in his April 19, 1649, sermon to Parliament, namely that God was currently "shaking" the civil powers of the nations which had given their allegiance to Antichrist, the most blatant example of which was "papal sovereignty."[15] Before the House of Commons in October, 1651, Owen termed these events "wonderful providential alterations."[16] Here, however, Laudian prelacy and Presbyterianism were the objects of Christ's "alterations."[17] Owen defined the kingdom of God as spiritual control of Christians which produced outward obedience and conformity to Christ.[18] This kingdom would soon supplant the Antichristian kingdoms being shaken and would triumph first among Jews.[19] Its outward form Owen summarized in six points:

> *1st.* *Fulness of peace* unto the gospel and the professors thereof. . . .
> *2dly.* *Purity and beauty of ordinances* and gospel worship. . . .
> *3dly.* *Multitudes of converts,* many persons, yea, nations. . . .
> *4thly.* *The full casting out and rejecting of all will-worship,* and their attendant abominations.
> *5thly.* *Professed subjection of the nations* throughout the whole world unto the Lord Christ. . . .
> *6thly.* *A most glorious and dreadful breaking of all that rise in opposition to him. . . .*[20]

Owen's New England counterpart was John Cotton, teacher of the first church of Boston. Cotton's leadership in establishing a Puritan theocracy was bound up with his millennial expectations. In 1642 he published three Biblical expositions defining the ideal church predicted for the millennium. It would consist of Jews and Gentiles united after the fall of Antichrist.[21] Although more literalistic than Owen on the era of glory as a thousand year reign, Cotton exegeted the "first resurrection" (Revelation 20 : 5-6) as "the rising of men from spiritual death to spritual life" and their consequent revitalization of the church.[22] Like Brightman he regarded the Song

---

tations. Conversely, "complex chiliasm" will be used as a synonym for the more complicated, systematized, generally more literalistic, premillennial positions.

15 John Owen, *The Works of John Owen, D.D.* (Edinburgh: 1862), VIII, 256-257.

16 *Ibid.,* 321.

17 *Ibid.,* 323.

18 *Ibid.,* 374.

19 *Ibid.,* 375.

20 *Ibid.,* 334.

21 John Cotton, *The Powring Out of the Seven Vials* (London: 1642). Cotton's anti-Roman Catholicism was also expressed in *An Exposition upon the Thirteenth Chapter of the Revelation* (London: 1655).

22 John Cotton, *The Churches Resurrection* (London: 1642), 9.

of Solomon as an allegorical prophecy of the church's history carried through an age of peace and rest to be born "after the destruction of *Leviathan* the great Turke." [23]

In both England and America the mild hopes popularized by Owen and Cotton assumed a nationalistic dimension in conjunction with political and social developments. They were a new version of Elizabethan expectations. Oliver Cromwell, from the initial victories of his band in skirmishes with royalists to his virtual dictatorship as Lord Protector, was forever guided by a sense of divine omnipotence's using him as the instrument for bringing England to her appointed glory and for overthrowing Antichrist.[24] His associations with counsellors and chaplains like Owen, Goodwin, Peter Sterry, and Philip Nye and correspondence with John Cotton gave his aspirations a definite millennial cast. "What is the Lord a-doing? What prophecies are now fulfilling?" he asked Cotton somewhat rhetorically in a letter written in October, 1651.[25] He urged members of the Nominated Parliament to "own" their calls as Christ's governing saints, working for the day when God would gather his church "out of the multitudes of nations and people of this world."[26] That Parliament shared Cromwell's hopes appears from a declaration it released in July, 1653.[27] Meanwhile Edward Johnson was claiming a similar election and mission for New England.[28]

The second major group of Anglo-American millennialists defended an early form of Anglo-American premillennialism or what can better be called the complex chiliasm of Mede and Alsted. Representatives of this group accepted much in common with the first group: the identification of Antichrist and the expectation of his fall, the conversion of the Jews and Gentiles, England as God's elect nation for bringing Christ's gospel and kingdom, the definition of that kingdom as an era of peace, joy, reformation in the church, holiness, and freedom from Satan and persecution. More basically, both groups shared a broader theological and confessional position. This deeper unity explains why men from both camps could lend mutual support to Anglo-American missions, endorse the same appeals for aid, support the same missionaries through the same agencies, and advance a basically common eschatological vision of and motivation for missions.

On several important points, however, the complex chiliasts differed from the first group.

First of all they were often engrossed in determining the dates of

23 John Cotton, *A Brief Exposition of the whole Book of Canticles, or, Song of Solomon* (London: 1642), 255. Toon unhesitatingly asserts Cotton's dependence on Brightman. (54)

24 Robert S. Paul, *The Lord Protector* (London: 1955), 59 *et passim.*

25 *Ibid.,* 251, n. 1.

26 As quoted by Paul, 279.

27 *V.R.G.,* V, 25. See 25-27 for an account of this declaration.

28 Johnson, 23 and 34.

millennial events. Their calculations were based on the principle that one day in the various periods mentioned in Daniel and Revelation was equal to one year. It became important for these expositors to find historical events from which they could date these various apocalyptic periods and thus determine the time when these periods would terminate and when a new era would begin. "Some say" that Antichrist's fall "will be about the year 1650 or 1656," said Thomas Goodwin in applying the year-day principle.[29] He accepted these dates as legitimate for the conversion of the Jews, but preferred to date Antichrist's fall at 1666.[30] Henry Archer, Goodwin's successor as pastor of the English-speaking church in Arnhem, Netherlands, made "a careful computation and comparison of Daniel with Revelation." His conclusions were virtually identical to those of Goodwin.[31] Peter Sterry, Cromwell's chaplain, dated the 1290 prophetic years of Daniel 12 : 11 and the 1335 prophetic years of Daniel 12 : 12 from the coronation of Constantine in 312. The former period expired with the coronation of James I in 1603 and the latter period of years ended as late as 1647.[32] The intervening forty-five years were years of preparation for the Commonwealth and Protectorate period. In a later work Sterry predicted "a great cataclysm" in 1656 which would be the sign of Christ's increasing rule.[33]

A second major difference from the mild millennial expectations of the first group hinges on the exegesis of the "first resurrection" mentioned in Revelation 20. In two sermons reprinted later under the Fifth Monarchy aegis in an attempt to "prove" Goodwin's allegiance to that cause,[34] Thomas Goodwin defended a physical resurrection of the saints before the millennium as the proper interpretation of that passage.[35] This position was held by virtually all followers of Mede and Alsted.

29 Goodwin, III, 72.

30 *Ibid.,* 158.

31 Louise F. Brown, *The Political Activities of the Baptists and Fifth Monarchy Men in England During the Interregnum* (Washington and London: 1912), 15. The best survey of Archer's position known to us is *V.R.G.,* V, 11-16. Koelman, 213, lists Goodwin, Archer, and Jeremiah Burroughs as the three Independents who in much earnestness revived the earlier ideas of the chiliasts. (213)

32 Peter Sterry, *The Comings Forth of Christ In the Power of his Death* (London: 1650), 10.

33 Peter Sterry, *England's Deliverance From the Northern Presbytery* (London: 1652), 44.

34 Nuttall, *The Holy Spirit . . . ,* 110. Nuttall calls it outright "pirating" of Goodwin's sermon. Koelman says Goodwin's sermon was taken over and misused by many English libertines. (216)

35 Thomas Goodwin, *A Sermon of the Fifth Monarchy* (London: 1654), 27-29; and *The World to Come* (London: 1655), 31-32. "Fifth Monarchy," of course, connoted something entirely different for Goodwin than the political program advocated by the sectarians of that name.

Representatives of this position also frequently advocated a literal or physical coming or appearance of Christ to establish the millennium. Archer said Christ would "governe as earthly *Monarches* have done," globally, in visible glory, peace, honor, and opulence.[36] He believed that Christ would come on the clouds, in his physical presence establish the reign of his saints, the center of which would be in a rebuilt Jerusalem, and return to heaven. In a milder vein, Goodwin and Mather doubted that Christ would reign physically on earth during the millennium.[37] Many advocates of a complex chiliasm expected some sort of physical appearance by Christ at the outset of the millennium, however.

Finally, those who accepted complex chiliasm stressed a literal, thousand-year millennium, an emphasis seldom mentioned by advocates of the first position we have considered.

The third group of Anglo-American millennialists defended various types of extreme or even fanatical millennialism and is relatively insignificant. They will be given brief consideration to complete our survey. They included those whose political and doctrinal positions put them, in the eyes of their contemporaries, on the fringe of the social pale. The Fifth Monarchy movement flourished in Cromwell's New Model Army.[38] As the Civil Wars progressed, the ideas of Mede, Archer, Goodwin, and other theologians and preachers took on immediacy for these Independents and Baptists who became convinced that they were God's instrument for defeating the fourth, Roman monarchy represented by the fourth beast of Daniel 7. In its place they would set up the fifth monarchy, which would be ruled by Christ and his saints. Incensed by Cromwell's rejection of its extreme views and by his increasing authoritarianism, which clearly precluded the rule of the saints, this group attempted to seize power in 1657. After a second attempt in 1661 little more was heard of this sect.

In addition to the Fifth Monarcy movement preoccupation with the Jewish motif produced several sects.[39] John Robins felt called to lead the army of one hundred forty-four thousand saints gathered from the tribes of Israel back to their homeland. His wife was convinced she would give birth to the Messiah, who would rule the blessed kingdom. In 1649 the London goldsmith Thomas Tany claimed to have received the revelation that he was a Jew of the tribe of Reuben. Then he was commissioned as a modern

---

36 Henry Archer, *The Personall Reign of Christ upon Earth* (London: 1642), 3. *V.R.G.*, V, 13-14.

37 Goodwin, *The World to Come*, 30.

38 Brown, 11-12. See also P. G. Rogers, *The Fifth Monarchy Men* (London: 1966), for a more recent survey of this sect.

39 In the second half of the seventeenth century European scholars manifested renewed interest in the Jews. Hans Joachim Schoeps, *Philosemitismus im Barock* (Tübingen: 1952), 1-3, relates the English dimension of this interest to its Continental counterpart, on which he concentrates.

Ezra to lead the Jews to their homeland and to rebuild the temple. To this end he established an encampment, arranged by tribe, for gathering the dispersed sons of Jacob. He solicited followers from as far as Holland.[40] A concoction of patriotism and millennial expectations was written by Arise Evans in 1656 and published eight years later. Directed at an Amsterdam rabbi named Menasseh Ben Israel,[41] the book urged Jews to recognize Charles II as the incarnation of the Messiah, who in the bloodless restoration to his throne would receive world dominion as Christ's vice-gerent. After the impending defeat of the Turks, twelve thousand Jews from each of the twelve tribes would march to Palestine under Charles' banner and repossess it.[42]

While the more radical movements of the third group of Anglo-American millennialists were in themselves self-contained "missionary" movements, the expectations of simple and complex millennialism evoked vigorous missionary effort in North America.

C. Mission Efforts

During this period English concern for the heathen and efforts to convert them were not restricted to Anglo-American missions in New England. English trading companies continued the policy of placing chaplains on their vessels and in their trading stockades. These men sometimes preached to the natives whom they contacted. Sir Robert Boyle, eminent scientist and devout Christian, used his position as a director of the East India Company in an attempt "to persuade it to convert the natives 'in whose countries we have flourishing factories.' "[43] He contributed to efforts aimed at distributing Scripture in the Turkish and Malayan as well as in the Irish and Welsh languages and was a pioneer in the Anglo-American missionary movement.[44] Most directors and members were more interested in profits, however, and the company chaplains were content to serve the English personnel for whom they had been appointed.

Ministers and theologians sometimes mentioned missions, as Robert Baillie, a prominent Scottish divine, and John Cotton did in their heated exchanges regarding church government and a number of other theological issues. In defending the mission zeal of the Independents against Baillie's charge to the contrary, Cotton indicated not only that New England pastors

---

40 For this information on Robins and Tany we are indebted to P. G. Rogers, *The Sixth Trumpeter* (London: 1963), 2-3.
41 *vide infra*, 58f.
42 Arise Evans, *Light for the Jews* (London: 1664).
43 Kellaway, 50.
44 *D.N.B.*, VI, 120.

Thomas Hooker and Thomas Shepard had written on effectual calling, justification by faith, and the soul's preparation for Christ, but that New England had sent the Reverends Knolles, Thompson, and James to convert the Indians of Virginia. Only unforeseen reverses have prevented New England from responding to a call from the Caribbean islands for ministers, continued Cotton.[45] John Oxenbridge argued for the propagation of Christianity by colonization in *A Seasonable Proposition of Propagating the Gospel by Christian Colonies in the Continent of Guaiana*.[46] But when a complete inventory of English efforts is made, it becomes apparent that the Indians of New England were the focus of English evangelism and that this was made possible by Anglo-American co-operation.

Individual New England pastors initiated evangelization of the Indians. Banished from Massachusetts Bay colony for refusing to acknowledge the spiritual jurisdiction of the civil magistrate, Roger Williams moved south, where he established close contact with the Narragansett Indians and gained unusual proficiency in the Algonquian language. In 1643 he published a handbook for helping the English learn that tongue. He hoped that it would be used by "the *Father* of *Mercies* to spread civilitie, (and in his owne most holy season) *Christianitie*."[47] Williams himself preached to the Narragansetts,[48] though he never made a concerted effort to establish a mission among them. More substantial work was begun by Thomas Mayhew after he and his father purchased the island of Martha's Vineyard off the southern coast of Cape Cod in 1641. A Congregational minister, Mayhew began learning the natives' language and gathering them into several groups around the densely populated island for preaching services. Between 1643, when he was gladdened with his first inquirer, and 1650 Mayhew had received twenty-two converts and catechized dozens of other Indians.[49] His place in the foremost American colony and the consequent attention his indefatigable work among the Indians received in New England propaganda have guaranteed for John Eliot his title as "Apostle to the Indians." He engaged the services of a clever young Indian as language teacher and interpreter and by the autumn of 1646 was able to conduct worship services in Algonquian in an Indian village. Soon he began to address the Indians of a second village. Several interested colleagues accompanied him and by assuming some of his regular pastoral responsibilities allowed him to preach in native settlements on a regular basis.

45 John Cotton, *The Way of Congregational Churches Cleared* (London: 1648), 75-77.

46 The title page of Oxenbridge's book gives no place or date for its publication. *D.N.B.*, XLIII, 8, suggests that it may have appeared in London in 1670.

47 Roger Williams, *A Key into the Language of America* (London: 1643), A3r.

48 Vaughan, 302.

49 *Ibid.*, 244.

The work of these pioneers was soon publicized in both New and Old England. When a synod convened in Cambridge in the summer of 1647, Eliot and his Indians demonstrated a service in Algonquian for the incredulous delegates. A series of eleven booklets now known collectively as the Eliot tracts was published in London between 1643 and 1671 to stimulate interest and support for mission work.[50] The first tract contained information on Harvard College as well as on the Indians and was edited by the Massachusetts colonial agents in London. The second, third, and fourth were devoted solely to reporting on mission work and were used by Edward Winslow, a new agent, to win a Parliamentary bill in 1649 establishing a missionary society. Officially known as The President and Society for propagation of the Gospel in New England, at the Restoration it was expanded and was given a new charter as the Company for Propagacion of the Gospell in New England.[51] The New England Company, as we shall refer to the body, was the first Protestant missionary society, and it gave to New England missions the secure financial basis which ensured their growth and stability.

In 1650 New England missions entered an era of expansion. Not only did interest in the cause spread through the wealthy Independent and Presbyterian merchants who served on the society in London and through the prominent commissioners who regulated her affairs in the colonies, but within a few short years many men in all the New England colonies were involved in missions and served that cause in a variety of capacities. Undoubtedly exaggerating, Robert Vaughan boldly states, "A combined roster of laborers in missionary and educational enterprises for the Indians would include almost every prominent name in Puritan New England." [52]

50 [Anonymous], *New Englands first fruits* (London: 1643); [Anonymous], *The Day-Breaking if not The Sun-Rising of the Gospell with the Indians in New England* (London: 1647); Thomas Shepard (ed.), *The Clear Sun-Shine of the Gospel Breaking Forth upon the Indians of New England* (London: 1648); Edward Winslow (ed.), *The Glorious Progress of the Gospel amongst the Indians in New England* (London: 1649); Henry Whitfield (ed.), *The Light appearing more and more towards the perfect Day* (London: 1651); Henry Whitfield (ed.), *Strength out of Weakness; or a Glorious Manifestation Of the further Progresse of the Gospell amongst the Indians in New England* (London: 1652); John Eliot and Thomas Mayhew, *Tears of Repentance. Or, A further Narrative of the Progress of the Gospel amongst the Indians in New England* (London: 1653); John Eliot, *A Late and Further Manifestation of the Progress of the Gospel amongst the Indians in New-England* (London: 1655); John Eliot, *A further Accompt of the Progresse of the Gospel amongst the Indians in New-England* (London: 1659); John Eliot, *A further Account of the progress of the Gospel Amongst the Indians in New England* (London: 1660); John Eliot, *A Brief Narrative of the Progress of the Gospel amongst the* Indians in New-England, *in the Year 1670* (London: 1671). Rooy, 176-220, gives a summary of the content of these tracts. We follow him in including the first tract in this series.

51 These official names are taken from Kellaway, 15 and 46.

52 Vaughan, 289.

The scope of the work also broadened. Like Williams, Eliot believed that the Indians had to "be *civilized* ere they could be Christianized," [53] and this commonly accepted principle was the basis of a comprehensive mission program. Inquirers or "praying Indians" were gathered into "praying towns" where they could be weaned from pagan culture and instructed in the rudiments of Christianity. Schools were erected in each of the six praying towns established in Massachusetts Bay before 1665. [54] Eliot completed his translation of the Bible in 1658. A number of Indian youth were enrolled at Harvard. The basic principles of agriculture and of Puritan civil and ecclesiastical government were taught. The goal through all these efforts, however, was the formation of covenanted native churches. To this end continual concern for the level of the Indians' faith was manifested, as is evidenced from the predominant place given to the Indians' confessions in the Eliot tracts of the 1650's.

Through these various efforts Anglo-American missions steadily expanded. Riding the crest of this success, Eliot wrote the English Presbyterian Richard Baxter in 1671,

> ...here be greater motions about the Indians y^n ever were since I began to teach y^m. I never found such violent opposition by Satan; and yet the L(or)d doth outwork him in all, & the Kingd(o)me of Christ doth spread and rise the more by his so violent opposition. [55]

In 1674 missionary Daniel Gookin reported that at the peak of the work on Martha's Vineyard there had been over fourteen hundred praying Indians, and in Massachusetts Bay, fourteen praying towns, two churches, and eleven hundred "souls yielding obedience to the gospel." [56] In that year Richard Bourne, Plymouth missionary, reported to Gookin that the eight praying centers in Plymouth sheltered four hundred ninety-seven praying Indians. [57] While Gookin claimed that there were thirty-six hundred [58] Christian Indians in New England, it is Vaughan's judgment that the total number just prior to the outbreak of King Philip's War approached twenty-five hundred, or twenty percent of the native population. [59]

Early in the summer of 1675, for motives still being debated by histori-

---

53 C. Mather, I, 560. Also see *The Day-Breaking* . . . , 16.

54 Vaughan, 285-286.

55 F. J. Powicke (ed.), *Some Unpublished Correspondence of the Reverend Richard Baxter and the Reverend John Eliot, the Apostle of the American Indians, 1656-1682* (Manchester: 1931), 62.

56 Daniel Gookin, *Historical Collections of the Indians in New England,* James Freeman (ed.) *(Collections of the Massachusetts Historical Society,* Series I, vol. I; Boston: 1792), 195.

57 Vaughan, 299.

58 Kellaway, 116.

59 Vaughan, 303.

ans,[60] the Wampanoag sachem known as King Philip and his allies from three other Indian tribes attacked the colonists and their Indian allies. In a savage, year-long war in which an estimated five thousand Indians and ten per cent of the colonial forces were killed,[61] over thirty years of mission work was damaged irreparably. "I must change my ditty now," wrote Eliot to Boyle in October, 1675. "I have much to write of lamentation over ye work of Christ among o^r praying Indians, of wch God hath called you to be nursing Fathers." [62] Hundreds of Christian Indians were killed in the war and countless others died from hunger and exposure suffered on Deer Island in Boston Bay, onto which they had been herded by apprehensive colonists. Only four of the fourteen praying towns survived the conflict. Although Eliot began the work anew in his mid-seventies, it never again achieved the scale in New England which had been reached by 1675.

D. *Missions and Millennial Expectations*

Taken collectively, millennial expectations were a prominent theological theme and created a strong motive for Anglo-American missionary efforts during the period covered by the present chapter. In the first section of the ensuing discussion we shall demonstrate the scope and character of these expectations in the thought of the strongest supporters of New England missions. Because the Eliot tracts were the missionary forum of these men, it becomes apparent that the eschatological texts found on the tracts' title pages were intended to convey the millennial expectations of the editors. These texts, which set the tone of the tracts and constructed the framework in which mission effort was seen, are examined in section two. Millennial expectations were among the most powerful arguments mustered to gain Parliamentary legislation supporting missions. The role of these expectations, particularly the hope for the imminent conversion of the Jews, in this campaign to obtain government funds will be analyzed in section three. In section four we shall treat the origin and influence of the theory that descendants of the ten lost tribes of Israel were to be found among the American Indians. John Eliot's interest in and the later history of that theory will be indicated in section five. But the more comprehensive and more basic expectations of the coming of Christ's kingdom as articulated by Eliot were ultimately of more significance in the rise of Anglo-American missions. His kingdom theology is the subject of the last section of this chapter.

60   *Ibid.*, 310-312, for a discussion of the theories involved.
61   *Ibid.*, 320.
62   John W. Ford (ed.), *New England Company: Letters from Eliot and Others, 1657-1714* (London: 1897), 52-53.

1. *Supporters of missions*

A cursory survey of the staunchest supporters of the budding mission work in New England yields at least a score of the most prominent advocates of simple and complex millennialism. The dedication to Parliament and the address to the reader of the 1648 Eliot tract, which was written by Thomas Shepard, were endorsed by twelve ministers, including both Presbyterians and Independents: Stephen Marshall, Jeremiah Whitaker, Edmund Calamy, William Greenhill, John Downame, Philip Nye, Sidrach Simpson, William Carter, Thomas Goodwin, Thomas Case, Simeon Ashe, and Samuel Bolton.[63] "To the Reader" in *Strength out of Weakness,* which was the sixth Eliot tract and which was compiled by Henry Whitfield in 1652, was signed by twelve Independents and six Presbyterians: William Gouge, Thomas Goodwin, Lazarus Seaman, John Owen, Edmund Calamy, Joseph Caryl, Jeremiah Whitaker, William Greenhill, George Griffith, Henry Whitfield, William Spurstow, William Bridge, Simeon Ashe, Sidrach Simpson, William Strong, Philip Nye, William Carter, and Ralph Venning.[64]

The influential writings of two of these men, Owen and Goodwin, have been treated in some detail in our survey of millennial views of this period.[65] The still earlier interest of Downhame and Gouge in millennial expectations has been indicated in the previous chapter.[66]

Several others delivered important millennial sermons prior to their endorsement of these tracts. These sermons merit consideration here. Not only do they demonstrate the wider concern of these signers with millennial issues, but they also represent a larger body of sermons which instilled in English politicians a sense of their instrumentality in bringing about the millennium, a consciousness to which the Eliot tracts appealed in requesting financial support for missions.

In 1641 William Bridge captured the exuberant hope of the hour in a sermon to Commons on Revelation 14 : 8, "a short, and sweet prophecy of Rome's ruin and destruction."[67] Seven years later events had proceeded to a point enabling him to broach the subject of "the kingdom and coming of Christ"[68] before that august group. Regaling Commons with visions of "helping Christ to his throne,"[69] whose visible coming on the clouds would cause the Jews and the fulness of the Gentiles to acknowledge him, and,

---

63 Shepard, alv.
64 Whitfield, *Strength out of Weakness* . . . , A6r.
65 *vide supra,* 37-42.
66 *vide supra,* 28-29.
67 William Bridge, "Babylon's Downfall," *The Works* (London: 1845), IV, 292.
68 William Bridge, "Christ's Coming Is at Our Midnight," *ibid.,* 404.
69 *Ibid.*

as Bridge judged, "is not far off," [70] the preacher reinforced John Winslow's appeal to Parliament for financial aid for New England missions. The appeal had been referred to a Parliamentary committee exactly two months earlier. While the Lord will not reign physically on earth for a thousand years because the "saints cannot spare him out of heaven so long," [71] his "*regnum potentiae*" will in those days be "from sea to sea." [72]

From the time he had published two works dealing with millennial expectations,[73] the renowned Presbyterian William Gouge had been interested in the conversion of Israel in the latter days of history. By the time he addressed the House of Lords in Westminster Abbey in 1645, he had placed this event in the context of history's final events. Dividing history into six periods or "days" followed by the seventh day or eternal Sabbath, Gouge applied his text to the sixth, which extends from Christ's ascension to his coming as final judge. For this period God promised through Ezekiel, "'I will doe better unto you then at your beginnings.'" [74] Recent events indicated to Gouge that history was proceeding according to God's plan. England had experienced God's increasing goodness under Edward III, Wycliffe, Henry VIII, Edward VI, and Elizabeth I. And now "yet another reformation," this one in church government, has begun, demonstrating the truth of God's promise.[75] Ezekiel's promise as well as that recorded in II Corinthians 5 : 17, "'Behold, all things are become new,'" [76] have not yet been completed, however. Indeed, Gouge spoke of "more particular promises concerning a future glory of the Christian Church" found in the Old Testament prophecies, the words of Christ and of his apostles, and especially in Revelation.[77] These do not apply to the world to come [78] but to the church's "glorious estate" before the day of judgment.[79] This "estate" will be characterized by the calling and conversion of the Jews and the fulness of the Gentiles into one, visible church.[80] Gouge believed with his fellow Puritans that he was living in or near the full brightness of the gospel day, when the

---

70 *Ibid.*, 421.

71 *Ibid.*, 409.

72 *Ibid.*, 410.

73 Neither work was written by Gouge, and both were printed without giving the authors' names. The first was *An Exposition of the Song of Solomon: called Canticles* (London: 1615) and was "perused and published by William Gouge." (A2r) For reflections on the Jews see 123f. The second work was *The Worlds Restauration. vide supra*, 28-29.

74 William Gouge, *The Progresse of Divine Providence* (London: 1645), 5. Gouge's reference is to Ez. 36 : 11.

75 *Ibid.*, 35.

76 *Ibid.*, 11.

77 *Ibid.*, 29.

78 *Ibid.*, 11.

79 *Ibid.*, 29.

80 *Ibid.*, 29-31.

gospel would be preached to men everywhere. God had reserved for them in "these later times . . . much matter of gratulation." [81] Where as Zechariah and Simeon had rejoiced to see the salvation of God (Luke 1 : 69; 2 : 30), "these old men saw but the Sunne-rising of the Gospel. We see it shining forth in the full brightnesse thereof." [82]

On May 17, 1648, the same day on which Bridge was addressing the House of Lords, his fellow Independent William Strong was preaching to the Lord Mayor and Aldermen of London.[83] He emphasized the triumph of the church over all her enemies. Her warfare will endure "till towards the end of the first 6000. years of the World." [84] Then "another condition" will prevail, which "may wel be stiled Triumphant and glorious." [85] Christ will establish dominion over land and sea (Revelation 10 : 5-6), giving his "'kingdom and dominion . . . unto the Saints of the most High.'" [86] The "last dayes" will be marked on the one hand by the fall of Rome, perfect reformation, and the church's deliverance from persecuting monarchies, and on the other hand by the most bitter opposition the devil can muster.[87] To his hearers in 1648 these prophecies were clearly recognizable in current events: episcopacy had given way to a truly reformed church, the power of the king was rapidly being depleted, and the devil was showing his tenacious resistance in the turmoil and rebellion in which England seethed. In this situation Strong came not with "ordinary supports" of God's providence and of his love for his children, but with those which were "more proper and peculiar to the enemies and sufferings of the last times, the cup that God hath reserved for you." [88] His consolation was that "these shalbe the last great suffrings of the saints, and they shalbe but short." [89] Then will come all the glorious events promised for the millennium:[90] the cessation of all persecution of the church, Christ's dominion over all kingdoms, the triumph of God's redemption over the sins of the saints, the impossibility of papacy's being restored, the indestructibility of the Reformed churches, the manifestation of God's special claim on his saints, and the final and complete destruction of God's enemies.[91] The ten kingdoms which constitute

81 *Ibid.*, 35-36.
82 *Ibid.*, 36.
83 The occasion was a day of thanksgiving for the victory of Col. Horton's forces in Wales.
84 William Strong, *The Vengeance of the Temple* (London: 1648), 1.
85 *Ibid.*
86 *Ibid.*
87 *Ibid.*, 18-19.
88 *Ibid.*, 42.
89 *Ibid.*
90 Although he does not here speak of this period as the millennium, earlier in his sermon he alluded to it as "the *thousand yeares* of the Churches Peace and glory." *Ibid.*, 26.
91 *Ibid.*, 42-46.

his enemies will be overcome not by physical force or destruction, but by "conversion." [92] The spiritual power, prayers, and praises of the saints are the weapons which will be employed in Christ's ultimate victory.[93]

Whether they expressed it in terms of Christ's reign, the renewal of all things, or the defeat of Christ's enemies, Bridge, Gouge, and Strong concurred on the nearness of the promised day of glory for the church. In this other signers of the Eliot tracts agreed with them. William Greenhill's millennialism was expressed some twenty years later in his preface to Increase Mather's study on Israel's conversion. Joseph Caryl and Jeremiah Whitaker endorsed the millennialism of Strong's Clavis Apocalyptica in the prefaces which they wrote for it in 1653. That same year Strong also addressed the Nominated Parliament on "State Prosperitie...," in which he expressed doubt concerning Christ's rule on earth in person during the millennium. He argued that the saints will be entrusted with this rule.[94] Strong preached to the Lord Mayor and Aldermen of London again in 1654, this time calling his hearers to separate themselves from "mystical Babylon" in a sermon Geoffrey Nuttall judges to be in the general tradition of John Jewel's homilies against Antichrist.[95]

The character of the pieces which they signed indicates that the other signers of the Eliot tracts were also advocates of a mild millennialism. The two pieces in Shepard's tract contain identical thought on this point. The signers underscored for Parliament the degeneracy of the natives and the necessity of giving the Indians English help. In his providence God had placed Englishmen in America. Driven there by Laudian cruelty, they had become God's "*instruments* to draw soules to him," to carry out "some farther Arrand" for their heavenly Father.[96] He has indicated this errand by "giving them some *Bunches* of Grapes, some *Clusters* of Figs in *earnest* of the prosperous *successe*" of their labor among these Indian "*outcasts*." [97] In the address to the reader the image of first fruits as signs of a successful harvest is replaced by that of the day-break which promises a bright day. Former tracts recorded the "*dawnings* of light, after a long and black night of darkness." [98] Now "*the sun is up*," and will scatter the "thick clouds of darknesse" and shine "brighter and brighter *till it come to a perfect day*." [99] The tract was designed to encourage the reader to wait and to pray for the accomplishment of this harvest, this bright day. The signers were

92 *Ibid.,* 46.
93 *Ibid.,* 31-35.
94 Nuttall, *Visible Saints,* 151. Nuttall emphasizes several of Strong's sermons included in his *Thirty-one Select Sermons* (London: 1656).
95 *Ibid.,* 58.
96 Shepard, [A4r-A4v].
97 *Ibid.,* [A4v].
98 *Ibid.,* a2r.
99 *Ibid.*

confident that the longed-for day would come. Not only are the ends of the earth promised to Christ for his possession, but he has sent his ministers to prepare for his coming. "Where the *Ministry* is the *Harbinger* and goes before, Christ and *Grace* will certainly follow after."[100] The writers gave a stirring vision of that perfect day, couched in the spirit and words of prophetic hope:

> This little we see is *something* in hand, to *earnest* to us those things which are in hope; something in *possession*, to assure us of the rest in promise, when the ends of the earth shall see his glory, and 'the King-domes of the world shall become the Kingdomes of the Lord and his Christ, when hee shall have Dominion from Sea to Sea, and they that dwell in the wildernesse shall bow before him.' And if the *dawn* of the *morning* be so delightfull, what will the clear day be? If the *first fruits* be so precious, what wil the *whole harvest* be? if some *beginnings* be so ful of joy, what will it be when God shall *perform* his *whole* work, when 'the whole earth shall be full of the knowledge of the Lord, as the waters cover the Sea,' and East and West shal sing together the song of the Lamb?[101]

Parliament, merchants, and all other Englishmen were urged to aid this beginning work in any way they could.

The epistle "To the Reader" in Whitfield's collection of letters issued four years later is even more explicitly millennial. It was asserted that these letters show the reader that Christ is going out to the ends of the earth as a light to the Gentiles — an incontrovertible fulfillment of Isaiah 49 : 6.[102] Although God's people have been impressed by Christ's riding forth on a red horse, destroying his enemies — undoubtedly a reference to the Roundheads' defeats of royalist forces and Scottish troops — his riding forth on a white horse to convert the heathen is even more impressive.[103] The converting work of Christ as depicted in this tract was commended to the readers in six points or thoughts. 1) This work is enlarging Christ's kingdom, fulfilling the promises made by the Father to the Son that all kingdoms of the earth will be his. 2) The work propagates Christ's gospel, the lifted scepter which draws the nations to their King. 3) The souls of the elect whom God has among these people are being rescued from the devil. 4) This work is completing the first fulness of the Gentiles. Under this point the writers cited their reliance upon Brightman and Mede,[104] the only post-Reformation commentators acknowledged in the epistle. 5) The Lord is prospering the New England work. 6) These *"first fruits"* of the Indians and this "day of

---

100 *Ibid.,* [A4v].
101 *Ibid.,* [A4v-alr].
102 Whitfield, *Strength out of Weakness...,* A4r.
103 *Ibid.;* see Rev. 6 : 2-4.
104 *Ibid.,* A5r.

small things" are not to be despised, for "the Lord hath opened a *great doore*, which we hope Satan shall never be able any more to shut." [105] In a final appeal for prayers and contributions for the work the writers referred to it as "one of the greatest workes that hath been upon the wheele in this latter age." [106]

The millennial context in which these signers of Whitfield's introductory epistle saw missions and on which they based their appeal for support was compelling not only for themselves and for their contemporaries but also for the staunch ally of Anglo-American missions of fifty years later, Samuel Sewall. Summarizing the contents of this epistle in his own book, he rejoiced that "there are no less than Six times Three very Credible Witnesses" [107] who testify that the conversions among the Indians fulfill the "glorious Prophecies" of Psalm 72 : 8 and Isaiah 49 : 6.

The tone that these supporters set for the mission work was sounded throughout the Commonwealth and Protectorate period. Joseph Caryl, who was a leading Independent and a good friend of Owen, proved to be one of the strongest campaigners for missions. His address "To the Reader" in the 1655 Eliot tract and his preface to the 1660 Eliot tract both have millennial overtones. In the former piece he spoke to all who "pray and wait" for the increase of Christ's kingdom to "the ends of the Earth." [108] Christ's glory is "increasing," as the spread of the gospel in New England shows.[109] Caryl told his readers that they had helped to realize the fulfillment of Biblical prophecies regarding this day.[110] In both pieces he emphasized that the converted Indians are only "first fruits" of a greater harvest.[111] The work of conversion among the Indians is related to "the work of Grace" in the lives of Englishmen and in the churches of England. The Indian example should spur them to holiness and to the practice of the presence of Christ. Then the new Jerusalem will descend from heaven. This is "the great thing" for which Caryl and his contemporaries, "upon whom the ends of the world are come," should "pray, endeavour and wait." [112] The founding of the New England Company, therefore, was a concrete step in realizing the climax of history, indicated Caryl.

Another introductory piece to the 1655 Eliot tract was signed by Whitfield, Ashe, Calamy, and John Arthur. Like Caryl they solicited prayers and contributions for the "finishing and perfecting of this blessed and glorious

---

105 *Ibid.,* A5v. These six points are given on A4r-A5v.
106 *Ibid.,* A6r.
107 Sewall, 46.
108 Eliot, *A Late and Further Manifestation . . . ,* "To the Reader," [A3r].
109 *Ibid.*
110 *Ibid.*
111 *Ibid.,* and Eliot, *A further Account . . . ,* A2v.
112 Eliot, *A further Account . . . ,* A4v.

undertaking." [113] This eschatologically defined goal of missions had theological, soteriological, and Christological moments for these men, since missions, they said, are conducive to "the Glory of God, the Salvation of soules, and the Inlargement of the Kingdome of Christ upon Earth." [114]

Edward Reynolds, who had been a Westminster divine and was preferred as Bishop of Norwich after the Restoration, wrote "To the Reader" in the 1659 Eliot tract. His prominence enhances the significance of his opening statement for our study.

> As it is the Ardent prayer of all that love the Lord Jesus in sincerity, that his Kingdome may be enlarged, and the glorious light of the *Gospell* may shine forth into all Na ions [*sic*], that all the ends of the world may see the salvation of our God, that the *Stone* cut out without hands may become so great a mountaine as to fill the Earth, that the *Idols* may be *utterly abolished,* and the *Gods of the Earth famished,* and that all the Isles of the Heathen may worship the only true God . . . , [115]

missions in New England should be given English support. As Owen had earlier, Reynolds read recent events as the shakings of the nations. These were "harbingers of the more glorious manifestations of Christ," [116] and had brought men to New England to sow the "seeds of the *Everlasting Gospel.*" [117]

Support for the work did not come only from England. In 1646 Richard Mather, who was an illustrious first generation New England divine, accompanied Eliot on one of his early visits to the Indians.[118] Mather saw the initial years of success in the context of Biblical promises for the growth of Christ's kingdom, as his opening sentences to the readers of the 1653 Eliot tract demonstrate.

---

113 Eliot, *A Late and Further Manifestation . . . ,* [A2r].

114 *Ibid.*

115 Reynolds, A2r. This paragraph contains references to no fewer than six passages: Ps. 63 : 3-5; 22 : 27; 98 : 3; Dan. 2 : 35; Isa. 2 : 18; Zeph. 2 : 11. Kellaway relates the New England Company's decision to publish the tract and their employment of Reynolds as editor as typical of the process by which other tracts were published. (23-24)

116 Reynolds, A2r.

117 *Ibid.* This is proof of the association of the concept *"Evangelium Aeternum"* with Anglo-American missions prior to Cotton Mather, an association Ernst Benz speculates might have existed. "Ecumenical Relations Between Boston Puritanism and German Pietism: Cotton Mather and August Hermann Francke," *Harvard Theological Review,* LIV, 1961, 173, n. 15. We have found no extended discussion of the missionary implications of this concept prior to Mather, however, and conclude that no more significance should be attached to it than to any of the many Biblical figures used to express contemporary hope for the glorious day.

118 Kellaway, 84.

The Amplitude, and large Extent of the Kingdom of Jesus Christ upon Earth, when 'the Heathen shall be his Inheritance, and the uttermost parts of the Earth his Possession; and when all Kings shall fall down unto him, and all Nations do him service, all contrary Kingdoms and Powers being broken in pieces and destroyed,' is a thing plainly and plentifully foretold and promised in the Holy Scriptures; *Psal.* 2.8 and 22.27. and 72.11. and 86.9. *Dan.* 2.35. 44, 45. and 7.26,27. *Zech.* 14.9.[119]

Mather conceded that neither he nor his fathers had seen the fulfillment of these promises, for paganism and opposition to Christ had been dominant. But "'the time is coming, when things shall not thus continue, but be greatly changed and altered'" in accordance with God's promises.[120] Christians who have desired and prayed for this day will rejoice when reading the ensuing Indian confessions and accounts of work among these pagans, he promised. "For hereby it will appear, That the Kingdom of the Lord Jesus ... is now beginning to be set up where it never was before." [121] God will not fail to complete the work now begun. Romans 11 teaches that God's mercy to the Gentiles "shall in time provoke the Jews" to jealousy and conversion.[122] Two subsequent generations of Mathers saw and supported Anglo-American missions in millennial terms.

We see, therefore, that many leading Puritans in England and America wrote and endorsed missionary propaganda in the 1640's and 1650's. Their support was predicated on the belief that through missions the glorious gospel day would dawn. It should be noted that this faith was based on many Old and New Testament passages of hope and not on a few select verses. Many Biblical images and figures of speech were used to describe the period that had already begun. After 1660, however, eschatological hope waned and the majority of these men, or those of them still alive, fell silent on the subject of missions and the millennium.[123]

2. Title page texts

That the hope for the latter days was the compelling motive behind Anglo-American missions in this period is evident not only from the dedicatory epistles and addresses to the readers but also from the Scripture texts displayed on the title pages of the Eliot tracts. These texts defined the perspective in which the work was seen. They were chosen for the hope

119 Eliot and Mayhew, B3r.
120 *Ibid.*
121 *Ibid.,* B3v.
122 *Ibid.,* C4r.
123 Nuttall notes that "especially between 1640 and 1660" millennial ideas abounded. *Visible Saints,* 157.

and promise which they contained for missions. Selected by the same men whose views we have just been considering, these texts must be understood in the millennial terms in which the tract editors and writers understood them if we are to gain a true conception of the impulse behind Anglo-American missions.

A notable development is discernible in the choice of texts. The texts of the early tracts emphasized the smallness of the beginnings of missions as boding something greater. "'And though thy beginnings be small, thy latter end shall greatly encrease'" (Job 8 : 7) and "'Who hath despised the Day of small things'" (Zachariah 4 : 10) [124] define the context in which New England efforts were discussed in 1643. The latter text also appeared on the title page of the 1647 tract, along with Matthew 13 : 13 and 33, which compare the kingdom of heaven to a grain of mustard seed and to leaven.[125] Although Shepard's tract of 1648 has no title page texts, the signers' two prefatory addresses are freighted with prophetic and apocalyptic imagery, terms, and quotations, as we have seen. These place greater emphasis on the character of the glorious day than the previous tracts. Winslow selected a text with a similar slant in 1649. It showed that the hope attached to Anglo-American missions had heightened: "'From the rising of the Sun, even unto the going down of the same, my Name shall be great among the Gentiles . . .'" (Malachi 1 : 11).[126] It was undoubtedly chosen because of Eliot's adaptation of it to the Indians, as related in one of his letters included in the tract. He preached on the text to the natives, reading it, "' . . . thy name shall be great among the Indians. . . .'"[127] Zephaniah 2 : 11 stresses the triumph of true worship over the entire world in the eschaton. It set the tone for Whitfield's 1651 tract: "'The Lord will famish all the gods of the earth, and men shall worship him, every one from his place, even all the Iles of the Heathen.'"[128] To the eighteen signers of the 1652 tract New England's dependence on England for prayer and support in her mission efforts made her appear as their "little sister" of Song of Solomon 8 : 8.[129] Apparently the day when God was speaking for America had arrived. By England's help she would become a beautiful bride. Hence Whitfield adopted the text as the theme of the tract: "'Wee have a little Sister, and she hath no breasts: what shall we doe for our Sister, in the day that she shall be spoken for?'"[130] Eliot and Mayhew, closer to the work than their English sponsors, realized that even in 1653 the work was still in its

124 *New Englands first fruits*, title page.
125 *The Day-Breaking* . . . , title page.
126 Winslow, title page.
127 *Ibid.*, 9.
128 Whitfield, *The Light appearing* . . . , title page.
129 Whitfield, *Strength out of Weakness* . . . , A6r.
130 *Ibid.*, title page.

beginning stages. Yet there was cause enough for hope for the future, for
" 'A bruised Reed shall he not break, and the smoking Flax, shall he not
quench.' " [131]

Although the subsequent Eliot tracts do not contain title page texts, they
are pervaded by the millennial expectations of the earlier tracts, for they
are replete with the same references to the apocalyptic and prophetic
passages on which this eschatology rested. Only Eliot's brief letter which
comprised the 1671 tract is an exception to this generalization.

3. Edward Winslow, John Dury, and the New England Company

Late in the 1640's millennial expectations were adduced by two persistent
defenders of missions to procure the stable basis which the fledgling missionary efforts required. The expectation of the imminent conversion of the
Jews was prominent in appeals for financial assistance from the English
Parliament. It was Edward Winslow, whom in 1646 the Massachusetts
General Assembly had appointed as its colonial agent in London, who kept
these appeals alive.

William Kellaway's argument for Winslow's carrying the manuscript of
the second Eliot tract with him to London and seeing to its publication is
convincing.[132] When the manuscript of the third Eliot tract, the work of
Shepard, arrived in London the following year, Winslow not only assumed
responsibility for its publication but also secured the endorsement — as we
have noted earlier — of twelve Presbyterian and Independent clergymen
for the work. These men signed the dedicatory address to Parliament and
the address to the English reading public, which were characterized by the
millennial expectations of the day.[133] The former is an outright solicitation
for Parliamentary support, an appeal Winslow pressed personally among
his many M.P. acquaintances. After Parliament responded by considering
the appeal and by referring it to committee for study and recommendations
on March 17, 1648, Winslow's advice to the committee influenced the final
form of the bill. However, for well over a year the proposal lay dormant.
Fifteen months after Parliament's initial action on the matter Winslow
published a collection of letters from Eliot and Mayhew geared to refresh
the M.P.'s memories and to revive their slackened concern. Entitled *The*

---

131   Eliot and Mayhew, title page.
132   Kellaway, 11.
133   Kellaway, 12, attributes both of these pieces to the twelve signers. So does
Rooy, 186-187. The internal evidence would warrant this conclusion not only because
of its millennial tone but also because of its jeremiad on English degeneracy and its
praise of New England's "prospects." Coming from either Shepard or Winslow this
would constitute a chauvinism hardly calculated to win the desired support of Englishmen.

Glorious Progress of the Gospel amongst the Indians in New England, this was the fourth Eliot tract. Because it was the crucial factor in winning the bill which established the New England Company, the millennial arguments it presented are worthy of closer consideration.

The millennial expectations present in Winslow's new tract were basically the same as those which had appeared in the earlier tracts. A significantly new element, however, was the theory that among the American Indians were descendants of the ten lost tribes of Israel. The source of this theory in the new tract can be traced to Thomas Thorowgood, a delegate to the Westminster Assembly who had been studying the question of the origin of the American Indians for a number of years. His interest in the subject had been revived by the debates regarding missions which Winslow had stimulated in the Long Parliament. By 1648 Thorowgood had written his speculations for publication.[134] He sent the proofs of the first sections of his book to his friend and fellow delegate to the Assembly, the peripatetic ecumenist John Dury.

Upon reading Thorowgood's proofs Dury remembered an account of Antonio de Montezinos which he had heard when in The Hague four years earlier. De Montezinos was a Portugese Jew who claimed to have had contact with a South American tribe which engaged in Jewish rites, including the recitation of the Shema. Not only had De Montezinos related his discovery to the Amsterdam rabbi Menasseh Ben Israel, but he had asserted its veracity under an oath taken before the synagogue in Amsterdam. According to Lucien Wolf Dury wrote to Menasseh Ben Israel for confirmation of the De Montezinos incident already in 1648.[135] A series of letters was exchanged between the two men, and the rabbi's initial confirmation arrived in time for mention in Winslow's tract, published in June of 1649. Aside from stimulating Menasseh Ben Israel to use millennial arguments in his eventually not unsuccessful plea for the revocation of Edward I's ban ejecting Jews from England, Dury's request produced the proof for the Thorowgood thesis which he sought.

Whether Dury and Thorowgood together contacted Winslow, or whether one of them initially approached the New Englander alone, or whether Winslow, hearing of Thorowgood's study, inquired about it from Thorowgood or Dury, is uncertain. Their respective activities brought all three men into the Whitehall-Westminster area with great frequency, where interest in one another's work would have provided sufficient opportunities for such

134 Thomas Thorowgood, *Jews in America, or Probabilities, that those Indians are Judaical, made more probable by some Additionals to the Former Conjectures* (London: 1660), 26.

135 We are indebted to Wolf for many of these facts, xxiv-xxvii. An account of De Montezinos' experiences can also be found in Ben Israel's "The Hope of Israel."

contact. Several references in the Eliot tracts hint at personal contact between Dury and Winslow, as will become evident in the course of the ensuing discussion. In any case, the latest that Winslow could have become aware of Thorowgood's work was late in 1648, the year when Dury received the proofs of the book for perusal. This is verifiable from Eliot's correspondence with Winslow. Winslow had written Eliot of Thorowgood's work. This letter apparently had not reached Eliot by December 2, 1648, for in the response Eliot addressed to Winslow on that date, he made no mention of the Thorowgood thesis.[136] His next letter to Winslow did. It was written on May 8, 1649 and was carried to England by Henry Whitfield, in whose tract it appeared in 1651.

About the time Eliot was responding to his letter, Winslow published *The Glorious Progress of the Gospel amongst the Indians in New England.* As already noted, unlike any of the previous Eliot tracts, this one demonstrated strong preoccupation with Thorowgood's theory and showed Winslow's continued infatuation with it after he had written Eliot. After recounting his reasons for publishing this collection of letters, his dedicatory epistle to Parliament immediately broached the problem of the Indians' origin.

> There are two great questions Right Honourable, which have much troubled ancient and modern writers, and men of greatest depth and ability to resolve: the first, what became of the ten Tribes of Israel, that were carried into Captivity by the King of Siria, when their own Countrey and Cities were planted and filled with strangers? The second is, what Family, Tribe, Kindred, or people it was that first planted, and afterwards filled that vast and long unknown Countrey of America? [137]

Winslow did not only pose the questions. He indicated that a London minister, whom we know to be Dury, had written Menasseh Ben Israel and had received at least one response from the Amsterdam rabbi.[138] Winslow said,

---

136 Along with two earlier letters from Eliot and one from Mayhew, Eliot's letter of Dec. 2, 1648 was published by Winslow the following May in *The Glorious Progress* ....

137 Winslow, A3v.

138 Ben Israel's response referred to by Winslow pre-dates his letters mentioned by G. H. Turnbull in his account of Hartlib's papers, *Hartlib, Dury and Comenius* (London: 1947). Turnbull speaks of "three letters to Dury from Menasseh Ben Israel, written from Amsterdam between November 1649 and July 1650...." (262) The November letter was published in Thorowgood's *Iewes in America, or Probabilities that the Americans are of that Race* (London: 1650), 129-139, contained an extensive account of De Montezinos, and closed with the cryptic note, "J. Dury Received this at London, 27 of Novem. 1649." (139)

> Now however I confesse questions are sooner asked then resolved, yet let me acpuaint [sic] your Honors, that a godly Minister of this City writing to Rabbi-ben-Israel, a great Dr. of the Jewes, now living at Amsterdam, to know whether after all their labor, travells, and most diligent enquiry, they did yet know what was become of the ten Tribes of Israel? His answer was to this effect, if not in these words, That they were certainly transported into America, and that they had infallible tokens of their being there.[139]

This comported with what Winslow and "many others in New England" had witnessed of Indian practices and beliefs. Here Winslow went into some detail for the M.P.s. Ceremonially, several of the Indians' practices, such as the "purification of weomen," were comparable to Mosaic ordinances. Their teachings concerning God, man's soul, his immortality, and eternal reward and punishment were striking in their similarity to Jewish teachings. They lamented the loss of the knowledge of God and the true worship possessed by their ancestors. In their traditions were included accounts of a great flood and of a man who was the only human ever to see God, "which certainly *I* believe to be *Moses.*"[140] It was remarkable that "the juncture of Time" in which the Indians were willing to accept the gospel corresponded so closely to what several renowned theologians had deduced from Scripture regarding the time when the Jews would be converted, indicated Winslow without explicitly adopting their position. Whether or not these suppositions were valid, "the work of communicating and encreasing the light of the Gospel is glorious in reference to *Jewes & Gentiles.*"[141] Making a deft appeal to Parliament's consciousness of being God's chosen instrument for extending Christ's reign, Winslow implied Parliament's responsibility for New England missions.

> And as God hath set a signall marke of his presence upon your Assembly, in strengthning your hands to redeem and preserve the civill Rights of the Common weale: so doubtlesse may it be a comfortable support to your Honours in any future difficulties, to contemplate, that as the *Lord* offered you (in this designe) an happy opportunity to enlarge and advance the Territories of his Sonnes Kingdom: So he hath not denyed you (as I am confident he will not) an heart to improve the same; and in as much as lies in you to make all the Nations of the Earth, the Kingdoms of the Lord, and of his Christ; that so your Honours may still preserve your interest in his favour, which is and shall be the prayers of   E.W.[142]

A lengthy appendix signed by "J.D." was clearly influenced by the Thorowgood thesis. It was written at "the request of the worthy Publisher

139 Winslow, A3v.
140 *Ibid.,* A4r.
141 *Ibid.,* A4r-A4v.
142 *Ibid.,* A4v.

60

of these precious papers," who "prevailed" upon the writer to contribute to this collection.[143] Fifty years later Samuel Sewall identified the writer as John Downame,[144] though he did not state on what authority he did so. Since Winslow had won Downame's endorsement as a signer of Shepard's tract,[145] Sewall's conclusion is a live possibility, though he showed little awareness of the origin and development of the Indian-Jewish theory in the Puritan tradition.[146] John Dury's interest in the theory, arising from his contacts with Thorowgood and Menasseh Ben Israel, his apparent relationship to Winslow, and the content of the appendix itself all argue for Dury being its author.

The times were pregnant with "palpable and present acts of providence" which "doe more then hint the approach of Jesus Christ," said J.D.[147] The writer, like Winslow, disclosed that many of the ablest contemporary theolgians felt that the conversion of the Jews "is at hand." Several "of the wisest Jewes now living" believed that about 1650 " 'either we Christians shall be Mosaick, or else that themselves Jewes shall be Christians.' " Pondering the letters included in Winslow's tract, he concluded that "at least a remnant of the *Generation of Jacob*" [148] was to be found in America, perhaps even descendants of the ten lost tribes. He found it significant that Eliot's first sermon to the Indians was based on Ezekiel 37 : 9-10, where the prophet speaks of the dry bones coming to life. The author of the appendix interpreted this, as did subsequent mission propagandists, as referring to the conversion of Israel as distinct from Judah. It seemed that God, "by a special finger," [149] first pointed Eliot to that text which directly concerned his hearers. J.D. then gave six "conjectures" as to why he agreed with "the *Jewes of the Netherlands*" that "a sprinkling at least of *Abrahams seed*" [150] might be found in America. These are similar, though not in all cases identical, to those given by Winslow. But, as did Eliot in his letter of May 8, which neither he nor Winslow could have seen until long after they had written their contributions for this tract, this writer admitted

143 *Ibid.,* 22.
144 Sewall, A2.
145 Shepard, a1v.
146 Modern historians have been mute on the question of the authorship of this appendix. While George L. Kittredge, *Letters of Samuel Lee and Samuel Sewall* (Cambridge, Mass.: 1912), 179, quotes Sewall uncritically, Rooy, 200, attributes it only to "J. D." and Kellaway, 14, leaves the impression that Winslow could have been its author. *D.N.B.,* XVI, 263, in J. Westby-Gibson's article on Dury attributes to Dury an " 'Epistolary Discourse [on Israelitish Origin],' 1649." This may well be a reference to the piece in Winslow's tract.
147 Winslow, 22.
148 *Ibid.*
149 *Ibid.,* 23.
150 *Ibid.*

that even if his conjectures "prevaile not with thee (Reader)," the mission work was worthy of support.

J.D.'s appeal then switched to the broader Scriptural promises regarding the coming of Christ in the glorious day, which we have treated earlier in this chapter and which were more commonplace expectations. No one who reads the missionaries' letters and rejoices " 'in the appearance of our Lord Jesus' " can deny that among the Indians "the *Sun of Righteousness* is risen, with 'healirg [*sic*] vertue under his wings.' " [151] All New England ministers were encouraged to participate in this work which God intended in "his carrying of them thither." [152] Unlike the work of the Spanish, the missions in New England are conducted in the full power of God's Spirit and the gospel. From the letters of the missionaries the writer cited many examples of this effectiveness. His application had five points. He urged his readers to study "the works of the Lord" to discover how God frustrates the plans of his enemies. Recent history afforded him a convincing illustration. The prime example is "the late Bishops persecuting of the Godly," [153] which drove them to America where they could take up God's work. This time of feeble beginnings was not to be despised. The response of the heathen to the gospel should shame lethargic Christians. Their zeal should also spur deeper reverence of the Sabbath in England. Finally, he made an appeal for aid for the work. Preachers must promote the work; the rich must contribute toward it; Parliament must pass the act that has been pending. In a blunt paragraph he urged the M.P.s to "rather steal from your sleep an houre, then suffer that good Ordinance to lye asleep so long." They would not deny a solicitation for a personal contribution to the work.

> How much lesse can you deny the passing of an Act to enable some to receive and dispose what others would gladly give. The work is so clear, that you need not many houres to debate it: And I hope you are so willing that I shall not need more words to presse it.[154]

The main thrust of Winslow's tract was both well executed and timely. It emphasized a theme of immediate relevance, while shrewdly not basing its appeal entirely on that theme. It did so the year after Parliament adopted *The Larger Catechism* laid before it by the Westminster Assembly. As we saw above, this document showed concern for the conversion of the Jews in its treatment of the second petition of the Lord's Prayer, which, according to the divines, implores that the reign of sin and of Satan may be destroyed, that the gospel may be propagated throughout the earth, that the Jews may be called, and that the fulness of the Gentiles may be brought

---

151 *Ibid.*, 24. Erroneously paginated "17."
152 *Ibid.*, 25.
153 *Ibid.*, 26.
154 *Ibid.*, 27.

in.[155] Furthermore, Winslow dedicated his tract to Parliament only a half year after "Prides Purge" in December of 1648, which ended the domination of the Presbyterians in Parliament. Winslow's use of Thorowgood's theme in his attempt to reactivate the legislative machinery stalled on his bill would have met with more sympathy among Independents, who were inclined to adopt 1650 and 1656 as dates for the conversion of the Jews.[156] The tract accomplished its purpose. By the end of the summer of 1649 the desired legislation had been passed. The New England Company was established. Its sixteen members were invested with the powers of a corporate body. They were authorized to collect, invest, and distribute funds for New England missions. The new missionary society authorized the Commissioners of the United Colonies of New England to superintend the use of Company funds in America.[157] The struggle to procure permanent support from England had been won.

4. Thomas Thorowgood's first tract

Thorowgood's speculations appeared in print the following year, 1650. Entitled *Iewes in America*, his booklet is significant and deserves our attention for a number of reasons. First, it contained the thought which had made such a deep impression on Dury and Winslow when in its proof form and which had helped to convince members of Parliament to assist New England missions financially. Secondly, Thorowgood's tract solicited support for New England missions from the English public. Finally, John Eliot himself gave the tract serious attention and for a time it stimulated his already strong optimism regarding his work.

Directed to "the honourable Knights and Gentlemen that have residence in, and relation to the County of *Norfolk*," [158] the dedicatory letter pleaded for their efforts in their "Spheres" in converting the Indians of America. Thorowgood reminded them of England's central place in God's plan for history and prayed that they might be found faithful at the imminent coming of Christ.[159] He indicated that his work was no plea for the readmission of Jews to England,

155 Müller, 641.
156 Nuttall's judgment on Parliamentary sympathy for admitting the Jews to England when that issue came up in 1653 applies *a fortiori* to their attitude toward aiding the conversion of the American "Jews": "There were many in that House who were sympathetic both to the plea and to the ground advanced for it; for it was the Parliament whose members had been nominated by the Congregational and Baptist churches of the country." *Visible Saints*, 145.
157 Kellaway, 12-16, gives a detailed account of the steps in the passage of the act. In 1643 Plymouth, Massachusetts Bay, Connecticut, and New Haven formed a confederation for mutual defense and other matters of common interest. Each colony elected two men as commissioners. See Kellaway, 62.
158 Thorowgood, *Iewes in America* . . . , A2.
159 *Ibid.*, B4.

which must be with sacred and civill cautions, that the *sweet name of our dearest Lord* be not blasphemed, but when will Christians in earnest endeavour their conversion, if the name of *Jew* must be odious everlastingly? I speak for their Gospelizing, though some suspect they are never likely to come again under that covenant.[160]

But "Scripture grounds," Thorowgood assured his readers, make plain that *"a time of love"* (Romans 11 : 23) is approaching when "the returne of that *Prodigall"* (Luke 15 : 32) will cause Christians to rejoice.[161] Therefore, "should wee beg for them" that God shed "'upon them the spirit of grace and supplication, that they may looke upon him whom they have pierced, and mourne for him as one mourneth for his onely sonne.'" (Zachariah 12 : 10) Even if these "poor Natives" are not part of the lost tribes of Israel, their conversion under the preaching of the *"Nov-angles"* will give cause for praising God. Therefore, "how should 'wee cast our mite into this treasury,' yea our *Talent*, our *Talents*, if wee have them? for certainly the time is comming, 'That as there is one Shepherd, there shall be one Sheepfold.' Io. 10.16."[162]

The work proper has three parts. In the first, the author reviewed the colonists' motives for leaving their homeland, various theories on the natives' origin, and his six "conjectures" on the Indians' Jewish origin.

Thorowgood was particularly intrigued by the problem of the Indians' ancestry. Already in the late 1630's he had begun investigating the possibility of their Jewish origin. This we know from John Dury's "An Epistolicall Discourse," where Dury marveled at the strange way in which God's Spirit had prompted Thorowgood to begin exploring this thesis "twelve or more yeeres agoe."[163] In explaining his position Thorowgood set his theory off against those of others. He noted that the opinions of scholars varied widely on the matter. Hugo Grotius said that the Indians had descended from Europeans who had passed to America from Norway. J. Lerius contended that their ancestors were Canaanites who had fled their homeland in fear of Israel. Johannes de Laet believed that they shared Tartar traits, while Emanuel de Moraes was convinced that the Carthaginians and Jews were their progenitors.[164] Thorowgood chose a version of the latter theory.

160 *Ibid.,* A3.
161 *Ibid.,* A3-A4.
162 *Ibid.,* A4.
163 *Ibid.,* D4r. Thorowgood was not the first to publish on the Indians' Jewish origin. The theory appears to have originated with Spanish Jesuits. In 1643 Roger Williams, A4v-A5r, listed several cultural similarities between the Indians and the Israelites but found more affinity between Greek and Algonquian than between Hebrew and the Indians' language. See Rooy, 234, n.l. As late as 1647 the theory was not even considered by the author of the second Eliot tract, who judged that " ... his reasons are most probable who thinke they are Tartars...." *The Day-Breaking ...,* 14.
164 *Ibid.,* 2-3.

Thorowgood's reasons for adopting the Jewish theory were couched in a list of six "conjectures." "The Indians doe themselves relate things of their Ancestors, suitable to what we read of the Jewes in the Bible." [165] Their "rites, fashions, ceremonies, and opinions" are strikingly similar to those of the Jews. [166] There are certain linguistic affinities between the two peoples. [167] The cannibalism of the Carib tribes is seemingly a fulfillment of God's curse on Israel recorded in Deuteronomy 28 : 53, where it is predicted that Israelites will eat the flesh of their sons and daughters. [168] "The people that have not yet received the Gospell of Jesus Christ are Jewes, but the Americans have not yet been gospelized," states the fifth conjecture, implying that the Indians could be the long lost Jews. [169] The heavy afflictions suffered by the Americans might well be the divine "plagues threatened unto the Jewes" for their sinfulness. [170]

In Part II Thorowgood refuted the arguments against his position.

Part III, which constitutes over one half of the entire book, is a forthright plea for missions addressed both to the "planters" or colonists and to residents of England. To the former Thorowgood reiterated the well-worn missionary motive for colonization. If men colonize with the intent of saving lost mankind, there will be benefits for both parties. "We may with more comfort expect and enjoy the externalls of the Indians, when wee pay them our spiritualls, for their temporalls, an easie and yet most glorious exchange." [171] A further inducement to missions is the vision that one day all America will hear and know the gospel. It is ripe for harvest, even though the laborers are few. Those who themselves have experienced much in the way of divine favor will want to assume the task of erecting this "Tabernacle for our God in America." [172] Violence, force, and cruelty must give way to learning the Indians' language, preaching, and teaching the Word. The colonists must be examples of holiness and piety and must pray for the conversion of the natives.

After leaving the colonists with a number of cautions, Thorowgood addressed his readers in England. They owe the colonists their "hearts and love" for the latters' risking of their lives and families in strengthening England's position overseas. [173] Confessionally, they are one with England. The charge that they are anti-monarchical is false. Therefore why should England not aid the colonists in missions to the Indians? Just as Pope Greg-

---

165 *Ibid.,* 3.
166 *Ibid.,* 6.
167 *Ibid.,* 14.
168 *Ibid.,* 17.
169 *Ibid.,* 20.
170 *Ibid.,* 26.
171 *Ibid.,* 59.
172 *Ibid.,* 68.
173 *Ibid.,* 77.

ory I sent his missionaries to pagan England, England should likewise make "solicitous endeavours that all the Natives of that New World, should be made a world of New creatures."[174] To that end prayers, promotional literature, and collections are in order. In his last two chapters Thorowgood cited Harvard College and the successes of extant missions as added incentives for English support for colonial missions. "'Up and be doing, and the Lord will bee with you,'" he concluded.[175]

Thorowgood's theory must have received added credibility for many English readers from the prefatory endorsement which was given it by John Dury. Dury admitted that when he had initially reflected on his friend's thesis, "it seemed... somewhat strange and unlikely to have any truth in it."[176] Only after he had considered wider issues did the truth of Thorowgood's claim become evident. Why had God brought to America so many men who believed that the tribes of Israel must be called to Christ before the end of the world? Did Scripture not prophesy the conversion of the Jews and their return to their homeland? How was the evidence received from such European Jews as De Montezinos and Menasseh Ben Israel to be interpreted? Were not God's recent dissolutions of world powers and empires another aspect of the culmination to which God was bringing history? These all became relevant questions for Dury.[177] As he pondered them he became convinced that Thorowgood's explanation would eventually become so evident as to stop even "the mouths of Atheists."[178]

> For seeing it is evident that the ten Tribes of Israell have been as it were lost in the world neare about the space of two thousand yeeres, if now they should againe appeare upon the stage, first as it were in another world by themselves, and then afterward speedily come from thence hither to the land of their ancient inheritance, where they shall be joyned to their brethren the Jews (which is clearly foretold by the Prophets shall come to passe) if (I say) those things should now begin to come to passe, what can all the world say otherwise, but that the Lords counsell doth stand, and that he hath fulfilled the words spoken by his Servants the Prophets concerning Israel.... The destruction then of the spirituall *Babylon* by the restauration of Israel, shall make out this to all the earth, that God alone is the Lord over all, and the Saviour of the people that put their trust in his name.[179]

The elating aspect of Thorowgood's thesis as far as Dury was concerned was not its theoretical elucidation of God's final acts in history, however.

---

174 *Ibid.,* 88.
175 *Ibid.,* 128.
176 *Ibid.,* D3.
177 *Ibid.,* D4.
178 *Ibid.*
179 *Ibid.*

Late in 1645 Dury had preached to the House of Commons that the "four chief heads of comfort" for the church were her deliverance from Babylon and particularly Rome, the coming of the Messiah to save his people, the enlarging of the church's bounds to include the Gentiles, and the eventual recalling of the Jews and their reunion with Gentile Christians in one church.[180] By his identification of American Indians as descendants of the ten lost tribes, however, Thorowgood had convinced Dury that the final and most glorious stage of history was in fact near. The sooner they could be converted, the sooner Christ would come into his full glory and men everywhere acknowledge him. So important did Dury deem it that others be convinced of Thorowgood's position and thus lend support to Anglo-American missions to the Indians, thereby hastening the end, that to Thorowgood's arguments he added his own corroborating evidence that the Indians were Israelites.[181] It was this enthusiasm that had been passed to Edward Winslow and which had influenced him in his struggle to gain Parliamentary support for New England missions.

It is of course impossible to determine both the extent to which Thorowgood's thesis was accepted by the reading public and the degree of success it had in winning public support for Anglo-American missions. Kellaway says it "did something to advertise" the work of the newly founded New England Company.[182] It evoked a negative response from the royalist governor of Lynn, Sir Hamon l'Estrange in 1652, who read it "with more diligence and delight for the Authors sake," but admitted, "as I sailed through the discourse, I fell upon many Sands and Rocks of reluctance to my sense." [183] He methodically rejected Thorowgood's "conjectures." However, among leaders in Anglo-American missions it produced both before — as we have seen — and after its appearance in print a degree of exhilaration and expectation which gave their work deeper meaning and heightened urgency.

5. John Eliot and the Thorowgood theory

John Eliot was one of the first to feel the impact of Thorowgood's thesis, as his letter of May 8, 1649 indicates. He addressed Winslow,

Much honoured Sir,

Your very loving acceptance of my Letters doth engage me very

180 John Dury, *Israels Call to March out of Babylon unto Jerusalem* (London: 1646), 2.
181 Thorowgood, *Iewes in America . . .*, D2-D3.
182 Kellaway, 24.
183 [Sir] Hamon l'Estrange, *Americans no Iewes* (London: 1652), A2r.

much unto you, but especially your cordial rejoycing in the progresse of this work of the Lord among these poor Indians. Sir, I shall first answer some material things in your Letter. First, for that opinion of *Rabbi-ben Israel* which you mention, I would intreat you to request the same godly Minister [*i.e.*, Dury, in all likelihood] (nay I hope he hath already done it) to send to him to know his grounds, and how he came to that Intelligence, when was it done, which way were they transported into *America*, by whom, and what occasion, how many, and to what Parts first, or what steps of intimation of such a thing may there be.[184]

Eliot admitted that he had already been inclined to investigate the question of the Indians' origin. However, his thoughts had run much farther back into Biblical history than to the tribe of Reuben, the tribe of the Jewish dispersion which De Montezinos thought he had discovered.[185] Basing his speculations on the genealogy of Noah in Genesis 10, Eliot decided that the Indians were descendants of Eber, a descendant of Shem. "If these people be under a Covenant and Promise as ancient as *Shem* and *Eber*, it is a ground of faith to expect mercy for them."[186] Had not Abraham paid tithes to Melchizedek, whom Eliot identified as Shem? And were not the Scriptures full of assertions that God is the God of the Hebrews? Following H. Broughton, Eliot theorized that Eber's descendants settled in eastern Asia, from which some crossed to America. The "sundry Prophecies in Scripture" which refer to " 'the goings down of the Sunne' " and which promise great blessings for the people of those regions undoubtedly apply to America, therefore.[187] God's fuller promise to Jacob, pledging to make him a great nation, has been accomplished partially "in the Nation of the Jewes"[188] (the two tribes). It will receive an even broader fulfillment among "the lost Israelites scattered in the world" (the ten lost tribes). Scattered among the descendants of Shem and Japhet, remnants of the ten tribes may also be found among the Indians. In finding and gathering the ten tribes, God will

bring in with them the Nations among whom they were scattered, and so shall *Jacobs* Promise extend to a multitude of Nations indeed; and this is a great ground of faith for the conversion of the Easterne Nations, and may be of help to our faith for these Indians; especially if *Rabbi Ben-Israel* can make it appeare that some of the Israelites were brought into *America*, and scattered here, or if the Lord shall by an meanes give us to understand the same.[189]

---

184   Whitfield, *The Light appearing . . .* , 14.
185   Wolf, 14.
186   Whitfield, *The Light appearing . . .* , 14.
187   *Ibid.*, 15.
188   *Ibid.*
189   *Ibid.*

Eliot found "comfort & encouragement" for his work not only in these but also in other promises such as, " 'That all Languages shall see his Glory, and that all Nations and Kingdoms shall become the Kingdoms of the Lord Iesus.' " [190] The remainder of his letter concentrated on practical aspects of his work and these broader prophecies. Eliot commended Owen and Parliament, Christ's instrument in establishing his kingdom, for their support of missions.

His closing paragraph referred to the "dry bones" motif of Ezekiel 37, though it is impossible that when he wrote his letter Eliot knew of the implications which J.D. saw in his earlier use of this text. He regretted that he had no time to convey some of the Indians' questions, "whereby you might perceive how these dry bones begin to gather flesh and sinnews." [191]

Between the writing of this and what was undoubtedly his following letter,[192] it appears that he had heard more from England on the Thorowgood thesis, for he responded, "Sirs, you tell me of one that will publish reasons to prove (at least) some of the ten Tribes are in *America*, it would be glad tydings to my heart." [193] He apparently relayed the information to a Mr. Dudley, who informed him of Captain Cromwell's observations of many Indians to the south who practiced circumcision. Eliot regarded this as "one of the most probable arguments" that he had yet heard for their descent from the ten tribes. His hesitancy to categorically identify the Indians among whom he worked as descendants of Israel was expressed in an earlier statement in the letter which shows that he had received a copy of *The Glorious Progress*... with J.D.'s interpretation of his earlier use of Ezekiel 37. "I allude to that in Ezekiel not because I have any light to persuade me these are that people there mentioned, only they be dry and scattered bones, if any be in the world." [194]

The following letter, written on October 29, 1649, while strongly emphasizing "the rising Kingdome of Jesus Christ" among the Indians,[195] left the Jewish theme untouched, save for one reference. Here Eliot expressed undaunted hope that Christ's kingdom would come to the Indians. But he saw England's reluctance to live by the Bible as detrimental to the conversion of the Jews. When "the Gentile Nations" adopt Scripture as "the foundation of all their Lawes, who knoweth what a door would be opened to the Jewes to come in to Christ." [196] In this letter he appeared to classify

---

190 *Ibid.*

191 *Ibid.,* 18.

192 Although this second letter from Eliot in *The Light appearing*... is not dated, Whitfield placed it between those dated May 8, 1649 and October 29, 1649, and our assumption is that it was written sometime between those dates.

193 Whitfield, *The Light appearing*..., 24.

194 *Ibid.,* 23.

195 *Ibid.,* 28.

196 *Ibid.,* 29.

both Indians and Englishmen as Gentiles, whose conversion would open the door for the conversion of the Jews. Into his last two letters included in the Eliot tract edited by Whitfield in 1651 Thorowgood's thesis did not enter at all. Nor did he mention the theory in his letters in subsequent Eliot tracts.

These sources, however, show Eliot's preoccupation with the theme of the nearness of Christ's kingdom, which he believed was being established among the Indians through his work. This was his dominant eschatological category used in reference to his work and will be treated in the following section. It was based on the broad prophecies of the Old and New Testaments. His interest in the ten tribes theory was guarded, and he reserved further comment on it for his correspondence with Thorowgood personally. The possibilities it proffered for immediate and widespread conversions among the Indians intrigued and excited him. But he realized that more concrete proof was needed before he could place more hope in these "conjectures."

Eliot sought that proof in the Scriptures. He was driven to them by the reading of Thorowgood's tract, which reached him after his initial responses to Thorowgood's theory based on the snatches in Winslow's letters. For several years he scrutinized Thorowgood's arguments and studied the relevant Biblical evidence — surely a tribute to his care and scholarship. Although Eliot wrote three letters to Thorowgood thanking him and his Norfolk patrons of New England missions for their gifts, he apparently withheld comment on Thorowgood's views.[197] He broke silence on October 16, 1656 in a letter addressed to Thorowgood personally. It was later woven into Thorowgood's argument in his second tract. Eliot expressed his dismay at having been prematurely drawn into the discussion. "Your labours and letters have drawn me forth further that way, than otherwise I should have gone."[198] He begged Thorowgood, who appears to have been pressing him for his opinion in these matters throughout their correspondence, "to spare me in this" and to permit him to listen to what others were inclined "to say in this matter."[199]

The evident regret expressed by Eliot in his October, 1656 letter to Thorowgood is highly interesting. It sets the historian searching for the expression of his opinion to which Eliot had reference. It is unlikely that he had his Eliot tract comments on the Jewish question in mind, for these had been written before Eliot had seen Thorowgood's first tract. Since he had restrained himself from commenting on the subject in his first three letters to Thorowgood, his dismay cannot have been regarding anything said in them. It must therefore apply to a third source. In all likelihood Eliot had

197 Thorowgood, *Jews in America*, 3. The three letters were dated March 18, 1653; June 27, 1654; and June 16, 1655.
198 *Ibid.*, 34. See Rooy, 234.
199 *Ibid.*

reference to what later appeared in Thorowgood's second tract as "The learned Conjectures of Reverend Mr. *John Eliot* touching the *Americans,* of new and notable consideration, written to Mr. *Thorowgood.*" This conclusion accords with Thorowgood's acknowledgment of having received Eliot's "Conjectures" after his first three letters.[200] Furthermore, Eliot's new piece had to be written before 1658, the year in which Thorowgood submitted his second tract to the New England Company for possible publication under their auspices. If indeed the comments in Eliot's 1656 letter to Thorowgood refer to "The Learned Conjectures . . . ," then Eliot's new piece must have been written before October of that year. A 1655 or early 1656 date for its composition is most likely, therefore. The significance of this date becomes apparent when the expectation of the conversion of the Jews in 1656, a view popularized by Thomas Goodwin and widely received in Independent and Congregational circles, is remembered. Eliot evidently succumbed to twelfth-hour excitement in writing his "Conjectures," for he said, "the time is even at hand" when God's people "do waite for the accomplishment" of prophecies regarding the discovery and the conversion of the ten tribes.[201] He noted the unprecedented prayer for their conversion and investigation concerning their whereabouts which occupied men at that time. Even before the fateful year ended Eliot realized that he had said too much. Nevertheless Thorowgood used Eliot's "Conjectures" to lend the prestige of Eliot's name to his second tract, published in 1660, and placed Eliot's piece before his own contribution.

In his new comments on the Indian's origin Eliot gave an extended restatement of the position he had taken in his letter to Winslow several years before. Indians, Chinese, Japanese, and Americans were all regarded as descendants of the sons of Eber. In addition he noted that when the ten tribes were later scattered, they were dispersed eastward, among a kindred people. Thus he conceded at the outset of his letter that fragments of the ten lost tribes "might be scattered even thus far, into these parts of America."[202] One thing was certain to Eliot. God had promised "to bind" and "to gather" the "dry and scattered bones" of the ten tribes.[203] This would occur in "the last daies."[204] In the search for these tribes in which many were engaged Eliot cautioned Thorowgood that "the surest thread to guid us" is the Scripture.[205]

It was Eliot's treatise, claimed Thorowgood, that rekindled his interest in the subject. Eliot's "new, but prevailing way and method"[206] occasioned

200 *Ibid.,* 1.
201 *Ibid.,* 1-2.
202 *Ibid.,* 1.
203 *Ibid.*
204 *Ibid.,* 20.
205 *Ibid.*
206 *Ibid.,* 27.

Thorowgood to re-evaluate his first tract and to analyze his subsequent notes on the subject. The result was presented in his second tract, which he hoped would stimulate further interest in and prayer for work among the Americans. Without claiming more than the "probabilitie" of his theory, he offered some additional "conjectures" which showed that he had read more deeply in the Spanish authors and consulted Menasseh Ben Israel's and Roger Williams' writings after he had produced his first tract. Once again his ultimate motive in writing was to win support for New England missions. Whether the Indians are Jews or not, Christianizing them is a "pretious work." [207] His second dedication, again to the "Noble Knights, Ladies, and Gentlemen of Norfolk," [208] commended Eliot and the American work to their further support. The promises of Scripture lent urgency to his appeal.

The New England Company realized the merit of the piece as promotional literature, for when Thorowgood requested in 1658 that it be published under its auspices, it gave it consideration in June and again in October. Although it ultimately was declined for the Company's sponsorship, its appearance in print on July 26, 1660 [209] was "useful" for the society, for it "spoke highly" of its work, judges Kellaway.[210] His judgment underrates the usefulness of the tract to the New England Company. Although the reaction it elicited from the new king is unknown, it is evident that Thorowgood's tract was deemed politically expedient in 1660 by prominent supporters of New England missions. The first dedication was addressed to Charles II and assured him that many who had left episcopacy for the more Reformed position, in spite of the danger which this act involved, were and would continue to be true to the king. New England missions were worthy of his support, it was suggested. Signed by Reynolds, Calamy, Ashe, and Dury, a note testifying that this dedication was originally written for the 1650 tract and addressed to the king's father was appended to the dedication. All four men had staunchly supported missions by lending their names to previous tracts, and it may have been judged that their political and ecclesiastical conservatism would stand missions in good stead with Charles II.[211] The efforts of the former three to insure that missions weathered the Restoration unscathed did not go unnoticed by the members of the Company, for they invited them to the September meeting to discuss the Company's future.[212] These four men used Thorowgood's tract in an effort to win

207 *Ibid.,* 51.
208 *Ibid.,* 1.
209 *Catalogue of the Thomason Tracts, 1640-1661,* 2 vols. (London: 1908), II, 325.
210 Kellaway, 25.
211 Reynolds conformed at the Restoration, and Ashe and Calamy were staunch Presbyterians.
212 Kellaway, 41.

political endorsement for missions, just as Winslow a decade before had utilized his ideas to win legislative support for missions. By 1660, however, Thorowgood's argument itself was of less importance than a show of fidelity to the monarch.

Whether it was the inability of theorists to do more than speculate on the Hebraic origin of the Indians, the passing of 1656, the death of the Lord Protector, or the Restoration of Charles II and the subsequent collapse of the more detailed millennial positions, in which the conversion of Jews played a dominant role, it is clear that in the 1660's and 1670's the Thorowgood thesis was in general disrepute among those groups to whom it had earlier proved so appealing. Joseph Caryl referred in passing to Indians as *"aliens from the Common-wealth of Israel"* [213] in the 1660 Eliot tract preface. Daniel Gookin speculated on the origin of the American natives from the "straits of Magellan" to "the most northerly part yet discovered," concluding that they were "originally of the same nations or sort of people." [214] The opinion that they are descendants of the ten tribes "doth not greatly obtain. But surely it is not impossible, and perhaps not so improbable, as many learned men think." [215] Gookin was in a lonesome minority, however. Even Eliot had fallen silent on the subject of the Indians' origin after his letter to Thorowgood. Cotton Mather later judged Eliot's speculations that the ten lost tribes might be found in America as a "wish" in which "he was willing to indulge himself." [216] This judgment is not wishful thinking on the part of Mather, however, who himself rejected the Thorowgood position. It accurately describes Eliot's position, which enabled him for a time to carry on his work "the more *cheerfully,* or at least the more *hopefully,* because of such possibilities."[217]

6. *Eliot on the kingdom*

An apparent ambivalence exists among scholars toward Eliot's eschatology. Rooy distinguishes Eliot from his contemporaries who defined the millennium "in a literal way and predicted the time of its beginning," while at the same time conceding that Eliot felt "the glorious kingdom on earth" was about to begin.[218] Staehelin speaks of a millennialist stamp on Eliot's hopes for the nearness of Christ's kingdom.[219] H. Richard Niebuhr readily asso-

---

213 Eliot, *A further Account . . .*, A3r.
214 Gookin, 144.
215 *Ibid.,* 145.
216 C. Mather, I, 560.
217 *Ibid.,* 561.
218 Rooy, 229.
219 *V.R.G.,* V, 118. He calls it a "chiliastischer Prägung."

ciates Eliot with a moderate form of millennialism.[220] All three correctly sense a chiliastic streak in Eliot's thought, while they hesitate to call him an outright millennialist. The apparent ambivalence and hesitancy are due to the inadequacy of current terminology regarding millennial views of the seventeenth century. A narrow, literalistic definition of "millennialist" disqualifies Eliot as such, for in fact he did not speak of his position in these terms, and even his elation regarding the prospects for 1656 were short-lived. He was not an advocate of complex chiliasm. Rather, he used the term "kingdom of Christ" in such a way as indicates that he shared the simple chiliasm or mild millennial expectations of a theologian like John Owen.

Eliot defined the kingdom of Christ not as a personal, physical reign of Christ on earth but as the condition which prevails "when all things among men, are done by the direction of the word of his mouth; his Kingdom is then come amongst us, when his will is done on earth, as it is done in heaven." [221] Broadly speaking, it has several dimensions: rule over individual Christians, over the church, over civil governments, and over his eternal kingdom in heaven.[222] Eliot anticipated a period of history prior to Christ's final return when in its first three dimensions Christ's kingdom would grow to proportions unknown before. In this he followed the order of events laid down by his fellow Congregationalists in England and America. Antichrist, whom Eliot identified with the church of Rome,[223] would fall, and in its place Christ's kingdom would be established to the ends of the earth. In an address to Cromwell he opined that the Lord Protector had been raised up by the Lord "to overthrow Antichrist, and to accomplish, in part, the Prophecies and Promises of the Churches Deliverance from that Bondage." [224] Cromwell has succeeded admirably, continued Eliot. But Christ's intention "in these daies is double." [225] Not only does he desire to overthrow Antichrist, but he also desires to establish his kingdom "in the room of all Earthly Powers which He doth cast down, and to bring all the World subject to be ruled in all things by the Word of His mouth." [226] While Eliot was grateful for Cromwell's accomplishments regarding the first point, he urged him to undertake the second as well by putting "Government into the hands of Saints" and by implementing "Scripture Government and Laws." [227] He offered Cromwell the "Comfort" that Christ's kingdom was also "rising

220 H. Richard Niebuhr, *The Kingdom of God in America* (Hamden, Conn.: 1956), 133.
221 John Eliot, *The Christian Commonwealth* (London: 1659), A4r.
222 See Rooy, 229.
223 *Ibid.*, 226.
224 Eliot and Mayhew, A2r.
225 *Ibid.*
226 *Ibid.*
227 *Ibid.*, A2v.

up in these Western Parts of the World." [228] Eliot continued, "the Lords time is come to advance and spread His Blessed Kingdom, which shall (in his season) fill all the Earth." [229] Anticipation of Christ's reign was the incentive which Eliot offered to Cromwell for following the Lord's plan.

Eliot reiterated this position six years later. It again stressed the two aspects of Christ's work: giving the saints his governing authority and reigning "over all the Nations of the earth in his due time." [230] To Christ he applied the apocalyptic figure of the stone in Daniel 2 : 34-35, which smashed the image and filled the entire earth. Christ will destroy all earthly monarchies, the last of which will be the Roman Antichrist, and his rule by his Word in Scripture will fill the earth in both civil and ecclesiastical affairs.[231] Eliot saw these events occurring in Britain,[232] and he rebuked a group of Cheshire and Lancashire ministers for resisting the beginning of Christ's reign through the godly rulers in power.[233]

Eliot saw his work in the context of the spread of Christ's kingdom to the ends of the earth. It stood at the beginning of the glorious harvest day and was a first step toward realizing the fulness of that day. He looked beyond the "day of small things" [234] to the fulness of Christ's kingdom. His results were only an "embrio" of that which would be furthered by the prayers of the churches.[235] His vision was captured in his favorite image, that of fields "white unto the Harvest." [236] He made a plea for more laborers,[237] for the Indians' responsiveness to the gospel indicated that God "is preparing a plentifull Harvest." [238] The harvest will ultimately be reaped in all fields of the world by men whom God will raise up through faith in his prophecies:

'. . . the Gospel shall spread over all the Earth, even to all the ends of the Earth; and from the riseing to the setting Sun; all Nations shal become the Nations and Kingdoms of the Lord and of his Christ.' [239]

A "weighty consideration" in reaping this harvest among the Indians was

228 Ibid.
229 Ibid.
230 Eliot, The Christian Commonwealth, A4r.
231 Ibid., B1r.
232 Ibid.
233 Ibid., A3v.
234 Winslow, 18. Eliot and Mayhew, B3r. Whitfield, Strength out of Weakness . . . , 1.
235 Winslow, 18.
236 Ibid., 10.
237 Ibid., 18.
238 Whitfield, Strength out of Weakness . . . , 8.
239 Eliot and Mayhew, B1r.

the type of ecclesiastical and civil government the converts should have.[240] Eliot discussed these matters with John Cotton and others and concluded as his "general rule" that, as in all other things relating to Christ's kingdom his Scriptural Word should be the guide. Then Christ will be the Indians' Law-giver, Judge, and King.[241] Although Eliot was concerned with establishing Christ's kingdom among the Indians, "the Lord will bring all the world"[242] to that state "ere he hath done."[243] He has promised through the prophets that Jews and Gentiles the world over will come to him. These prophecies "are in part begun to be accomplished"[244] by the conversions of many Indians. It will be particularly difficult for nations that have lived under Antichrist's rule to leave their false wisdom and to accept Christ's reign. Yet, this is Christ's 'great designe... in these later dayes."[245] In subsequent letters and writings Eliot reasserted the principle that Scripture is the one great standard or norm for Christ's dawning kingdom among the Indians and the other nations.[246]

By adopting this vision of the ultimate extent of Christ's kingdom, Eliot was led to suggest and to support the comprehensive work of New England missions. Indians needed to be educated in order to read the Scriptures. Schools were established. Those Scriptures had to be translated into the native language. Eliot employed an interpreter, learned the language, and reduced it to writing; paper, presses, and a printer were sent from England. Christ's reign had to be felt in civil affairs. Settled, secure, orderly native communities were built. Christ's reign demanded an ecclesiastical dimension. Natives were catechized and evangelized; they were converted and confessed their faith; some were even trained as pastors and evangelists. Seen logically, therefore, Eliot's total program for missions was a grand effort to realize the kingdom of Christ among the Indians which he felt was so near. Although he was not primarily a theoretician of missions, his vision and his efforts formed a consistent whole and ultimately rested on his millennial hopes for the glorious reign of Christ.

7. Summary

The organized Anglo-American mission program that was born in the 1640's was the fruit of generations of theologizing about the course of

---

240 Whitfield, *The Light appearing...*, 23.
241 *Ibid.*
242 *Ibid.*, 24.
243 *Ibid.*, 23.
244 Eliot and Mayhew, B2v.
245 Whitfield, *The Light appearing...*, 24.
246 *Ibid.*, 28-29, 41. Eliot and Mayhew, B2v-B3r. Eliot, *The Christian Commonwealth*, B3r.

history, England's role in it, and the future of Catholics, Jews, and pagans. While Brightman and Mede taught the conversion of the Jews by supernatural means, events in the Civil Wars indicated to their successors that God deigned to use his saints in establishing his kingdom in England and America. As the anticipated dates 1650 and 1656 neared, therefore, appeals to participate in the establishing of Christ's kingdom were made with increasing frequency. God's use of Cromwell and the army of saints confirmed the validity of this theological modification which had special relevance for missions. The spiritual power, prayers, and praises of the saints would be used by God to convert Christ's enemies, Strong instructed his hearers in London in 1648. Winslow urged Parliament to be active instruments in extending Christ's kingdom. Eliot felt the gospel ministry was a "harbinger" of Christ's coming in the glory of his kingdom.

Events in the 1640's afforded all proponents of an optimistic view of history, no matter how extreme or mild their millennial position, a basis for their hope. These Englishmen, including colonists, shared at least four general premises regarding the future which all had a long tradition in English thought and which were all interrelated. First, they anticipated the fall of Rome or Antichrist. When the prelacy upheld by the compromising monarch and Archbishop Laud — only one step from papacy — was subverted, it seemed certain that God was beginning the final "shakings" of the nations which would climax in Rome's complete destruction. Second, once the Antichristian forces had been disarmed Jews and Gentiles would swarm into the true church. English contact with the heathen through commerce and colonization was interpreted as the further unfolding of the divine plan. Third, Englishmen awaited an era of true faith and blessing among all men. Westminster's reforms in church government and the passing of government to Cromwell and the saints were seen as initial endeavors in this direction. Fourth, and of a slightly different genre, Englishmen felt divinely mandated to guide history to her appointed ends in these matters. It seemed, therefore, that England was in the vortex of history in the 1640's. On all four counts the times were pregnant with a new age.

Anglo-American missions were the fruit of these enlivened expectations, especially, though not exclusively, of the second. Presbyterian and Independent millennialists were her strongest supporters and leaders in the propaganda and financial drives on her behalf. The title page texts of the Eliot tracts prove that missions were seen as crucial in realizing the fulness of those hopes which had already begun to be fulfilled. Uncountable guarantees of this glorious day were found throughout the Old and New Testaments and were used throughout the missionary literature to amplify the understanding of and quicken desires for it. The early work was seen as leaven, a mustard seed, a bruised reed and smoking flax, a day of beginnings and small things, the harvesting of first fruits. All these figures guaranteed greater things to follow. Christ, the Sun of Righteousness, was seen as riding forth to victory on a white horse. Knowledge of the Lord was being spread to all nations, from sea to sea, to the ends of the earth. He was claiming the nations as his heritage. Fields were white unto harvest. The everlasting gospel was being proclaimed. The stone cut out of the mountain was crushing earthly kingdoms and would soon fill the earth with Christ's kingdom. Clearly the first fulness of the Gentiles was being completed and would be followed by widespread conversions of both Jews and Gentiles. Eliot's thought and work was captivated by the hope of establishing the fulness of Christ's kingdom.

Although the distinctive positions of complex chiliasm find little place in the missionary literature, the anticipation of 1650 and 1656 heightened interest in the fall of Antichrist and the conversion of the Jews as those dates neared. Coupled with Thorowgood's thesis that the Indians might be Jews, these hopes won vital legislation and financial support for missions, and for a time Eliot himself entertained the same hopes.

These eschatological expectations fueled and fanned missions into a bright blaze throughout the 1650's. At the Restoration much of the historical basis for these hopes disappeared. Significantly, the promotion of missions through the highly effective method of tracts virtually died out at the moment that the new king returned to England. By then, however, Anglo-American missions were well enough established to burn brightly until the devastation brought by King Philip's War in 1675.

Chapter III

The new Jerusalem
(1675-1735)

A. *General Background*

The latter half of the seventeenth century saw the birth of the Age of Reason. For men like Sir Robert Boyle and Sir Isaac Newton there appears to have been little interplay between faith and reason. Among others the new spirit soon made its influence known, however. Moderates, Latitudinarians, and Cambridge Platonists were all affected by rationalism.[1] The Cambridge Platonists and the Latitudinarians emphasized the role of reason in religion, though the latter lacked the mystical piety of the former.[2] A tendency toward Arianism and Deism were products of this era which provoked rebuttals from conformists and nonconformists alike.

Nonconformists steadily gained recognition and after 1688 enjoyed an easier lot than during the early years of the Restoration. The established church was afflicted with pluralism and absenteeism among the clergy and with moral looseness and spiritual indifference among the laity. In reaction to these conditions and in conjunction with German Pietism[3] religious societies sprouted in and around London. Eventually they contributed to the rise of Anglican and Scottish missions and the Methodist movement.

English Protestants were solidly united in their opposition to Roman Catholicism. While Charles II was only suspected of papal sympathies, James II admitted his Catholicism outrightly. The Popish Plot of 1678 and provisions of the secretly signed Treaty of Dover hardened anti-Catholicism. James II awarded known Catholics key positions in government and issued declarations of indulgence to all non-Anglicans. After Parliament responded to widespread fear of the king by giving the throne to James' daughter Mary and her Calvinist husband, William of Orange, the presence of the non-juring element of the clergy became the cause of sustained fear of Jacobian intrigues. Armed clashes in 1707 and 1715 marked the eruption of antipathies which had never been far below the surface of English life since the Reformation. Louis XIV's empire-building and his revocation of the

---

1 Moorman, 254f.
2 *Ibid.*
3 Martin Schmidt, "Das hallische Waisenhaus und England im 18. Jahrhundert," *Theologische Zeitschrift*, VII, 1951, 39.

Edict of Nantes were chief contributing factors in the English fear of Roman Catholicism.

The Calvinism of William III assured James II's successor of an even warmer welcome in Presbyterian Scotland than in Anglican England. The sufferings of the Covenanters during the "killing times" were relieved by the Revolution, and in 1690 Presbyterianism once again replaced Episcopalianism as the official form of Christianity in Scotland. It remained so even after the unification of England and Scotland into one kingdom in 1707, a union which fostered Scottish contact with the English colonies.[4] According to Andrew Campbell, while the rationalism of the age did not produce extensive Arianism or Deism in the Scottish church, it evoked a moderation akin to the humanism of several earlier Scottish divines.[5] When the Marrow Men reacted to this lethargy and fostered a renewal of a more evangelical spirit by reprinting the *Marrow of Modern Divinity*,[6] they undoubtedly opted for the warmer piety and fervor previously represented in the sacramental gatherings and praying societies, religious groups honoring the theology of Westminster and the covenanting tradition.[7]

In New England trouble and introspection characterized the two decades following King Philip's War. Cotton Mather cited hunger and war as the two chief spoilers.[8] Boston was ravaged by two major fires and an epidemic between 1676 and 1679. The colonial charter was revoked in 1684, and Sir Edmund Andros' policies as governor were a source of constant irritation to colonists until Increase Mather won a measure of colonial self-government in 1691. Trade stagnated. Financial peril impended. New England searched her soul in the light of these judgments from God. Comets were read as portents, and the Reforming Synod of 1680 was summoned in an effort to set the Congregational house in order and to lift the hand of divine wrath from the colonies.[9] The witch trials in 1692 were a less acceptable manifestation of the reforming spirit, though they must not be explained solely in terms of this spirit.[10] The chief object of this spirit, however, was the merely nominal religion of the average New Englander. His dominant interests appeared to be pleasure and wealth. Moral laxness

4 Andrew J. Campbell, *Two Centuries of the Church of Scotland, 1707-1929* (Paisley: 1930), 23.

5 *Ibid.*, 34-35.

6 Van den Berg, 36.

7 Campbell, 30-32.

8 Cotton Mather, *Magnalia Christi Americana*, I, 88.

9 *Ibid.*, II, 316-339; and Kenneth Ballard Murdock, *Increase Mather: The Foremost American Puritan* (Cambridge, Mass.: 1925), 114-115, 151.

10 When he claims that the conclusion that the witch trials were "the direct effect of the political and religious disturbances" is "unwarranted," William Warren Sweet fails to do justice to the obsession for reform which drove many New England leaders in this period. *The Story of Religion in America* (New York, Evanston, and London: 1950), 61.

and doctrinal liberalization inevitably followed. Connecticut attempted to combat these tendencies centered in Massachusetts by founding Yale College in 1701. Solomon Stoddard chose to use communion as a means of softening the unregenerate for conversion. During his ministry his Northampton congregation experienced five "harvests" or revivals, precursors of the Great Awakening, which began in that church under his famous grandson, Jonathan Edwards.

The middle colonies began receiving a great influx of colonists during these years: Quakers, a number of German groups, Scotch-Irish Presbyterians, Anglicans, and New Englanders. As had New England, this area became the locus of mission activities.

B. Millennial Expectations

Interest in eschatology persisted throughout this period in both Britain and America. The same basic themes that were found earlier recurred: the fall of Antichrist, the conversion of the Jews and the Gentiles, and the millennial era with its various characteristics. These themes did not all receive equal attention, nor were they always discussed in the same terms as they had been earlier. The Jewish motif received considerably less attention, and the era of glory was regularly discussed in terms of "the beloved city" or "the New Jerusalem." The conversion of the nations began to be considered in terms of the pouring out of the Spirit.

Complex chiliasm was as prevalent during this period as at any other time in seventeenth and eighteenth century England and America. It had gained ground in New England since the days of John Davenport.[11] The works of Joseph Mede were still held in high esteem. They were used by men as influential as Henry More, the Cambridge Platonist,[12] and Isaac Newton, who refused to date the inauguration of the millennium.[13] More spent the latter part of his life dating and explaining the sounding of the six trumpets, which he believed would precede the last phase of world history.[14] And Samuel Sewall, hinting that the demand for editions of Mede's works exceeded their supply, expressed obvious delight in having a copy within his reach.[15] One writer considers the complex chiliasm of Sewall and Increase and Cotton Mather "the high-water mark in colonial exposi-

11   *P.F.F.*, II, 563; and Frank E. Manuel, *A Portrait of Isaac Newton* (Cambridge, Mass.: 1968), 107.

12   Frank E. Manuel, *Isaac Newton, Historian* (Cambridge, Mass.: 1963), 145-146; and Manuel's later work, *A Portrait of Isaac Newton,* 366-367.

13   Cotton Mather, *Magnalia Christi Americana,* I, 331.

14   Mullinger, III, 656.

15   Sewall, 52.

tion" of prophecy.[16] One searches the writings of these three men in vain, however, for some of the more extreme practices of millennialists such as date-setting, a practice engaged in with frequency by Richard Baxter's London antagonist, Thomas Beverley. In several of his writings Beverley argued that the millennium would begin on August 27, 1697.[17] Writings of men such as Hanserd Knollys [18] and activities of others like John Mason undoubtedly kept alive whispers of Fifth Monarchy movements.[19]

Even so, the less sensational and consequently harder-to-trace simple chiliasm was probably far more widespread. Even Cotton Mather admitted as much in his biographical sketch of Thomas Walley. Walley believed that "the first resurrection" spoken of in Revelation 20 would be corporeal, a fact, "which it may be many good men will count worthy rather of *reproach* than *applause.*" Mather consoled himself with the hope that "in the times of more illumination learned men must and will" come to the position of Mede and Walley.[20] And, writing particularly of the latter part of this period, a modern scholar concludes that the chiliasm which expected upheavals in nature and a general conflagration before the millennium "seems not to have persisted as a widely acceptable formula."[21] Writing in 1734, a New England representative of this position espoused by the Mathers dolefully "acknowledged that the contrary opinion generally prevailed: the earthly Kingdom was foreseen this side of judgment and cataclysm."[22]

Simple chiliasm, which had permeated Reformed theology on both sides of the Atlantic since the days of Owen, was given new life by a new generation of commentators. William Lowth, chaplain to the Bishop of Winchester, wrote his *Commentary on the Prophets* in published installments between 1714 and 1725.[23] Son of a refugee Huguenot minister, Charles Daubuz wrote *A Perpetual Commentary on the Revelation of St. John,* which went through a number of editions after its initial appearance in

16 *P.F.F.,* III, 124f.
17 Thomas Beverley, *The Prophetical History of the Reformation* (London: 1689), title page; *A Fresh Memorial of the Kingdom of Christ* (London: 1693), 21f.; *A Sermon Upon Revel.* 11.11 (London: 1692), title page; and many others. This little known chiliast kept London printers occupied in the 1690's. We have seen approximately twenty separate works written by him and conveniently bound in one volume by the staff of The British Museum.
18 Knollys wrote *The World that Now is; and the World that is to Come* (London: 1681), and *An Exposition Of the whole Book of the Revelation* (London: 1689).
19 P. G. Rogers, *The Fifth Monarchy Men,* 131-132; and Alan Heimert, *Religion and the American Mind* (Cambridge, Mass.: 1966), 60.
20 Cotton Mather, *Magnalia Christi Americana,* I, 601.
21 Heimert, 60.
22 *Ibid.*
23 *D.N.B.,* XXXIV, 216-217.

1720.[24] The commentary of an Anglican rector named Daniel Whitby, who was famous for advocating rapprochement with nonconformists, was very influential in spreading simple chiliasm. Entitled *Paraphrase and Commentary on the New Testament*, it included an appendix called "A Treatise of the Millennium." On the basis of this appendix Whitby has generally been regarded as the father of postmillennialism,[25] a conclusion which must be qualified in the light of the widespread simple chiliasm which preceded him. He influenced the thought of later commentators such as Daubuz and Moses Lowman, a Presbyterian minister, and of missionary thinkers such as Jonathan Edwards.[26] Philip Doddridge, a famous Independent divine and hymnwriter of the next generation, considered his commentary "preferable to any other." [27]

Across the North Sea Herman Witsius of the Netherlands predicted the calling of the Jews to Christ and their return to Palestine, which would be followed by abundant spiritual and physical blessings.[28] His writings long influenced English and Scottish commentators and missionary leaders.[29]

One form of chiliasm which developed in the Age of Reason deserves attention before we complete this survey. Reconciling their Christian faith with their scientific theories and findings, the apocalyptic physicists developed the idea of a catastrophic end to the present age, which will be followed by the millennium. Their thinking developed within the complex chiliastic tradition. Thomas Burnet's scientific explanation of the creation, flood, and the forthcoming consummation appeared in 1681. The present earth will be purged by fire, and the purified, millennial state will follow, he claimed.[30] Less than a decade later Sir Isaac Newton's writings on mathematics and his discoveries regarding gravity made Burnet's cosmology obsolete. However, the theological presuppositions underlying the cosmology of both men are the same.[31] Neither Newton's nor Burnet's mathematical work can be understood apart from their theological thought. Newton's lengthy discussions with Henry More, his private research on Daniel and Revelation, his abiding interest in chronology and the millennium as the capstone of world history, and his flirtations with Fatio de Duillier and perhaps even with the French prophets contributed to his total view

24 *D.N.B.*, XIV, 95-96.
25 Goen, 37; and *P.F.F.*, II, 649f.
26 Goen, 37.
27 See *D.N.B.*, LXI, 29. Whitby's commentary first appeared in 1703.
28 Jan van Genderen, *Herman Witsius* ('s-Gravenhage: 1953), 127.
29 *Ibid.*, 236-240. Witsius was a contemporary of Jacobus Koelman, *vide supra*, 27, n. 136. Simple chiliasm had been current in the Netherlands among leaders of the so called Second Reformation, of which both Koelman and Witsius were sons. Van den Berg, 20-21, suggests the significance of this eschatology for early Dutch missions.
30 Miller, 223; *D.N.B.*, VII, 409; *V.R.G.*, V, 105.
31 Miller ignores this fact in his treatment of the apocalyptic physicists.

of reality.[32] Newton believed that history was moving toward the cataclysmic events predicted in II Peter 3:6, 7, 10-12, events which would be followed by the new heaven and new earth promised in Isaiah 65:17 and Revelation 21:1.[33] His thinking was modified by his former friend and successor at Cambridge, William Whiston. In *A New Theory of the Earth,* 1696, Whiston explained creation, the flood, and the beginning of the millennium on a fire-purged earth in terms of a comet whose passing within close proximity to the earth did affect and would affect its gravitational stability. Until the middle of the eighteenth century he busied himself with prophecies, the identity of the ten lost tribes, and the date of the inception of the millennium.[34] The theories of the apocalyptic physicists received widespread attention in Britain and America and fostered speculation on the significance of each new celestial or terrestrial sign of the times.

C. *Mission Efforts*

New England missions struggled forward in the last quarter of the seventeenth century. The work was stunted by the war of 1675, impaired by subsequent Indian attacks, slowed by Eliot's age, and eclipsed by more urgent colonial affairs. John Cotton, Jr., informed Increase Mather of Eliot's lament that "he hath none to betrust the work with after his death but myselfe."[35] Both the New England Company in London and her board of commissioners in the colonies were afflicted with complacency until an infusion of new blood into both bodies gave the work new life. Part of the problem was that there simply were not many friendly Indians left in Massachusetts to be converted. Those who had not been killed in hostilities had been Christianized. The Mathers and Nehemiah Walter reported to London that at the turn of the century there were thirty Indian congregations, thirty-seven Indian preachers and seven or eight Englishmen able to preach in the Indian tongue, and only two pagans among one hundred eighty Indian families on Martha's Vineyard.[36] The repeated proddings of

32 Manuel, *A Portrait of Isaac Newton,* 361-362, 349f., 206f. As early as 1950 H. McLachlan's *Sir Isaac Newton: Theological Manuscripts* (Liverpool: 1950) made an appeal for understanding the forgotten Newton. The recent books by Manuel meet this need. Henceforth it will be impossible to agree with a former generation of scholars whose views are reflected in the *D.N.B.*'s article on Newton, which asserts that his theological and historical manuscripts "are of no great value." *D.N.B.,* XL, 390.

33 Manuel, *A Portrait of Isaac Newton,* 378-379.

34 *D.N.B.,* LXI, 10-14; Miller, 231; *V.R.G.,* V, 112.

35 John Cotton, Jr., Letter to Increase Mather dated September 10, 1688 *(Collections of the Massachusetts Historical Society,* Series IV, vol. VIII; Boston: 1868), 258.

36 Increase Mather, Cotton Mather, and Nehemiah Walter, *A Letter about the*

some of New England's chief leaders failed to launch a concerted missionary drive into virgin territory during the first thirty-five years of the new century. Pragmatic colonists were obviously not willing to expose themselves to the cruelties of savages constantly subject to French Catholic manipulation. It would take the self-sacrifice of David Brainerd and the pen of Jonathan Edwards, living in a later period and motivated by new forces, to rekindle sustained mission fervor in American Calvinists.

A flourish of missionary organization in Britain at the turn of the century brought the established churches of both England and Scotland into corporate mission activity for the first time. This had been preceded by individual appeals such as the carefully drafted scheme for missions in India which Humphrey Prideaux submitted to Archbishop Tillotson in 1695.[37] But only when Thomas Bray and a number of his friends organized the Society for Promoting Christian Knowledge in 1699 did Anglicans establish the machinery which would eventually include missions to non-Christians within its scope. The Anglican communion did not officially enter mission ranks until 1701, however, when the Society for the Propagation of the Gospel in Foreign Parts was incorporated and granted a royal charter.[38] Both societies ministered to Anglicans overseas. Already in 1700 August Hermann Francke became a corresponding member of the S.P.C.K., a relationship which blossomed into co-operation between German Pietists and the S.P.C.K. in missionary enterprises in America and India.[39] The S.P.G. sponsored extensive work among American Indians and Negroes. The general assembly of the Church of Scotland initiated steps toward missions to combat Roman Catholicism and ignorance in the Highlands in 1706. Two years later Queen Anne granted her sanction to this society which eventually supported missions to the American Indians.[40]

Individual Quakers emulated the example of John Foxe, who preached to Indians during his 1667 tour of the American seaboard. But organized missions were not begun until the 1790's, and records of preaching before that time are virtually non-existent. One historian of Quakers judges that his subjects were not as zealous in preaching to the Indians during the one hundred fifty years prior to 1800 as were Catholics, Congregationalists, Anglicans, and Moravians.[41]

Present State of Christianity among the Christianized Indians of New England (Boston: 1705), 4-5.

37   See William Brown, *History of the Propagation of Christianity among the Heathen since the Reformation*, 3 vols. (3rd. ed.; London: 1854), III, Appendix II, 476-478.

38   These two societies are henceforth abbreviated S.P.C.K. and S.P.G.

39   See Schmidt, "Das hallische Waisenhaus . . . ," 39-41.

40   Henceforth S.S.P.C.K.

41   Rayner W. Kelsey, *Friends and the Indians, 1655-1917* (Philadelphia: 1917), 35.

D. *Missions and Millennial Expectations*

In the ensuing sections of this chapter we shall first investigate the place of millennial expectations in the rebirth of missionary efforts in New England, where King Philip's War had been followed by twenty years of indifference and even antipathy to that cause. This will be done in the first four sections. Section five will treat the effects of eschatological thought on Anglican missions. Although Anglicans were by far the most active evangelists of this period, millennial expectations played only a relatively minor role in their missionary motivation. Hence our treatment of the vigorous Anglican mission work is limited to only one section. Scotland's contributions to the eschatological vision of missions were of both immediate and long-range significance. They will be treated in the final section of the chapter.

1. *The call for reform*

The ideals of the Edward Johnson generation haunted Increase Mather and his contemporaries. New England was not living up to the ideal set for her by her founders, who had stressed inner spiritual renewal. Only in a formal sense was she a "city set upon a hill," whose light shone for all to see. Rather than calling England to repentance and reformation, she was whoring after the heathens' gods. Her problem was not primarily that her ideals had been shattered by the toleration which her Independent colleagues had allowed in England under Cromwell and that she, finding her audience gone as Perry Miller suggests, capitulated in psychological defeat.[42] Had she been true to her original pledge she would have found in both the "apostasy" of the Independents and in the restored Anglicanism added incentives to preserve true doctrine and polity. But New Englanders themselves no longer believed in their own cause. The half-way covenant proved that. Her problem was that she had broken her covenant with her God.[43] The jeremiads of the ensuing decades were preached by leaders who saw that New England must reform herself before she could preach reform effectively to others.

Because New Englanders believed that the millennium would be the fruit of global reform, it is necessary to devote some attention to their unceasing appeals for reform in New England.

The evidence that New England had forsaken her faith was damning. The leaders at the Reforming Synod cited it: a laxness in combating

42 Miller, 12-13.
43 For a survey of the half-way covenant in American Puritanism see Peter Y. De Jong, *The Covenant Idea in New England Theology* (Grand Rapids: 1945), 110-176.

Quakerism, liberalization in the dress of both sexes, drunkenness, profanity, desecration of the Sabbath, employer-employee friction, dishonesty, lust, disinterestedness in ecclesiastical matters, pride, family tensions, unwillingness to reform, and general worldliness.[44]

Whether or not the situation was as critical as the leaders reported is difficult to confirm or to contradict since we are dependent mainly on their accounts. But these men did combat the above-mentioned evils. Appeals for conversion occurred with frequency in the preaching of Cotton Mather, especially during his first years in the pulpit. These sermons are typical:

> Invitation to Christ (ten sermons on Mt. 11 : 28), Be ye Reconciled, Almost Persuaded, Effectual Calling, and the 'Works, by which the Holy Spirit praepared men for the Lord Jesus' — Election, Vocation, Marks, Preparation, Conviction, Contrition.[45]

In preaching on these themes Mather was simply following a pattern in New England homiletics to which his father had contributed much.

Increase Mather constantly warned his hearers to repent or suffer the judgments of God. These judgments, which would reach into eternity, began in the present. He saw them in the troubles of his day, and he read them as signs that the times of God's impending wrath had arrived. A survey of his most important publications and activities shows this dominant theme in Mather's thought. Murdock finds that already in Mather's study on the conversion of the Jews there was "effective use of references to current affairs, to the Great Fire of London, to the latest comet, and to church dissensions in Boston." [46] In 1674 "this vigilant Watchman and wise Discerner of the Signs of the Times," as President Urian Oakes of Harvard billed him in the introduction, published *The Day of Trouble is Near*. It complained that New England had spurned the religion "which did distinguish us from other *English Plantations*," and once again interpreted current ills as harbingers of divine judgment.[47] He endorsed a friend's treatise on reformation by writing a preface for it, pressed the General Court of Massachusetts to convene the Reforming Synod — of which he was chosen moderator — and stepped up his literary campaign.[48]

> From his sermons he prepared a series of little books, and between 1675 and 1683 the list of his writings includes 'The Times of Men are in the Hand of God,' 'The Wicked Man's Portion,' 'Renewal of Covenant the Great Duty,' 'Pray for the Rising Generation,' 'A Discourse Concerning the Danger of Apostasy,' 'Returning unto God,'

44 Rooy, 267; and Murdock, 114-115.
45 Rooy, 244.
46 Murdock, 94-95.
47 These citations from *The Day of Trouble is Near* are from Murdock, 101-102.
48 *Ibid.*, 103 and 151.

'Heaven's Alarm to the World,' 'The Latter Sign,' 'A Sermon Wherein is shewed that the Church of God is sometimes a Subject of Great Persecution,' and a series of 'sundry sermons' under the title of 'Practical Truths Tending to Promote the Power of Godliness.' Five of these books were printed more than once, two of them appearing in three impressions.[49]

One work of Mather during this period treated millennial themes.[50]

It is not hard to imagine the general tone of New England preaching when it is remembered that the Mathers were New England pacers. A clergy that concentrated on decadent parishoners did not devote much attention to hostile pagans.

We can draw several conclusions regarding the two Mathers prior to 1688. Their interest in missions was apparently minimal. Their dominant concern was in warning wayward colonists against impending judgment and in calling New England to reform.

In 1688 Increase Mather embarked for England to plead for the renewal of the colonial charter. His three year stay was something of a turning point, for his interest in both missions and millennial expectations was stimulated. It was an interest he appears to have communicated to his son.

Early in his stay in London Mather wrote a cryptic account of New England missions to Professor John Leusden, a Dutch Hebraist at the University of Utrecht.[51] The account delighted Leusden, who reciprocated by dedicating a Latin-Hebrew edition of the psalter to Mather.[52] Mather was equally delighted by the widespread reception given the letter, for it appeared in Latin, German, French, and English editions.[53] Kellaway suggests that the success of the letter was a factor in Mather's appointment as commissioner for the New England Company in 1690. He was "the most renowned" of several new appointees.[54] Undoubtedly his personal visits with Boyle,[55] then serving his last years as Governor of the Company, and his introduction to various members of the Company assured his appointment. Mather's attention was also drawn to missions by the communications he received from John Cotton, Jr., and his defenses must have been alerted by rumors current in London of attempts to subvert the Indians to Roman

49 *Ibid.*, 130.

50 *Diatriba de Signo Filii Hominis, et de Secundo Messiae Adventu; ubi de modo futurae Judaeorum Conversionis* (Amsterdam: 1682).

51 Entitled *De Successu Evangelij apud Indos in Nova-Anglia*, this letter was translated by Cotton Mather and included, with a lengthy commentary on it, in his acount of the life of Eliot. *Magnalia Christi Americana*, I, 562-575.

52 The impact of Mather's letter in the Netherlands is described by Rooy, 274, n. 5.

53 Murdock, 272.

54 Kellaway, 202.

55 Murdock, 266.

Catholicism.[56] Richard Baxter, who had corresponded for decades with Eliot and had also received Mather into his home, must have engendered enthusiasm for missions in his guest.

The visits with Baxter were often devoted to discussions on eschatology. It was during these years that Baxter was debating Thomas Beverley. Mather was diplomatic as well as learned, for he could speak with both men. Among his library books on the interpretation of prophecy and the millennium was Beverley's *Thousand Years Kingdom of Christ*, inscribed "Mr. I. Mather . . . *Ex dono Authoris.*"[57] In his discussions with Baxter his mediate position between his host and Beverley appeared. On the basis of his talks with Mather Baxter dedicated his assault on Beverley's position, *The Glorious Kingdom of Christ*, to Mather. Regarding Mather's treatment of the conversion of the Jews he confided, "I have read no man that hath handled it with so much Learning and Moderation as you have done. . . ." He went on to tell his American friend,

> I know no man fitter, if I err, to detect my Errours. And as your Candour is rather for my publishing, than suppressing these Papers; so truly I am so far from disliking a true Confutation of this (or any Errour that I shall publish) that I therefore direct these lines to you, to intreat you, to write (whether I be alive or dead) your Reasons against any momentous or Dangerous Errour which you shall here find: That as we thus friendly consent to such a Collision, or rather Communication, as may kindle some further sparks of light, the Readers may be helpt by comparing all, the better to seek out the truth.[58]

The letter is as much a tribute to Baxter's passion for truth as to his esteem for Mather.

The fruits of Mather's trip appeared soon. While it may be true that "he did not take more than passing interest in the Company's work,"[59] his interest was sufficiently sustained and visionary to initiate steps toward further mission activity. His name heads the list of distinguished signers of a letter to Governor Phips and the Council of Massachusetts, who were solicited "to encourage a design of propagating the Christian faith" among the Indians.[60] Slightly over three years later he expressed his continuing distress over the plight of missions. Since Eliot's death "there has been a signal blast of heaven on ye Indian work."[61] Many of the most devout

---

56 Kellaway, 200-202.
57 Murdock, 269, n. 29.
58 *Ibid.*, 266-267.
59 Kellaway, 207.
60 A letter to Governor Phips, October 2, 1693 (*Collections of the Massachusetts Historical Society*, Series III, vol. I; Boston: 1825), 134.
61 Ford, 81.

converts, both preachers and laymen, had died, and the younger generation of Indian Christians were not of equal mettle. Writing to Sir William Ashurst, Governor of the Company, Mather informed him of a plan to send two ministers capable of addressing the Indians in their tongue on a tour of all the praying towns. They were presumably sent in order to reverse this downward trend. The next year he reported that the tour was in process: Mr. Rawson and Mr. Danforth were visiting "all the Indians throughout ye province."[62]

Mather's concern for the continuation and improvement of the Indian work is further demonstrated by a second problem which he broached in these years. Only three of the colonial commissioners enjoyed the health and opportunity to meet their obligations to the Company. Another was indisposed, and new appointments to replace several who had died had not been made. Speaking for himself and commissioner William Stoughton, Mather recommended a number of replacements. Among them were Judge Samuel Sewall of Boston and Mather's son Cotton. These men were readily appointed, and through their contributions "a more vigorous period in the Commissioners' affairs" began.[63] Increase's activity on behalf of missions continued into this new period.

An assessment of the forces which constrained Mather's mission activity after 1688 must acknowledge the note of millennial expectancy, however faint it was. By 1693 there were indications that God's anger was lifting from New England and that a more favorable period, particularly for missions, lay ahead.

> Inasmuch as the peace, by the good hand of God lately restored in the eastern parts of this province, affords a return of the opportunity to gospelize the Indians in those parts; the former neglects whereof, 'tis to be feared, have been chastised in the sore disasters, which the late wars with the salvages have brought upon us,

Massachusetts must "by all fit methods" encourage missions.[64] Thus could the original pledge of the colonial charter be realized and French missions be challenged. By thus seeking the kingdom of God, trade would undoubtedly be blessed as well.[65]

Admittedly, much of the old concern with God's judgment and blessing as responses to Congregational faith and conduct shines through here. There is an attempt to discern the signs of a better era. But just the fact that Mather and his fellow ministers could speak hopefully about prospects for the future and could suggest that a part of New England's destiny as

---

62 *Ibid.*, 82.
63 Kellaway, 203. Also see Vaughan, 307.
64 Letter to Phips, 133-134.
65 *Ibid.*

expressed in the Massachusetts charter was within reach indicates renewed interest in millennial themes.

Cotton Mather gave motifs like signs of the times, judgments, and reformation a millennial emphasis in a number of writings in the 1690's. He was influenced by, even "shaken by," [66] the views of the apocalyptic physicists. Furthermore, he followed men like Mede, Goodwin, and even Beverley in anticipating a judgment and the dawn of the millennium sometime near the turn of the century. In 1692 he wrote, "I am verily perswaded, 'The Judge is at the Door'; I do without any hesitation venture to say, 'The Great Day of the Lord is Near, it is Near, and it hastens Greatly.'" [67] That same year he preached *A Midnight Cry*, in which he calculated that Christ's coming would occur "about an Hundred and Fourscore Years" after the first Reformation, which began in 1517.[68] Although his calculated date is actually 1697, he, like Increase, was unwilling to commit himself to an exact date as had Beverley.[69] But he knew that 1697 could not be far wrong. Cotton wishfully conceived of himself as a second John the Baptist, "an Herald of the Lord's Kingdome now approaching, and 'the Voice crying in the Wilderness,' for Preparation thereunto." [70]

This modern prophet warned his hearers to be in constant expectancy and preparation for "that Glorious Revolution." At that time Christ would conduct a judgment in the earth's atmosphere. He would accomplish two objectives: "both dispossess the *Divels* of our *Air*, making of it a *New Heaven*, filled with the *New Jerusalem* of his Raised Saints; and also by a terrible Conflagration make a *New Earth*, whereon the *Escaped Nations* are to walk in the *Light* of that *Holy City*." [71]

The spiritual victory of the forces of Christ in the heavens would be followed on earth by "a REFORMATION more Glorious, more Heavenly, more Universal far away than what was in the former Century." [72] Opponents of the new reformation will be utterly desolated, continued Mather. He was living near the dawn of the day when God would "vouchsafe a marvellous Effusion of His own *Spirit* upon many Nations" and when piety and charity would "gain the Ascendent, over those Men and Things, that for many Ages have been the Oppressors of it." [73] "A Wonderful STATE

---

66 Miller, 227.

67 Cotton Mather, *Preparatory Meditations Upon the Day of Judgment*, as given in Thomas James Holmes, *Cotton Mather, A Bibliography of His Works*, 3 vols. (Cambridge, Mass.: 1940), II, 839.

68 *Ibid.*, 840, n. 5.

69 *Ibid.* In 1708 Increase called such date-setting "too much Boldness and Presumption."

70 Cotton Mather, *A Midnight Cry*, as given in Holmes, II, 680.

71 *Ibid.*, 683.

72 *Ibid.*

73 *Ibid.*, 684.

of External PEACE" would spread over the whole earth. Delight in the slaughter of Protestants by such Roman Catholic powers as Louis XIV of France, the consistory of cardinals, and the Duke of Alva would be surpassed. Only good and just magistrates would rule.[74]

Until the peace of the new reformation dawns, said Mather, the saints should strive to realize "as much of it *Now* among our selves, as may be Consistent with our present Circumstances."[75] Pure churches should be planted and maintained in all places. But at this stage in his thought *plantatio ecclesiae* meant primarily the planting and preservation of Reformed, English congregations. Rooy's conclusion from analyzing the *Magnalia,* which was written in 1702, is applicable here: Mather's chief concern was "not the conversion of the heathen, though this takes its place in the larger whole."[76] Mather regarded the Indians as "capable of giving sore Annoyances unto us."[77] These savages strongly resembled the ancient Philistines in the cruelty with which they laid waste New England countryside and tortured her inhabitants. If they are not Canaanites, they must at least be Sythians, he concluded.[78]

Nor did missions receive overt attention in the eschatology advocated in Mather's 1696 election day sermon, views he still defended in 1702, when he included the following paragraph from his sermon in the *Magnalia.*

> The tidings which I bring unto you are, that there is a REVOLUTION and a REFORMATION at the very door, which will be vastly more wonderful than any of the deliverances yet seen by the church of God from the beginning of the world. I do not say that the *next year* will bring on this *happy period*; but this I do say, the bigger part of this assembly may, in the course of nature, live to see it. These things will come on with horrible commotions, and concussions, and confusions: The mighty angels of the Lord Jesus Christ will make their descent, and set the world a *trembling* at the approaches of their almighty Lord; they will *shake* nations, and *shake* churches, and *shake* mighty kingdoms, and *shake once more, not earth only, but heaven also.*[79]

Only after the great Reformation got under way would the Jews and the Gentiles accept the gospel. Meanwhile New Englanders had to demonstrate good faith in God's promises by doing what they could for the conversion of the unbelievers. Mather's own good faith was stimulated by his appoint-

---

74 Cotton Mather, *Things to be Look'd for,* as given in Holmes, III, 1082 and 1084.

75 *Ibid.,* 1084.

76 Rooy, 253.

77 Cotton Mather, *Things to be Look'd for,* as given in Holmes, III, 1084.

78 Cotton Mather, *A Midnight Cry,* as in Holmes, II, 682.

79 Cotton Mather, *Magnalia Christi Americana,* II, 653.

ment as commissioner, by the appearance of a novel little book written by Sewall, and by his contact with Pietism.

2. Phaenomena quaedam Apocalyptica

One theme in New England discussions regarding her meaning and her future was "the New Jerusalem" as described in Revelation 21. Twisse's letter to Mede had originally raised the question whether or not New England might be the location of the city prophesied as descending from heaven.[80] Mede's answer had chagrined the planters, and debate on the issue had never entirely died. It had received attention in the Eliot tracts.[81] Mather's *Magnalia* associated it with incidents in earlier New England history,[82] though the possibility that Sewall rejuvenated Mather's interest in the idea must be considered. As the credibility of the theory that the Indians were Israelites waned,[83] however, the redman received correspondingly less missionary attention as a prospective citizen of the New Jerusalem. Indian wars confirmed his kinship with Canaanites. When the celestial city descended, the New England contingent entering its gates would be Congregational saints, the spiritual Israel.

It fell to Samuel Sewall to restore the Indian to a place beside the white man in colonial thinking on the new Israel. He was well-read in the writings of first generation colonial ministers and theologians, and he understood and believed their vision of New England like few of his contemporaries. Taking seriously the commitment in the charters to gospelize the natives, Sewall stressed missions in a millennial context. Moreover, as the new century neared, he saw himself and his contemporaries in that same context. His insights were published in *Phaenomena quaedam Apocalyptica ad Aspectum Novi Orbis configurata*, a conglomeration of jumbled exegesis, speciously fortifying historical examples, and forthright, sometimes brilliantly worded, appeals. But its main thrust was unmistakable. The realization of the New Jerusalem in New England and America was bound up with the conversion of the Indians. The Boston judge was challenging his fellow citizens to renew missions. His ideas are worth summarizing.

Some think Asia will be the scene of the New Jerusalem, he begins. Wherever it will be, it "will not straiten, and enfeeble; but wonderfully

---

80   *vide supra*, 25-26.
81   *vide supra*, 53.
82   Rooy, 261.
83   One indication of the low estate to which the Thorowgood theory had fallen is Samuel Lee's response to the queries of a London medical man. The prominent New England pastor thought the Indians were a mixture of Tartars and Phoenicians. Sewall, who forwarded the letter to London after Lee's sudden death, remained deferentially silent about his own views. See Kittredge, 178-179.

dilate, and invigorate Christianity in the several Quarters of the World; in *Asia*, in *Africa*, in *Europe*, and in *America*." [84] As an American Sewall asks why America, perhaps New Spain, can not be the location of the New Jerusalem. If Eliot's opinion that the American natives are descendants of the ten tribes of Israel can be proven true, "the dispute will quickly be at an end." [85] The city may well descend behind Antichristian lines, to a region possessed by Satan for many ages. For Christ can easily enter the strong man's house and overpower him.

In a chain of expositions of four key Scripture passages Sewall builds his case. Psalm 2:8 reads, "'Ask of me, and I shall give thee the heathen for thine inheritance, and the *Uttermost* parts of the earth for thy possession.'" [86] America has a stronger claim to this charter of Christ's government than any other part of the world, for, as the last major area to be discovered, she is in fact the "uttermost" part of the earth. The ferocity of the Spanish conquistadors fulfilled verse 9, "'Thou shalt breake them with a rod of iron, thou shalt dash them in pieces like a potters Vessel,'" [87] and the fall of arrogant Montezuma, king of the Aztecs, was predicted in verse 10. Relying heavily on the Eliot tracts, Sewall applies Ezekiel 37, the prophet's vision of the valley of dry bones, to America. "Certainly, no part of the habitable World, can show more *Bones*; or bones more *dry*, than these vast Regions do." [88] For his third passage Sewall turns to Daniel 11:45. "And he shall plant the tabernacles of his palace between the sea and the glorious holy mountain; yet he shall come to his end, and none shall help him." "Plant" obviously refers to "American plantations"; "tabernacles," the temporariness of Antichristian settlements there; "palaces," the Spanish emphasis on pomp and wealth; "between the seas," the Central American isthmus. And although the adjective "holy" in the phrase "glorious holy mountain" hardly seems to fit Spain, does not Exodus 15:13 and 17 refer to wicked Israel as dwelling in God's holy habitation? [89] Finally, Revelation 6:8f., the account of the opening of the fourth and fifth seals, applies to America. The four first seals are local in application, referring to Asia, Africa, Europe, and America in that order. The fourth is chilling. "'And I looked, and behold, a pale horse; and his name that sat on him was Death, and hell followed with him: and power was given to them over the Fourth part of the earth, to kill with sword, and with hunger, and with death, and with the beasts of the earth.'" [90] The cruel slaughter of millions of Indians by the Spanish fulfilled this prophecy. The opening of the fifth seal, when John

84 Sewall, 2.
85 *Ibid.*
86 *Ibid.*
87 *Ibid.*, 3.
88 *Ibid.*, 4.
89 *Ibid.*, 5-6.
90 *Ibid.*, 8.

saw the souls of those martyred for their Christian witness, Sewall also blithely applies to pagan Indians. Following a long excursus on Protestant martyrs in Europe and Indian martyrs in America, two classes of martyrs are distinguished. "The first were slain because they were *Christians;* the latter were slain because they were *Not Papists.*" [91]

Having proven America's place in apocalyptic events to his satisfaction, Sewall describes the extent to which these events have transpired. He jumps, therefore, to a consideration of the pouring out of the sixth vial, Revelation 16 : 12-16. Believing that "no less than Five ANGELS have already poured out their Vials" [92] against the Roman Catholic establishment, Sewall senses that the sixth is about to flow. Like each of the former, this one has its particular objective.

> And the Sixth Angel seems now to stand ready with his Vial, waiting only for the Word to be given for the pouring of it out. The pouring out of this Vial will dry up the Antichristian Interests in the New World: and thereby prepare the way for the Kings of the East.[93]

By these kings Sewall understands the Jews. Today there are many Jewish families throughout the Americas. "Probably, these *Jews* will be converted, before any great Numbers of the *Indians,* shall I say, or *Israelites,* be brought in," for such seems to be the order prophesied in Zechariah 12 : 7.[94] When Christ converts the inhabitants of America, he will break the dominion which Satan has so long held on this continent. Therefore, the "Americans are, at this Time, very Emphatically Concerned" in the divine apocalyptic drama.[95] Englishmen should not balk at Mexico's being the location of the New Jerusalem, for they can reach it as conveniently as they can the old Jerusalem.[96] As irrefutable English evidence of God's present activity in America Sewall cites the "no less than Six times Three very Credible Witnesses" who testified in *A Glorious Manifestation of the Further Progress of the Gospel* that Psalm 72 : 8 and Isaiah 49 : 6 were being accomplished in the conversion of the New England Indians.[97]

Sewall focuses the bulk of his remaining discussion on missions. "It may be hoped that Christ will be so far from quitting what He hath already got in *New-England;* that He will sooner enlarge his Dominion, by bringing on a glorious Reformation in *New Spain.*" [98] Hence he not only chides Twisse

---

91   *Ibid.,* 17.
92   *Ibid.,* 21.
93   *Ibid.,* 26.
94   *Ibid.,* 39.
95   *Ibid.,* 45.
96   *Ibid.*
97   *Ibid.,* 46. *vide supra,* 48.
98   *Ibid.,* 54.

for changing his initial opinion about America as the location of the New Jerusalem,[99] but he also reminds his readers of what the founders of New England said about the Indians. Did not John Cotton, Joseph Caryl, Richard Mather, and John Endicott all firmly believe that the Indians would be converted according to many Biblical promises and that Christ's kingdom would be established here?[100] Did not John Oxenbridge in *A Plea for the Dumb Indian* explicitly and convincingly argue for Indian missions? He gave two motives: the command of Christ, based on Mark 16 : 15, and the desire for the Lord's return, based on Matthew 24 : 14. Paraphrasing Oxenbridge, Sewall makes a rousing appeal for support on the basis of the second motive.

> I need not again rescue this Text to the sence that favours the *Indians* Gospelling: but rather imploy it in this Service. Christians, Would you not gladly have Christ come? Do you not long for such a Day of his *Presence*, as will never be obscured by a Night of *Absence* or Withdrawing? Do you not look out sharp for Him, to end the Violences and Abuses of the sons of Wickedness? To dispatch this Vain and Vexatious world? What say you? Do you so love Christ, as to say with the Bride, by the same Spirit, 'Come Lord Jesus! Come quickly!' Are you in good earnest that hear this? Desire then, Pray and Labour that the Gospel may be preached in all the World; in this *Indian* End of it. For till then, Christ himself tells you, He will not, He cannot come. The Door is, as it were, shut against Him. How do you desire Him to come in, and yet ly drowsing and turning on your Bed, as a Door upon the hing? You are trying near hand, how you can shift for your *Selves;* and so in effect, shift off CHRIST, who is all this while kept without door. For Love, or Shame, Get Up! and Open the Door! 2 *Peter,* 3.12. 'Looking for, and hasting unto the coming of the day of God.' Sit not then still: but as we use to. do with desirable and welcom Guests, go out to meet Him, and bring Him in....[101]

Sewall left no chance for misunderstanding. "Let Protestants now, for shame, arise, and shew that they have some breathings of a true Apostolical Spirit in them."[102]

Like two strategically aimed shots, the two dedications of Sewall's book were addressed to Sir William Ashurst, Governor of the New England Company, and to William Stoughton, Lieutenant Governor of the Massa-

---

99 *Ibid.,* 54-56.

100 *Ibid.,* 56-57. Sewall gives excerpts from the writings of these men which mention Ps. 2 : 8-9 (three times); 22 : 27; 72 : 11; 86 : 9; Dan. 2 : 35, 44-45; 7 : 26-27; Zech. 14 : 9 (twice); Acts 1 : 7; Rev. 18 : 21; 12 : 7-9; 15 : 8.

101 *Ibid.,* 59. For broader background on the work of Oxenbridge in Guiana see J. M. van der Linde, *Het Visioen van Herrnhut en het Apostolaat der Moravische Broeders in Suriname, 1735-1863* (Paramaribo: 1956), especially 19-23, "De Engelse handelskerk."

102 Sewall, 60.

chusetts colony and treasurer of the board of commissioners. Ola E. Winslow does not have an adequate basis for her suggestion that in his dedication to Ashurst Sewall "was placing himself in line for appointment as one of the American commissioners." [103] His motives were much nobler than petty personal ambition. He was deeply concerned for New England's future, and he was preaching a largely forgotten lesson to his fellow Puritans: New England will share in the blessings of Christ's imminent kingdom only if she pursues missions in covenant obedience to her original pledges. He had seen a new vision, and he directed his message to two people capable of taking effective action on it. Its appearance in 1697, a year when expectations were running high, was no accident. Referring to the work of the 1650's, he addressed Stoughton,

> The sorrowful Decay and Languishing of the Work in many places, since that time; and the little Faith that is now to be found in exercise concerning it: are so far from being a ground of Discouragement; that it gives us cause to expect that the set Time draweth very near for our blessed Lord Jesus Christ to be Recognised and Crowned KING of Kings & LORD of Lords.[104]

America would assist in the coronation ceremony. Most likely she would be the stage of the New Jerusalem. In her God had begun "to form a People for Himself." [105] They were undoubtedly the lost descendants of Jacob. Sewall wanted to "show the Company that he was deeply interested in the Indians' conversion," [106] through which God would perfect that work already begun.

No one in his generation in America was a more dedicated servant of missions than Sewall. His personal acquaintance with the Eliot family and visits to Roxbury undoubtedly stimulated his early interest in missions. In 1699 he was appointed as a commissioner. The next year he assumed responsibilities as secretary of that body and the year after that as treasurer. "At no other time in its history had the Company been kept so well informed of its affairs and interests in New England as it was" by Sewall.[107] He held his offices until 1724. His interest in the natives' welfare is seen in his suggestion to set aside large reserves guarded from the relentless encroachment of the white man both by natural boundaries and by legislation.[108] The scope of his contributions can be ascertained from the extensive references to him in Kellaway's study. In Sewall's funeral sermon

---

103   Ola E. Winslow, *Samuel Sewall of Boston* (New York: 1964), 157.
104   Sewall, B1r.
105   *Ibid.,* B2r.
106   Kellaway, 204.
107   *Ibid.,* 204-205.
108   *Ibid.,* 216f.

Thomas Prince eulogized, "He is Eyes to the Blind, and Feet to the Lame: a Father to the Poor — to the Poor *Indians* I might especially say, for whom He has the tenderest Compassions." [109]

Throughout his long career as commissioner Sewall was quickened by his eschatological vision. In 1713 he published some further reflections on several prophecies. He considered them "an Appendix to the *Phaenomena*."[110] Once again he suggested that Daniel 11 : 45 referred to the American colonies of the Catholic powers.[111] When once the Jews were received "into Favour again," the Gentiles would be brought from death to life.[112] The theme of the gospel day in America comparable to those which had preceded on other continents received a new basis from Sewall's interpretation of the parable of the sower, Matthew 13 : 3-9. Sewall interpreted the four types of soil as Asia, Africa, Europe, and America. "Why may we not, without being Envied, or derided, hope that the *Americans* shall be made the good Ground that shall once at last prove Especially, and Wonderfully fruitfull?"[113] Even the mighty angel who descended from heaven to plant his left foot on the land and his right foot on the sea (Revelation 10 : 2) foretold the eventual superiority of American over European churches, which were respectively the sea and land according to Sewall's interpretation. For "*Justus Heurnius* supposeth that the Churches Planted in those Regions termed *Sea*, shall Excel in Glory; as the Right Foot in common acceptation excels the Left."[114] The most striking feature of the booklet is the poem with which it concludes. Composed on January 1, 1701, it conveys the main features of Sewall's theology:

> Once more! Our GOD, vouchsafe to Shine:
> >Tame Thou the Rigour of our Clime.
> Make haste with thy Impartial Light,
> >And terminate this long dark Night.
>
> Let the transplanted *English* Vine
> >Spread further still: still Call it Thine.
> Prune it with Skill: for yield it can
> >More Fruit to Thee the Husbandman.
>
> Give the poor *Indians* Eyes to see
> >The Light of Life: and set them free;
> That they Religion may profess,
> >Denying all Ungodliness.

---

109 Thomas Prince, *A Sermon upon the Death of the Honourable Samuel Sewall, Esq.* (Boston: 1730), 33.

110 Kellaway, 206.

111 Sewall, *Proposals Touching the Accomplishment of Prophecies Humbly Offered* (Boston: 1713), 1-2.

112 *Ibid.*, 4.

113 *Ibid.*

114 *Ibid.*, 8.

From hard'ned *Jews* the Vail remove,
    Let them their Martyr'd JESUS love;
And Homage unto Him afford,
    Because He is their Rightfull LORD.

So false Religions shall decay,
    And Darkness fly before bright Day:
So Men shall GOD in CHRIST adore;
    And worship Idols vain, no more.

So *Asia*, and *Africa*,
    Europe, with *America*;
All Four, in Consort join'd, shall Sing
    New Songs of Praise to CHRIST our KING.

In 1727 New England was rocked by an earthquake which provoked numerous sermons on God's judgment, his anger, and the nearness of the end.[115] Sewall's complacency was plainly shaken as much as that of anyone. Perhaps the conflagration which would introduce the gospel era had occurred. He reprinted, with an appendix by his own hand, a sermon first published in 1700 by his deceased pastor Samuel Willard. He felt that the subject, the national conversion of the Jews, was both important and seasonable.[116] The same year and undoubtedly for the same reasons he republished his *Phaenomena*. Once again Sewall seized a time of excitement and expectancy to lift the eyes of New England citizens to the blessings stored in the Scriptures for themselves and the Indians.

3. *Descent of the dove*

When in 1698 Cotton Mather was appointed as commissioner with Sewall, a second distinguished career in American missions began. He had shown earlier interest in missions through his contact with the Dutch missionary to the Iroquois tribe, Godefridus Dellius,[117] but only after his appointment did it fully blossom.[118] It was also during his tenure as commissioner that Mather began speaking of missions in eschatological terms. Several motifs are clearly discernible in his eschatology during this period. They are of different origin, or were at least quickened by different contacts he enjoyed.

115 See the references in Charles Evans, *American Bibliography* (Chicago: 1903f.), I, the relevant categories in the index. Some of these sermons reached two or three editions.
116 Samuel Willard, *The Fountain Opened* (3rd. ed.; [Boston]: 1727), 16.
117 See Holmes, I, 50-52; and Rooy, 249, n. 4.
118 The fruits of Rooy's combing of Mather's *Diary* for references to missions and related themes are found in his footnotes on pages 244-248. Dated, these references are almost wholly from 1700f. The same is true of Mather's publications on behalf of missions. See Rooy, 248-252.

At different times one or another of these motifs was dominant, though none was ever entirely absent. We shall trace their importance for his views on missions as it appears in his relevant writings.

Mather's accent on the need for reform in the churches was inherited from the widespread Puritan discussions on the subject. Although in at least one instance in the *Magnalia* he appealed for missions on the basis of the nearness of Christ's appearance,[119] when he wrote this study the reformation problematic was dominant in his thinking. He surveyed the mighty acts of God in New England for his contemporaries that they might become faithful in realizing the goal for which New England had been founded. He was concerned with what Rooy calls "the primary and foundational mission" of founding and maintaining the pure church in America, and only very secondarily with "the secondary and ancillary mission" of evangelizing the Indians.[120] Hence, "direct reference" to the ancillary mission "is made rarely" in the *Magnalia* and even then is often overshadowed by the former.[121] Even the section on Eliot is construed as "The Triumphs of Reformed Religion in America."[122] His many uses of such terms as "New Jerusalem" lack the missionary context and connotation of Sewall's understanding of that term.

As he became more active in the Company's work, however, his writings began to place missions in the context of a renewed Christianity. He published an appeal in 1702 "for regular intercession for the revival of the churches and conversion of Jews, Muslims, and pagans."[123] The following year he wrote that "all Ecclesiastical History, down from the Book of, *The Acts of the Apostles,* to this Time, are fill'd with admirable Examples, of a *Zeal* flaming in the Hearts of *Christians,* to *Christianize* the rest of the World." He found that zeal for the conversion of Negro slaves absent from America: "*Christianity,* Whither art thou fled!" And he prayed that it might return to New England.

> *Return, Return,* O Beautiful Daughter of Heaven, *Return, Return, that we may look upon thee.* What shall we then see, but a vast company of *Christian Householders,* filled with zealous contrivance and agony, to see their *Houses* become *Christian Temples,* and a glorious CHRIST worshipped and obeyed by all their *Households!*[124]

---

119 Beaver, "Eschatology . . . ," 63.

120 Rooy, 275. Although Rooy has shown that the primary and the ancillary mission were "the double thrust" of the one "New England Mission" and must be seen in relationship to one another, New England generally emphasized the former.

121 *Ibid.,* 269.

122 Cotton Mather, *Magnalia Christi Americana,* I, 530.

123 Beaver, "Eschatology . . . ," 63. The reference is to *An Advice to the Churches of the Faithful.*

124 Cotton Mather, *The Negro Christianized* (Boston: 1706), 10-11.

Several years later he articulated the relation of reform and missions still more sharply. "It is the opinion of some Seers, that until the Temple be cleansed, there will be no general appearance of the nations to worship in it." [125] Part of this cleansing must be a willingness on the part of many working under the societies for propagating Christianity to relinquish their pet fancies and interests. "Let us therefore do what we can towards the *reformation* of the Church, in order to its *enlargement*."[126] Men would be converted to and united in the truth when the Holy Spirit was poured out. On the basis of his understanding of the prophets Mather gave a three-point plan for his day: 1. revive primitive Christianity; 2. convince European powers to abandon papacy; 3. form and quicken "the people who are to be 'the stone cut out of the mountain.' " [127] The note of reform and revival was never absent from his later writings, but Mather turned increasingly to the message of the prophets regarding the millennial period itself.

In 1710 he dedicated *Theopolis Americana* to Sewall. *"My Pray'rs and Hopes for* America, *are* Yours; *and I must Acknowledge, that* you *first gave me some of the* Hints, *which my* SERMON *brings for the Grounds of them."* [128] The book dealt with the New Jerusalem, which would follow the seven vials about to be poured out against Antichrist, which would probably be a literal rebuilding of the old Jerusalem, and whose influence would reach men in the entire world.[129] This sermon, originally preached to the Massachusetts General Assembly, was based on Revelation 21 : 21, "The street of the city was pure gold." "Street" Mather interpreted as "marketplace" or place of business, and "gold" as the Golden Rule. On this allegorization he based his explanation of the ethic of the New Jerusalem. It would be inhabited by good and righteous men; it would suppress all oppression, dishonesty, and drunkenness; its churches would be the markets of truth.[130] That the site of the city would be in America Mather was not ready to acknowledge. "All I will say, is thus much. There are many Arguments to perswade us, That our Glorious LORD, will have an Holy City in AMERICA." [131] That God would allow America to remain "a *Place for Dragons"* while Satan would be bound was unimaginable.[132]

> Has it not been promised unto our Great Saviour? Psal. 2,8. 'I will give thee the uttermost parts of the Earth for thy Possession.' And,

125 Cotton Mather, *Essays to do Good* (London: 1807), 156. This work first appeared under the title *Bonifacius* (Boston: 1710).
126 *Ibid.*
127 *Ibid.,* 159.
128 Cotton Mather, *Theopolis Americana* (Boston: 1710), A2v.
129 *Ibid.,* 4.
130 *Ibid.,* 7-41.
131 *Ibid.,* 43.
132 *Ibid.*

Psal. 86,9. 'All Nations whom thou hast made, shall come and worship before thee, O Lord, and shall glorify thy Name.' And, has it not been promised? Mal. 1,11. 'From the Rising of the Sun even unto the going down of the same, my Name shall be great among the Gentiles.' AMERICA is Legible in these Promises.[133]

As a great mountain Christ's kingdom would fill the earth, including America (Daniel 2 : 44). The truths for which men were martyred in America would triumph in her. Had not even Augustine predicted that the church of Christ would flourish in all four parts of the earth? The parable of the Sower proved that the gospel would bear much fruit on the good, American soil, and the fact that Jesus entered a ship after teaching that parable proved to Mather that the gospel would reach America by navigation. When the seventh trumpet would sound and the vials would begin to flow on Antichrist in America and Europe, it would be impossible that the Spirit-filled men who would bring the gospel to the ends of the earth would ignore America. New England was "a *Seisin*" of Christ, which guaranteed his claim to the rest of America.[134] Christ's dominion would be from sea to sea, and the ambassadors of the holy city would have their work also in New England.[135]

The fact that Mather was not immediately concerned with the evangelization of the Indians in his sermon on the New Jerusalem is understandable in terms of his opinions concerning the whereabouts of the ten tribes and the sequence of millennial events. While the two tribes were scattered to all corners of the earth, the remnants of the ten tribes might be found "in the very Places whither *Salmanassar* so long ago transported them."[136] With the ten tribes still in the Middle East, it was only logical for Mather to conclude that the New Jerusalem would be rebuilt in Palestine. Only then would her emissaries be sent to all nations, and only then would the Indians be converted en masse. Mather, therefore, was awaiting the great earthquake, the pouring of the seventh vial, which would signalize the fall of Antichrist. After Antichrist's fall the ten tribes would return and rebuild Jerusalem. Thus, while his ultimate hopes for America were similar to Sewall's, Mather looked to Europe and the Middle East for act one in the millennial drama.

During the second decade of the eighteenth century Mather began corresponding with leaders in the Pietist movement. These contacts were a third source of his interest in missions, and they provoked his thought on other eschatological motifs.

In 1714 Francke wrote to Mather regarding his father's letter to Leusden. He desired to be more fully informed about Eliot and the present state of

133 *Ibid.,* 43-44.
134 *Ibid.,* 50.
135 *Ibid.,* 44-51.
136 *Ibid.,* Appendix, [53].

the work in America, and he related to Mather the beginning of the Pietist work in Tranquebar. In his response, addressed to the missionaries in Tranquebar, Mather spoke highly of the missionary vocation and deplored the fact that Roman Catholic missions were outstripping Protestant missionary exertions.[137] He encouraged the Danish-Halle men to preach only "the *Pure Maxims* of the *Everlasting Gospel*" which he summarized as the doctrines of the Trinity and redemption in Christ and as the ethic of the Golden Rule.[138].

Just as his thinking on the Golden Rule, which he had treated in *Theopolis Americana,* Mather's views on the everlasting gospel appeared in other of his writings. The year after he wrote his letter to the missionaries, 1715, he published *The Stone Cut out of the Mountain. And the Kingdom of God.* The teachings of the everlasting gospel are like "*a Sweet-scented Liquor,*" which, when sprayed upon warring bees, obliterates all differences in odor by which they distinguish friend from foe, Mather wrote.[139] The everlasting gospel would become the basis of unity for Christians in the coming kingdom of God, which would eventually spread through all the earth as the stone cut out of the mountain. But it would also become the message brought to non-Christians as that kingdom spread. [140]

Other eschatological themes entered Mather's correspondence with the Pietists in his letter to Anton W. Boehm in 1716. In it "Mather dared think that 'vital piety and Franckian charity' needs must unite the people of God, and when this occurred the Papal empire would fall and the Kingdom of God would come." [141] When Francke suggested, following the common European notion, that America was the "worthless servant" who would be thrown "into the outer darkness" (Matthew 25 : 30), Mather praised her "true and genuine Christianity." [142] Denying the Eastern Orthodox tradition associating the West with Antichrist, Mather contended, "We have now seen

137 Benz, 179.
138 *Ibid.,* 180-181.
139 Holmes, III, 1038. Also see Benz, 173-174. While we have found no theological elaboration on the concept "*Evangelium Aeternum*" to this point in the Anglo-American missionary tradition, we have found such on the concept of the stone cut out of the mountain. *vide supra,* 54.
140 Benz correctly recognizes the role of the "*Evangelium Aeternum*" idea in Mather's ecumenical and missionary thought. He overextends himself, however, by calling it "the basic element" in both. (185)
141 Beaver, "Eschatology . . . ," 63.
142 Benz, 166. It is grossly in error to cite Mather's responses to the Pietists, and this response in particular, as the source of "the soteriological self-understanding of the American churches." (167) See also 168. The studies of Rooy and Blanke, to mention only two, quite disprove this and Benz's later allegation that Mather's *India Christiana* in "one of the earliest expressions of that missionary self-consciousness of American Christianity which has influenced so deeply the historical self-understanding of the American people." (182)

the *Sun Rising in the West."* [143] American missionaries have brought pure religion to the Indians.

The pouring out of the Holy Spirit was the last and possibly most significant eschatological motif which entered Mather's correspondence with Pietists. "'Tis indeed with a very Trembling Heart, and not without the most profound Submission, that I would now hint a matter to you," he wrote to Ziegenbalg.[144] Reputable scholars

> are of this Perswasion; That the *Reformation* and *Propagation* of *Religion*, will be accomplished, by Granting over again, those *Extraordinary Gifts of the Prophetic Spirit*, by which the Holy Spirit watered the Primitive Church, and at first spread and confirmed the *Christian Religion* in the World.[145]

The Spirit had lived in the early church for more than two centuries, only to be succeeded by the spirit of Antichrist. After twelve hundred sixty years it was likely that "the *Dove"* would return again. What if God's kingdom would come "with the Joy of the Holy SPIRIT, working with such *Gifts* and in such *Ways*, as He has promised, for both the *Internal & External* Propagation of His Gospel?"[146] Joel's prophecy of the pouring out of the Spirit on all flesh must still be fulfilled *"in the Latter Days."* [147] It might even be that Antichrist would be destroyed by men wielding gifts given them by the Spirit. Mather suggested to Ziegenbalg that in answer to prayer God might supply him with such gifts of the Spirit as were consonant with the new age and which would facilitate his mission work.

> Whether the Time appointed by GOD for such an Effusion of the Holy Spirit, may quickly come on, & the *Kingdom of GOD be suddenly to appear?* For my part, I do not Know. But that it is not very far off, I do Believe. Whether You, who are such Devout Worshippers of GOD, and who with so much of Charity and Self-denial, may Enjoy (what I wish for you) the *First Fruits* of this Effusion; I confess, 'tis what I know not. But that GOD may favour you with Plentiful Successes, This is what I constantly & fervently Pray for, and what upon some good Grounds I hope for.[148]

When the commissioners of the New England Company assembled at

143 As quoted by Benz, 168.

144 Cotton Mather, *India Christiana* (Boston: 1721), 69. The letter was dated Dec. 31, 1717.

145 *Ibid.* Mather may have had in mind Solomon Stoddard, who experienced a number of awakenings in his Northampton congregation. *vide infra,* 124. Interestingly, Stoddard's fourth "harvest" occurred just several years before Mather addressed this letter to Ziegenbalg.

146 *Ibid.,* 71.

147 *Ibid.,* 72.

148 *Ibid.,* 74.

Judge Sewall's home several years later, Mather delivered an address which was later published with a portion of his Pietist correspondence. Choosing Psalm 89 : 15 as his text, he focused on the words "joyful sound," which he interpreted as "gospel." Following his extended account of the coming of that sound to America after centuries of Satan's dominion there is an appeal for prayer for current work in America and in Tranquebar. Striking the same note he had sounded to Ziegenbalg, Mather suggested that prayer for the Spirit was the most effective weapon with which to arm missionaries. "I despair of any very Great Matters to be done, for the Spreading of the Gospel, thro' the World, until the *Israelitish Nation* be Returned unto their Land, and Converted unto their GOD." [149] Therefore, prayers "for that Happy Revolution" should be fervent, and he and his colleagues should "be doing what we can." [150] If the prayers were answered and the work blest, both the Jews and the Gentiles would be converted.

> Yea, who can tell, but the Holy SPIRIT promised upon the *Asking* for it, would make such a Descent, as to *do Wondrously*, and the *Holy Arm of the Lord* would be *made bare in the Eyes of all the Nations*, and *all the Ends of the Earth, should see the Salvation of our GOD;* and the *Dove* would so Return to us as to Tarry with us, and the *Flood* of Ignorance and Wickedness, wherein the Earth is now over-whelmed, shall be carried away.[151]

Scarcely fifteen years later it appeared that those prayers were answered in the Great Awakening. Then, however, the outpouring of the Spirit was interpreted in the simple chiliastic framework of Jonathan Edwards rather than in terms of Mather's complex chiliasm.[152]

4. Heirs of the vision

During the Mather-Sewall era of New England missions others also declared that God's plan for the end of history required that his people pray and work for the conversion of the non-Christian.

In 1700 Samuel Willard preached the doctrine, "THERE will be a more peculiar Opening of CHRIST as a Fountain of Life, when the JEWS shall be

---

149 *Ibid.*, 46.
150 *Ibid.*, 47.
151 *Ibid.*, 48.
152 Mather's final chiliastic views were recorded in his manuscript for *Triparadisus*, which unfortunately was misplaced before the book could be published. Samuel Mather gave a summary of its contents in *The Life of the Very Reverend and Learned Cotton Mather, D.D. & F.R.S.* (Boston: 1729), 140-146. Holmes, III, 1123-1124 also summarizes and outlines the manuscript, which was recovered after Mather's death.

Called." [153] Days of spiritual felicity for the church would follow "*her wilderness-state*" and would be contemporary with "*the Calling of the* Jews," "*the fulness of the* Gentiles," and "*the destruction of* Anti-Christ." [154] Effecting conversions and Christian vitality, the mighty pouring out of the Spirit in those days would accompany preaching.[155] What action did Willard enjoin on his hearers in the light of these truths? Christians should practice prayer and diligence in equipping their children for that day.[156]

Samuel Danforth, minister of Taunton and itinerant missionary, preached on the need for using all possible means for obtaining a "divine visitation." Centering his thoughts around past and future outpourings of the Spirit, he proclaimed that "the fresh Breathings and Pourings out of Gods Spirit on His People... is a Prognostick that Christ hath a Marriage Day at hand, wherein He will Espouse some Other People to Himself, Even such as knew Him not, and that called not on His Name." [157] Meanwhile, the propagation of the gospel in unevangelized settlements and colonies may foster preliminary revivals, he continued.

Solomon Stoddard, who had had harsh words for the Indians earlier,[158] warned New England of God's impending wrath against her for neglecting missions since the days of Eliot. For in the light of the many promises in Scripture regarding their conversion, "*it is a very desireable thing that the Heathen be brought to the Faith.*" [159] He cited two of the best known promises: "It was foretold of Christ, that 'all nations shall call him blessed,' Psal. 72.7. GOD promised to Him that He 'would give Him the Heathen for his Inheritance,' Psal. 2.8." [160]

The same spirit of lamentation characterized "An Attestation by the United Ministers of Boston" several years later. Since Eliot's death, they complained, there has been "a growing occasion" for complaint against the neglect of missions.[161]

In a series of sermons on "the desire of the nations" (Haggai 2:7),

---

153 Willard, 3.
154 *Ibid.*, 8-9.
155 *Ibid.*, 11.
156 *Ibid.*, 13-15.
157 Samuel Danforth, "An Exhortation to All," in *The Ministry of Taunton,* Samuel Hopkins Emery (ed.), 2 vols. (Cleveland: 1853), I, 213-214. This sermon was originally delivered in 1714. See Kellaway, 233-234, for an account of Danforth's missionary activities.
158 See Kellaway, 206-207.
159 Solomon Stoddard, *QUESTION Whether God is not Angry with the Country for doing so little towards the Conversion of the Indians* (Boston: 1723), 11.
160 Solomon Stoddard, *An Answer to some Cases of Conscience Respecting the Country* (Boston: 1722), 11.
161 See Experience Mayhew, *Indian Converts* (London: 1727), xiv-xviii. Mayhew indicated that the style of the "Attestation" "appears to indicate the hand of Cotton Mather." Also see Holmes, I, 58.

Benjamin Coleman, a prominent Boston minister, reported that as yet many nations had not made Christ their desire. But, "we look for the days, when the blessed Saviour of men shall be *more* the desire of the nations than he yet has been." [162] Coleman anticipated the days when true converts would increase in number, when the church would be enlarged by the pouring out of the Spirit, when she would be pure and holy, when Antichrist would fall, and when the Jews and Gentiles would be converted.[163] In response to these truths Christians should lament the darkness of the nations, especially of the Jews, and should pray for Christ's speedy coming.[164] Prayer became action five years later, when Coleman participated in the ordination of three full-time missionaries to the Indians.[165]

In spite of sporadic interest in missions to the Indians, however, the cause languished in New England during this period. Only a handful of leaders was interested in it. Even they were unable or unwilling to devote themselves to missions with the selflessness of Eliot. Genuine involvement occurred only on the administrative level. Internal colonial problems and English-French friction, in which the Indian tribes became pawns manipulated in a European struggle for supremacy in America, were the two major deterrents to missions. It is significant, however, that the evangelistic activity and interest that appeared were largely the results of the several millennial expectations of the age. Missions were considered as belonging to the last and glorious age of the church on earth, and that age was at hand.

5. *To the Gentiles first*

The Pietist initiative which led to the Francke-Mather correspondence was shown much earlier toward the English religious societies movement. At an early meeting of the S.P.C.K. two of Francke's envoys explained the Pietist schools to men looking for precedents for their charity schools scheme.[166] Francke later promoted knowledge of the S.P.C.K. and the S.P.G. among his German friends, trained English lads at his famous orphanage, and had Pietist propaganda translated into English.[167] *Pietas Hallensis* was a translation of Francke's account of the orphanage by Anton Wilhelm Boehm, chaplain of the German-speaking Lutheran congregation in London. After 1706 there were several editions, some with a foreward by Joseph Woodward, the first historian of the religious societies movement. The book

162 Benjamin Coleman, *Twenty Sacramental Discourses* (London: 1728), 199.
163 *Ibid.,* 199-200.
164 *Ibid.,* 202-203.
165 See Beaver, *Pioneers in Mission,* Chapter II, *passim.*
166 W. K. Lowther Clarke, *A History of the S.P.C.K.* (London: 1959), 13.
167 Schmidt, "Das hallische Waisenhaus...," 40.

was "extremely important in the spreading of pietism throughout the Anglo-Saxon world."[168] Appreciative even of Roman Catholic instances of benevolence, it represented a faith concerned not first of all with creedal statements and the defense of dogmatic positions, but with realizing the spirit of Christianity in the daily life of the believer.[169]

Pietism's emphasis on benevolent action as the fruit of renewed piety was formally similar to the humanitarianism and moralism which motivated much of the Anglican mission activity of the period.[170] In the S.P.C.K., for example, the goal of spreading Christian knowledge was pursued via the founding of schools and libraries, via literature production and distribution, via efforts to reform morals and manners, and via evangelization. It was felt that the light of the kingdom of God would be diffused through such efforts to lift men to the truths of Christianity.[171] The S.P.C.K. annual sermons deal with such topics as the education of the ignorant, aid to the poor, and compassion to the fatherless and to the handicapped. "An almost uniform characteristic is the apology for educating the poor, which the preachers felt obliged to make."[172] The work of the society was not integrally related to the realization of God's promises regarding the latter days, as the work of the dissenters in the New England Company had been.

If she could overlook the theology of Rome in appreciation of Catholic benevolence, Pietism could also co-operate with Anglican benevolence in spite of the Latitudinarian and humanitarian soil out of which it grew. Such co-operation was realized when the S.P.C.K. extended aid to the Danish-Halle mission in Tranquebar in 1710 and to German immigrants in the American colonies in the 1730's. On the other hand, the broad objectives of the British society readily allowed her to participate in such joint enterprises.

The S.P.G. presents a different picture from the S.P.C.K., however. Not only did she restrict her work to specifically Anglican projects, but paralleling the emphasis on benevolence and morality in her annual sermons is the interpretation of her work as fulfilling the Scriptural promises of the

168   Benz, 163, n. 7.
169   Schmidt, "Das hallische Waisenhaus . . . ," 44 and 45. Francke's Pietism "fragt nicht nach äusserlichem Bekenntnis." (44) "Immer wieder bietet er das Lebensmotiv an entscheidener Stelle auf—entsprechend der pietistischen Grundkonzeption, die die Rechtfertigung, ein juristisches Bild für den Heilsvorgang, durch die Wiedergeburt, ein biologisches Datum, ersetzt. Hier entdeckt der Pietismus aus seiner Frontstellung zur Orthodoxie den grundsätzlich geschichtlichen Charakter des Christentums, wenn auch noch nicht der christlichen Botschaft selbst." (45-46)
170   For an analysis of the forces which stimulated Anglican philanthropy and benevolence see Van den Berg, 36-40; and Clarke, 13-14.
171   Van den Berg calls efforts to realize the kingdom through benevolent enterprises directed at a human race capable of moral betterment the "Erasmian line" of thought. (39)
172   Clarke, 31.

conversion of the Gentiles. Van den Berg correctly asserts that Latitudinarianism was hardly the milieu in which the eschatological motive for missions could thrive. He discovers, however, that "the expectation of the coming Kingdom" did stimulate S.P.G. interest in missions.[173] This anomaly is explainable when it is remembered that such highly esteemed Anglicans as Mede, Ussher, and More had established the reputability of chronological and millennial investigations. Eschatology did receive some attention in Anglican theology, therefore, and its missionary implications were expounded as the central theme in at least one-fourth of the sermons — always presented by a bishop or other leading churchman — delivered to the S.P.G. between 1701 and 1735. It always took the form, however, of very mild millennial expectations, which looked toward the fuller gospel day predicted in both testaments.

The conversion of the nations was seen as guaranteed by Biblical promises. George Stanhope, Dean of Canterbury, set the tone for subsequent sermons on the fulfillment of prophecy when he preached on Isaiah 60 : 9 in 1713. "Whatever Views this Prophecy might have, of any Events peculiar to the *Jewish* Nation; The glorious Increase, and future Fulness of the Christian Church, have generally been thought the main Intention of it."[174] The Dean applied the text to lands still undiscovered. Psalm 67 : 2 is "an earnest Prayer for the Enlargement of the Church, to the Joy of all Nations, and the Increase of God's Blessings," declared the Bishop of Clogher the following year.[175] Everyone who prays for the coming of the Lord's kingdom by reciting this prayer should support mission work, he continued.[176] His closing paragraph typifies as well as any the spirit of Anglican expectations:

> God, in his own due Time, will undoubtedly cause the Fulness of the Gentiles to come in; and how glorious and comfortable a Presage of that happy Time, would a generous Encouragement be of this Undertaking now? What a distinguishing Honour is it, to be thought worthy to be his Instruments in bringing to pass such his gracious Purpose; to be subservient to him in making good his Word, in fulfilling the Promises that he has made, and in so setting forth the Glory of his Goodness and Truth? May the good God inspire us all with such true Christian Zeal and Evangelical Charity, as may prove effectual to the Enlargement of his Kingdom, 'that His Way may be known upon Earth, His saving Health among all Nations.'[177]

Having selected as his text the parable of the mustard seed (Matthew

---

173 Van den Berg, 65.
174 George [Stanhope], S.P.G. (a.s.) (London: 1714), 3.
175 George [Ash], S.P.G. (a.s.) (London: 1715), 3.
176 *Ibid.*, 14.
177 *Ibid.*, 27.

13 : 31-32), another preacher proclaimed that Christ's kingdom would succeed the four monarchies of Daniel 11 : 44 and would eventually fill the whole earth. In the small number of converts in America he saw "the day of small things" which was not to be despised,[178] and he sensed that Old and New Testament promises of the fulness of the Gentiles might be nearing their fulfillment.[179] Likewise Isaiah 49 : 6, 9 : 9, Galatians 4 : 4, Malachi 1 : 11, Luke 2 : 32, Psalm 22 : 27, 67 : 5, and Ephesians 3 : 5-6 were all interpreted in subsequent sermons as promising the fulness of the Gentiles and as inducements to further S.P.G. efforts. The preacher in 1732 predicted, after analyzing a number of prophecies, that after widespread Gentile conversions the Jews would also acknowledge Christ.[180]

Throughout the S.P.G. annual sermons there occur numerous incidental eschatological motifs. These indicate both that the preachers were acquainted with the missionary associations of these themes in earlier Anglo-American missions and that these men gave credence to only the mildest versions of these expectations. English sea power as the divinely appointed means to spread the gospel to the ends of the earth and therefore England's privileged position in God's plans for history were themes which received some mention.[181] There was some inclination to look for signs that the promised spread of Christianity was near. Present zeal for converting the Gentiles was one such sign.[182] Edward Waddington hoped that "the late Frenzy of the Nation" brought on by the bursting of the South Sea Bubble would serve as a sign of God's anger with English avarice and as a premonition of the "glorious Day" of Gentile conversions.[183] Conversely, the Bishop of Lichfield and Coventry, seeing such "present bad Circumstances of the *Christian* World" as the spread of infidelity and the strong anti-Jansenism of the bull *Unigenitus,* concluded that there could be no sudden and imminent approach of a happy state of the church.[184] The westward march of the gospel was cited as an indication that God's plan to evangelize all the earth before the end of history was being fulfilled.[185] Finally, the period of universal knowledge of Christ was spoken of as "Christ's future Kingdom," [186] "the Ends of the World," [187] "that glorious Day," and *"the perfect Day."* [188]

---

178 Edward [Chandler], S.P.G. (a.s.) (London: 1719), 17.
179 *Ibid.,* 21
180 Richard [Smallbrooke], S.P.G. (a.s.) (London: 1733), 16-17.
181 [Stanhope], *passim;* [Ash], 27.
182 [Chandler], 21.
183 Edward [Waddington], S.P.G. (a.s.) (London: 1721), 34, 38-39.
184 [Smallbrooke], 26-27.
185 Zachary [Pearce], S.P.G.(a.s.) (London: 1730), 26.
186 [Ash], 3.
187 [Chandler], 20.
188 [Waddington], 34 and 37.

Only on one occasion did a S.P.G. preacher carry more specifically apocalyptic thoughts into the pulpit. He cautioned against being "so very sanguine as some among us are in their Expectations" that in three or four years the world would be miraculously converted to Christianity, Christianity would be purified, and the church would enter an era of unprecedented happiness.[189] The calculations of others had been erroneous. He did acknowledge, however, that the fall of Antichrist would overcome Jewish animosity toward Christianity, that the conversion of the Jews would effect Gentile conversions, and that miracles of some sort might possibly be used by God to facilitate these conversions.[190] His is the only S.P.G. sermon admitting this sequence of millennial events, which had become so standard in dissenting circles.

In conclusion it can be said that of the two Anglican societies only the S.P.G. appears to have been influenced in her work by mild millennial expectations. Even then, the benevolent spirit of the age was undoubtedly a more significant factor in motivating her undertakings than were eschatological considerations. The latter were of the mild or what we would term the simple, unsystematized variety, and they were so general in nature that they added little urgency to the society's undertakings. The Biblical promises functioned as a guarantee that Anglican efforts would not be fruitless and as an incentive to begin and support initial steps toward the day when all nations would acknowledge Christ. Hence, although Anglican missions sponsored by far the bulk of Anglo-American mission activity during this period, we give them proportionately less treatment than dissenting efforts.

6. *Scottish stirrings*

As had been true in England and in the American colonies before her, in Scotland the provision of an organization responsible for mission work was preceded by years of intensive analysis of the prophecies regarding the latter days. Names like Forbes and Durham were recorded in boldface type in the annals of Scottish exposition. Toward the close of the seventeenth century two Scottish divines again focused attention on the place of the conversion of the nations in the sequence of events predicted for the last days. Their names were Robert Fleming, Sr., and Robert Fleming, Jr. While neither man was directly involved in mission activity, the father typifies the generally accepted eschatology of Scottish Calvinists of the period, and the son made astoundingly accurate predictions which were significant for the rebirth of missions in the 1790's.

Fleming, Sr., who had received his tutelage under Samuel Rutherford,

---

189 [Smallbrooke], 25.
190 *Ibid.*, 30-34.

has been regarded as the author of a study on earthquakes as a sign of the fall of Rome.[191] His major literary effort was *The Fulfilling of the Scripture,* which was begun in the 1660's and republished several times before his death. The elaborate 1726 edition bears such notable names as Isaac Watts and Daniel Neal in its list of subscribers — some indication of Fleming's reputation. The book is basically an apology for the reliability of Scripture. Former instances of the fulfillment of Scripture had to be taken as guarantees that the unfulfilled prophecies would also be realized. The fall of Babylon, the conversion of the Jews, a united and flourishing Gentile-Jewish church, the fall of the Turkish empire, and finally, the battle of Gog and Magog all remained to be fulfilled.[192] His discussion of these points was marked by caution and a reluctance to speculate beyond what is said in Scripture. He believed that the fall of Antichrist was well advanced; that the Jews would return to Palestine, where they would be converted and where the purity of their faith would be emulated by the Gentiles; and that the first resurrection of the saints who would reign with Christ had to be taken figuratively.[193] The spread of Reformed Christianity since the Reformation indicated to Fleming that the victory promised to the church was gradually being secured.[194]

Robert Fleming, Jr., abandoned his father's caution with respect to establishing the dates of the rise and fall of the papacy. By establishing 606 and 758 as the earliest and latest possible dates for its rise, Fleming calculated that Antichrist must be overthrown between 1848 and 2000.[195] He preferred the later of the two dates. Furthermore, Fleming attempted to determine the dates of the pouring out of the seven vials. Their flow would gradually sap Roman Catholic power. The church of his day was living under the fourth vial, which would be emptied by 1794. "I cannot but hope that some new Mortification of the *chief Supporters* of *Antichrist* will then happen; and perhaps the *French Monarchy* may begin to be considerably humbled about that time." [196] The fifth would run until 1848. The Mohammedan Antichrist would be the object of the sixth vial, which would destroy the Turkish monarchy by 1900. The seventh vial would be poured out between 1970 and 2000, when the millennium would dawn. Apart from his interest in dates, Fleming, Jr., closely followed the position of his father.

It was left to Robert Millar of Paisley to articulate the missionary

191 *P.F.F.,* credits the father with this work. *D.N.B.,* noting that Hew Scott gives it to the father, attributes it to the son. (XIX, 285)

192 Robert Fleming, Sr., *The Fulfilling of the Scripture* (5th ed.; London: 1726), 157.

193 *Ibid.,* 157-163.

194 *Ibid.,* 171f.

195 Robert Fleming, Jr., *A New Account of the Rise and Fall of the Papacy,* in *Discourses on Several Subjects* (London: 1701), xxvi-xxvii and xxxii-xxxiv.

196 *Ibid.,* lxiv.

implications of Scottish theology's position on the prophesied spread of Reformed Christianity to the ends of the earth. He did so in *The History of the Propagation of Christianity*, which first appeared in 1723. Judged to be "one of the earliest books in the English language written with a concern for the evangelization of the world," [197] Millar's book treated the spread first of Roman Catholic and then of Protestant Christianity as the progressive fulfillment of the prophecies of the enlargement of Christ's kingdom. To the present surge in missions Millar added his prayers "that 'the earth may be full of the knowledge of the Lord, as the waters cover the sea'; 'that all the kingdoms of the world may become the kingdoms of our Lord and of his Christ'; 'that he may reign for ever and ever.' " [198] Some prophecies of the conversion of the Gentiles and of the fall of Antichrist have already been fulfilled, said Millar. Those regarding the fulness of the Gentiles and the conversion of the Jews have not.[199] With Pierre Jurieu, Huguenot professor at Sedan and later in Rotterdam, Millar thought that God had reserved the arts of printing and modern navigation for the Christian West.[200] Through them true Christianity would be spread around the globe.[201] Since "the time is near" when the promised enlargement of the church "shall be fully accomplished," missions should be supported with prayer and fasting, said Millar,[202] thus anticipating the concerts of prayer held twenty years later.[203] In the "happy days" ahead, when Roman Catholic error and denominationalism would be abolished, all Christians would unite in propagating true Christianity among the Gentiles.[204] Among his recommendations Millar included an appeal for reform. Reform would enable "a holy warmth of sincere piety" to flourish and would foster missions.[205]

Mission interest in Scotland did not originate with Robert Millar. A full decade earlier the S.S.P.C.K. had been issued a patent instructing it to employ its assets in "instructing the people in the Christian Reformed Protestant Religion." [206] The society's efforts were concentrated on erasing illiteracy and papacy from the Highlands. Millar's study was quickened in part by these efforts. He was also indebted to Cotton Mather, from whose

197 John Foster, "A Scottish Contributor to the Missionary Awakening: Robert Millar of Paisley," *I.R.M.*, XXXVII, 1948, 138.

198 Robert Millar, *The History of the Propagation of Christianity*, 2 vols. (3rd. ed.; London: 1731), I, vii-viii.

199 *Ibid.*, I, 72; II, 227.

200 The life and thought of Jurieu has recently been given attention by Frederik R. J. Knetsch, *Pierre Jurieu* (Kampen: 1967).

201 Millar, II, 229-230.

202 *Ibid.*, 355.

203 Foster, 142.

204 Millar, II, 365.

205 *Ibid.*, 377.

206 As quoted by Maclean, 6.

Magnalia account of missions in America he excerpted almost verbatim.[207] But Millar's contribution was significant in its own right. He opened to his countrymen the missionary dimensions of the eschatology that most of them shared, and he urged them to act accordingly. The spirit represented by Millar sparked the evangelical awakening and interest in missions in the following decade.

7. Summary

Between 1675 and 1735 Anglo-American mission activity and thought were concentrated in the old New England Company and three new societies, the S.P.C.K., the S.P.G., and the S.S.P.C.K.

Millennial expectations affected the New England Company through her three leading commissioners, Increase and Cotton Mather and Samuel Sewall. During the last twenty-five years of the seventeenth century the Mathers, anticipating a cataclysmic arrival of the millennium or glorious reformation, urged New England to repent, reform, and realize as many traits of the millennium as possible before its arrival. Though they believed that the complete conversion of the nations belonged to the millennium, the Mathers nevertheless promoted missions as one of many tokens of preliminary reform. Cotton even contended that reform, the cleansing of the temple, was a prerequisite for the further spread of Christianity. Sewall's eschatology differed from the Mathers' on two points, both of which gave his concern for missions more urgency than theirs. The old notion that the Indians were descendants of the ten tribes of Israel and the idea that the New Jerusalem would be located in America caused him to promote missions as the means for converting the Indian "Israelites" and for beginning the millennium. Faithfulness in missions would hasten Christ's coming; inactivity would delay his return, said Sewall. After 1700 Sewall's urgency and Pietist contacts quickened Cotton Mather's interest and activity in missions, though he never conceded Sewall's two chief tenets. Mather increasingly emphasized the effects of the pouring out of the Holy Spirit on the nations during the millennium. Holding up Pietist missions as an example, Mather continued to promote missions as a sign of Reformed faithfulness, which would eventually be blest with a great effusion of the Spirit on all men. He spoke of the kingdom of Christ as a growing mountain which would gradually fill the earth. It would spread by the proclamation of the eternal gospel, that is, by true doctrine and morality.

Unfortunately the conceiving of missions in eschatological categories, which led these commissioners and other prominent New England preachers

---

207 See Samuel Mather, 70. Compare, for example, the passage from Millar cited on page 140 of Foster's article with *Magnalia Christi Americana*, I, 556.

to commit themselves to that cause, never evoked a similar sense of obligation below the administrative level. Several English preachers addressed the Indian congregations at the most twelve times a year, and few new preaching posts were opened. Religious and political conditions in the colonies were partially responsible for blocking the practical fruition of the eschatological hopes of the commissioners and the first generation New Englanders. Candor demands the admission, however, that on a deeper level there simply was not the prevalent faith in the fulfillment of Biblical promises that would have nurtured a renaissance in Puritan missions no matter what the external obstacles might have been. At the same time, what interest and activity did exist was owing to the eschatological expectations of the period.

In Britain the S.P.G. relied on the Biblical promises that all nations would acknowledge the Christians' God as an incentive and as a guarantee for her work. Even here the urgency and immediacy of the New England eschatology was absent. Both the S.P.C.K. and the S.S.P.C.K. undertook extensive charity school programs and literature campaigns in the conviction that the dissemination of Christian knowledge would promote morality and alleviate social ills. In that sense they were working for a better age in the history of mankind. But this vision apparently was not based on nor expressed in terms of Biblical eschatology. Even their strong anti-Catholic polemic was not linked to the Biblical notion of the Antichrist's fall. In Scotland a mild millennial eschatology prevailed in circles which held more firmly to the traditional Westminster theology than to the newer Latitudinarianism which infused the S.S.P.C.K. The Flemings articulated these hopes. Robert Millar showed their implications for missions.

To hazard a generalization on this period, we can say that although millennial eschatology provided new insight into the understanding of missions, it could not motivate large-scale evangelistic efforts. That would come only with the evangelical awakenings.

Chapter IV

A great effusion
(1735-1776)

A. *General Background*

The four middle decades of the eighteenth century were a time of contrasts and extremes. Culturally, the primitiveness of the Highlands and of the American frontier contrasted with the early inventions of the Industrial Revolution. Politically, American colonists demanded their rights from the crown and won them in the Revolutionary War. Religiously, the emotionalism and personal piety of the awakening movements countered the formalism and intellectualism of much Anglican and Presbyterian faith. Unitarians challenged trinitarians. Deists clashed with the orthodox. Old Lights and New Lights, factions formed during American revivals, crossed swords over the significance of the Great Awakening and did battle on such issues as itinerant preaching, the marks of conversion, and lay exhorting. In Scotland the secession finalized in 1740 was the result of theological differences aggravated by the Patronage Act of 1712, which landed gentry frequently used to bar evangelical preachers from like-minded congregations. Patronage also provoked the formation of the Relief Church twenty years later. In the south, cells of English evangelicals reacted to the coldness of Anglican piety and became the components of the Evangelical party.[1]

In this turmoil the factor having the greatest bearing on millennial expectations and missions was the awakenings in Britain and America, although, as we shall see, such recalcitrant opponents of revival as Charles Chauncy were also among the most dedicated advocates of missions construed in eschatological categories. The significance of the revivals warrants a closer look at these phenomena.

Predecessors of the large-scale evangelical awakenings abounded. Griffeth Jones addressed outdoor crowds as early as 1714 and is regarded as the "patriarch of the Welsh revival"[2] and as a social and religious reformer.

---

1 All who stressed conversion and a strongly experiential Christianity and who generally advocated revival are designated "evangelicals." Capitalized, "Evangelicals" refers to those evangelicals who remained within the Anglican church and who eventually became identifiable as a distinct party.

2 John D. Walsh, "Origins of the Evangelical Revival," in *Essays in Modern English Church History*, G. V. Bennett and J. D. Walsh (eds.) (London: 1966), 134.

Howell Harris and Daniel Rowlands spread revival in the same area through their itinerant preaching in the mid-thirties. Already in the seventeenth century local revivals were known in the American colonies and must be understood as responses to the repeated appeals for repentance and reform sounded by men like Solomon Stoddard. By 1725 Dutch Reformed colonists in New Jersey were being awakened by the preaching of Theodore J. Freylinghuysen. William Tennent achieved the same results among Presbyterians, and his sons and his disciples eventually spread the movement throughout the middle colonies. Several years of sermons on the evangelical doctrines of Calvinism and the reform of behavior led to the transformation of Jonathan Edwards' Northampton parishoners in 1735.[3] The English edition of Edwards' account of this awakening probably was instrumental in quickening the Cambuslang revival in 1742 under the direction of the leading Scottish evangelicals. The large rallies and campaigns of the Wesley brothers and George Whitefield co-ordinated and disseminated revival on a wider scale, however. Beginning in 1738 Whitefield's overpowering oratory and ceaseless travels and John Wesley's superb organizing skills sustained a movement which otherwise would not have generated the proportion of personal piety, social reform, and dissension that it did.

Perry Miller summarizes various explanations of the Great Awakening. It has been explained as "agrarian protest, . . . an uprising of debtors against creditors, . . . the common man against the gentry, . . . the sheer panic resulting from a sore-throat epidemic," and an outpouring of the Holy Spirit.[4] Miller interprets it as a crisis provoked by the democratization of Puritan religion. J. D. Walsh's conclusion regarding the British revivals is the most convincing basic explanation of not only the British but also the American awakenings. Noting that these movements were found in many places simultaneously and that they "can be traced back to no single source," Walsh suggests that they were similar reactions by persons facing common intellectual and religious issues.[5] Local situations and factors determined the time when revivals occurred and contributed to their varied characters but should not be confused with the more basic explanation. Anglicanism and dissent had a common heritage of theology and piety which made mutual influence possible and which created the possibility for a similar reaction to the same stimuli. John Wesley is a case in point. Not only was he a convinced Anglican, but he "absorbed Puritan influences with his mother's milk." [6] His respect for Puritan theology grew during subsequent

3 Ola E. Winslow, *Jonathan Edwards, 1703-1758* (New York: 1941), 158-165, tells the story of the Northampton awakening in a graphic way.

4 Miller, 153.

5 Walsh, 135-136.

6 John A. Newton, "Methodism and the Puritans," eighteenth lecture of the Friends of Dr. Williams's Library (London: 1964), 7.

study. In Latitudinarianism, Deism, and Arianism the revivalists had common enemies, whom they fought with an essentially common weapon. They all preached repentance and renewal of heart and life.

With the coming of the awakenings Anglo-American religion entered a new era. Thereafter the "religious affections," as Edwards called the Spirit-quickened movements in the hearts of the awakened, were defined as the essence of a supra-denominational form of religion. This evangelicalism was construed as the antithesis of all forms of religious rationalism.[7] The bond between evangelicals, which was already strong, became even stronger as they fought their common enemies with their new, revival-forged weapons. Whitefield spread information about the various evangelical parties. Edwards became a major influence on Scottish evangelicals and they on him.[8] The day after his dismissal from Northampton Edwards wrote his good friend Thomas Gillespie, and two days later he sent off a letter to John Erskine.[9] In his correspondence with Isaac Watts and John Guyse, Benjamin Coleman hinted at the Northampton revival. When they pressed him for details, he forwarded a lengthy description drafted by Edwards, which they in turn published for the benefit of fellow Englishmen. Personal and written contact between evangelicals is graphically illustrated in a sketch of Thomas Prince's life with which Erskine many years later prefaced a Scottish edition of Prince's sermons. On his deathbed the Congregationalist Prince is quoted as expressing his debt to an Anglican and a Presbyterian: " 'O dear Mr Whitfield! That great and good man was the means of my conversion and Mr Tennant of carrying it on.' " [10]

The contact effected among evangelicals by the revivals soon produced concerts for prayer as a means for sustaining and spreading revival. Philip Doddridge, probably out of interest in the work of the Moravians and of the Wesleys in Georgia, preached a sermon in 1741 urging Christians to assemble at least four times a year to pray for missions.[11] Its printed form, which appeared the following year, may well have found its way to Scotland. For in 1744 Scottish evangelicals proposed that Christians assemble locally on Saturday evenings, Sunday mornings, and the first Tuesday of every quarter to pray for the outpouring of the Spirit among Christians and upon all nations. The original proposal made this a two-year project. When an appeal to renew the plan for seven more years was issued and circulated abroad, Edwards supported the idea with his widely received *An Humble Attempt.* The book "provided the power for this movement on both sides

---

7 Heimert, 3.
8 Henderson, Chapter X, "Jonathan Edwards and Scotland."
9 Ola E. Winslow, *Jonathan Edwards...*, 365, n. 15.
10 Thomas Prince, *Six Sermons,* John Erskine (ed.) (Edinburgh: 1785), x.
11 Ernest A. Payne, "Doddridge and the Missionary Enterprise," in *Philip Doddridge,* Geoffrey F. Nuttall (ed.) (London: 1951), 89.

of the Atlantic." [12] Its eschatological orientation gave both a short-range and a long-range boost to missions.[13] A strongly eschatologically oriented concern for missions flowed directly from the revivals, therefore.

B. *Millennial Expectations*

It is generally conceded that the Great Awakening promoted discussions on and interest in the millennium. H. Richard Niebuhr says, "It is remarkable how under the influence of the Great Awakening the millenarian expectation flourished in America." [14] Speaking of millennialism several pages later, he continues, "Yet the Awakening and the revivals seem above all to have made it the common and vital possession of American Christianity." [15] After 1740 hardly any of the evangelical Calvinists' statements "can be fully comprehended" unless seen as somehow expressive of the prevalent hope for the immediate dawn of the millennium, says Alan Heimert.[16] Calvinistic millennialism "controlled the mind of the period." [17]

It would be quite wrong, however, to attempt to explain either the awakening or millennialism solely in terms of the other. As we have seen in the previous section, revivals deserve a much more complex and basic explanation. And millennialism has a history in the Anglo-American tradition that predates talk of revival as an outpouring of the Spirit. That they were not only compatible but also mutually advantageous is undeniable, however. Each flourished in the presence of the other. The revival was often regarded as a sign of the nearness of the millennium, if not as the arrival of that era itself. Millennialism, on the other hand, had always taught that a time of increased spirituality would crown the course of earthly history. This had been defended by early English Calvinists, the denials of Niebuhr and, in an earlier era, of Samuel Hopkins notwithstanding.[18] The New England expectations of the teens and twenties had sharpened interest in revival. And thirdly, the writings of Daniel Whitby and of those influenced by him had been widely accepted. The millennialism produced in New England,

---

12 Beaver, "Eschatology ... ," 66.
13 John Foster, "The Bicentenary of Jonathan Edwards' 'Humble Attempt,' " *I.R.M.*, XXXVII, 1948, 375. See also R. Pierce Beaver. "The Concert for Prayer for Missions," *Ecumenical Review,* X, 1957-1958, 420-427.
14 Niebuhr, 135.
15 *Ibid.,* 143.
16 Heimert, 59.
17 *Ibid.,* 66.
18 Niebuhr, 143. Hopkins, who wrote at the end of the eighteenth century, was oblivious of the scope of seventeenth century chiliasm. He dated its general acceptance from Whitby and Edwards. See his "A Treatise on the Millennium," appended to vol. II of *The System of Doctrines* (Boston: 1793), 6.

which was based on all three sources, heightened anticipation of revival as the emergence of the promised day.

The same factors were at work in America and in Britain, especially in Scotland. In England millennial ideas receded into the background. Even there, however, "the idea of a *spiritual* Millennium" was supported by both Whitefield and Wesley.[19] Their eschatology was the same type as that of Edwards, though it did not assume the importance for them that it did for him. The same cannot be said of Scotland. It was deeply impressed by Edwards and molded by the same tradition as he. In fact, Scottish evangelicals like John Erskine and John Willison had published widely received works on millennialism before Edwards' eschatological thought had had an opportunity to permeate Scottish theology. Edwards' contributions in this area should be seen as supporting and reinforcing indigenous Scottish writing, therefore.

The awakenings were the occasion of the widespread acceptance of simple chiliasm, which later became known as postmillennialism. Men realized that the new era could dawn through the natural means of gospel proclamation blessed by the pouring out of the Spirit. The doctrine of the catastrophic introduction of the millennium as taught by the apocalyptic physicists and the Mathers became passé. At this time New England's Calvinistic eschatology was purged of such "symptoms of cosmic despair."[20] Johannes Bengel was almost simultaneously expounding postmillennialism to German theologians and preachers. The popularization of this eschatology in America and Britain during the revivals, however, is based on the long tradition of simple chiliasm which had been perpetuated by the documents of Westminster and the Savoy Declaration. The writings of Whitby and his students gave new life to that tradition, as we have seen in the previous chapter. Edwards, for example, relied heavily on this school of expositors, especially upon Moses Lowman's commentary on Revelation, published in 1737.[21] Doddridge also praised the study,[22] indicating the influence of the Whitby school on evangelical dissenters in England. The Scottish evangelicals almost without exception followed this line of eschatology. When the returns are tabulated, therefore, we, rejecting his bitter value judgment, can conclude with Froom that postmillennialism "swept like a scourge over a large percentage of the churches."[23] Throughout the remainder of the eighteenth and the beginning of the nineteenth centuries this position grew "to formidable proportions."[24]

---

19 Van den Berg, 82.

20 Heimert, 64.

21 Goen, 37.

22 *D.N.B.*, XXIV, 208.

23 *P.F.F.*, II, 640. Whitby becomes Froom's whipping boy, which further indicates his widespread influence. (II, 649-655).

24 *Ibid.*, III, 254.

This is not to deny that there were still men who anticipated a catastrophic end to the present age, who read the signs of the times in an attempt to pinpoint the date of Christ's physical return and of the resurrection of the saints from the dead, and who defended the other notions of complex chiliasm. David Imrie, who corresponded with John Erskine, read Isaac Newton and Christopher Love, a mid-seventeenth century millennialist, and sounded a warning subtitled "An Account of a dreadful Judgement that is to be inflicted upon the World beginning at the Year 1754."[25] Thomas Prince continued to hold some elements of the chiliasm of the Mather era, and, although he did not agree with these doctrines, John Erskine published Prince's sermons unexpurgated.[26] As was Imrie, Jonathan Parsons, a former student of Edwards, was disturbed by the Lisbon earthquake of 1755 and calculated that the judgment day was near. Unlike the quake of 1727, however, this one was generally ignored by evangelicals.[27] Only with the French Revolution would complex chiliasm recoup some of her earlier losses.

To leave the impression that the intense millennialism which developed through the awakenings was the only chiliasm current in England and America in this period would be an unforgivable oversight, however. Both inside and outside the Church of England a more detached and generally more scholarly form of expectation existed. It too was of great importance for the missionary movement. Charles Chauncy supported missions from eschatological incentives. Many occupants of the bishops' bench, abhorring the emotionalism of the revivals, gave their considered opinions on prophecy and its past and future fulfillment. Bishop Thomas Newton, Bishop of Bristol, wrote a three-volume *Dissertation on the Prophecies* which appeared in 1754 and which was marked by strong opposition to Rome. When his friend Warburton, Bishop of Gloucester, founded a lectureship at Lincoln's Inn, the purpose of which was to prove the validity of revealed religion, especially from fulfilled prophecies, the post was filled by Richard Hurd, who later became Bishop of Lichfield. Hurd produced *An Introduction to the Study of Prophecy* in 1772. Likewise Robert Lowth, Bishop of London, enjoyed a long and illustrious career as a student of Hebrew poetry and prophecy and awaited the fulfillment of Isaiah's messianic predictions.[28] The detached mood in which these men investigated prophecy pervaded the sermons of their colleagues delivered to the S.P.G.

25   The title is *A Strange and Wonderful Prophecy* ([n. p.]: 1756). For a discussion of the Erskine-Imrie correspondence see Henry M. Wellwood, *Account of the Life and Writings of John Erskine, D.D.* (Edinburgh: 1818), 226-231.

26   Prince, *Six Sermons*, xv-xvi.

27   Heimert, 68-69.

28   For information regarding the Anglican bishops mentioned in this paragraph we are indebted to S. C. Orchard, who kindly allowed us to read the rough draft of his unpublished doctoral dissertation, *English Evangelical Eschatology, 1790-1850*, presented to Trinity College, Cambridge, 1968. The relevant section, "The Protestant Establishment," may be found in Chapter I.

C. *Mission Efforts*

The major societies dutifully continued their earlier work: the S.S.P.C.K. in the Highlands, the S.P.G. in the colonies, and the S.P.C.K. in America and in South India in conjunction with German Pietists. When Thomas Thompson of the S.P.G. volunteered to carry the gospel to Africa, home of the slaves among whom he was working in America, he did not foresee that his work would yield for the Anglican communion her first African clergyman in Philip Quaque, ordained in 1765. The work in Africa was destined to bear little fruit until the missionary awakenings of half a century later, however. The S.S.P.C.K. also ventured into a new area by assuming support for work among the American Indians in 1732. Some of the most illustrious names in American missions during this period were associated with the S.S.P.C.K.

Since the work of the New England Company and of the S.S.P.C.K. in America was closely associated with millennial expectations, it is necessary that we consider it in greater detail. Both societies funneled funds to American missionaries through their boards of commissioners in Boston, which had "an interlocking membership."[29] Furthermore, the S.S.P.C.K. established another body of commissioners for the middle colonies. The New England Company complained of the embarrassing problem of having more money available for missionaries' salaries than it could spend.[30] Nevertheless, a good many more men than during the previous period stepped forward to offer their services in missions. John Sergeant began work at the famous and sizeable Stockbridge mission in 1734. He was succeeded by Jonathan Edwards, Stephen West, and John Sergeant, Jr., in that order. Gideon Hawley served well as schoolmaster at that post. The Brainerd brothers, David and John, and Joseph Bowman made forays into Indian territory on the Pennsylvania frontier. In 1741 Azariah Horton was appointed by the S.S.P.C.K. to work among the Long Island Indians. Like much of this interest in missions, Eleazer Wheelock's ambitious scheme for educating Indian and white youth for missionary service was conceived in the womb of revival. In 1743 he began instructing the Indian lad Samson Occum. By 1755 he had established Moor's Indian-Charity School, out of which grew Dartmouth College. Eventually graduates of Wheelock's school such as Joseph Brant, Occum, and Samuel Kirkland became missionaries. Wheelock also prepared a number of men to serve as schoolmasters in Indian settlements.[31] Taken *in toto*, therefore, the appearance of so many full-time ordained men in Anglo-American missionary ranks indicates nothing

29 Beaver, *Pioneers in Mission,* 216.
30 Kellaway, 177-178.
31 The best source of information on many of these American missions is Beaver's *Pioneers in Mission.*

short of a renaissance in missions. For the most part, however, it utilized existing missionary structures.

Interest was by no means confined to the ranks of the full-time missionary. The wide acceptance of Edwards' edition of the diary and life of David Brainerd, which first appeared in 1749, tells us as much about Edwards and the mind of the reading public and their receptivity to such a study as the book itself tells us about Brainerd. Without doubt it made a contribution to "a new era of missionary labor." [32] But just as important, it was a product of that new era. If the main motive of men like Brainerd and Hawley had been the pursuit of sainthood, as Ola E. Winslow suggests,[33] the diary would never have rung a responsive chord in the hearts of so many others. The truth is that the new era in missions was the result of a new vision of the fulfillment of God's promises for the universal spread of Christianity. The revivals had given that vision to countless Britons and Americans, and their united support of missions was an effort to realize it. Missions "subsequently became, at times, the most prominent of the many devices by which Calvinism sought to accomplish the millennium." [34] The self-sacrifice of Brainerd epitomized the dedication through which it would be realized and became the prototype of what was demanded of all Christians. Support for missions was forthcoming from the public.

It is in the same spirit that Edwards sent his ten-year-old son into the forests with Hawley to learn the Oneida language.[35] It is the same awakened urgency that characterized Doddridge's 1741 proposal for a Northamptonshire missionary society. It is the same revived zeal that stirred Samuel Hopkins, earlier a colleague and confidant of Edwards, to promote his scheme for educating two Negroes as missionaries to Africa.[36] However, it took another generation of reflecting and writing on the missionary implications of the eschatology which the revivals did so much to promote in Calvinistic circles before missions to Asia, Africa, and the South Sea islands were undertaken. This occurred in the face of a new revival and radical changes on the political scene.

It was during this period that Moravian missionaries undertook work in the Caribbean and steadily pushed westward through Pennsylvania into eastern Ohio, where their flourishing mission villages were devastated during the Revolutionary War. Although their work was an inspiring example for Anglo-American efforts, its story belongs to the German church

---

32 Ola E. Winslow, *Jonathan Edwards . . .* , 240.

33 *Ibid.,* 274.

34 Heimert, 82.

35 See Samuel Hopkins, "Appendix III" to his "Memoirs of the Late Rev. Jonathan Edwards, A.M.," in *The Works of Jonathan Edwards,* 8 vols. (London: 1817), I, 104.

36 Dick L. Van Halsema, *Samuel Hopkins: New England Calvinist,* an unpublished dissertation presented to Union Theological Seminary, New York in 1956, 252.

and was prompted by different theological and religious forces.

D. *Missions and Millennial Expectations*

In studying the relationship of mission efforts and millennial expectations we shall once again use the method of subdividing our material into pertinent topics. In the first section we shall trace the development of this relationship in Edwards' writings produced during the revival years. He must be seen as representative of the development in the lives and minds of many of his contemporaries. Secondly, it will be shown how American Old Lights and New Lights co-operated in missions. Next, the Scottish evangelicals will be viewed as to the effects which their eschatology had on missions. A similar assessment will be made of the English ecclesiastical scene.

1. *In the crucible of revival*

When revival came to Northampton in 1734 and 1735, the first inclination of Jonathan Edwards was to explain it as another in the series of miraculous conversions begun during the ministry of his grandfather. Not only had Edwards labored side by side with the venerable Stoddard for two years, but his congregation included a number of reputable witnesses of the last of the Stoddard awakenings who testified that the present work was of "the same spirit" and "the same nature." [37] Edwards thought of it primarily as the *"renewing, strengthening, edifying,"* and *"converting"* operations of the Holy Spirit.[38] And although he acknowledged in *A Faithful Narrative of the Surprising Work of God*, written more than a year after Northampton hearts had cooled, that the conversions had stimulated in many a readiness if need be to die for the conversion of others,[39] Edwards related the revival neither to the promises of Scripture regarding the last days nor to any broader dimension of the church's life than renewal within established colonial congregations.

A number of years later, probably during or immediately following the Great Awakening, Edwards reflected on his earlier interest in the spread of Christ's kingdom.[40] He confided that during a stay in New York in 1723

37 Edwards, III, 52.
38 *Ibid.*
39 *Ibid.*, 46.
40 The exact date when Edwards wrote these reflections on his early life is unknown. Samuel Hopkins' calculations would place them in the early 1740's. After giving excerpts from an early diary of Edwards, whose latest included entry is Nov. 22, 1724, Hopkins' "Memoirs" of Edwards' life incorporates this later document, which "was written near twenty years after, for his own private advantage." (*Ibid.*,

he had experienced "great longings for the advancement of Christ's kingdom in the world." He continued, "my secret prayer used to be, in great part, taken up in praying for it." [41] Any news of events favorable to its spread had encouraged him, and it was in the hope of finding such news that he had read "public newsletters." His conversations with a friend had often revolved around the spread of the kingdom "and the glorious things that God would accomplish for his church in the latter days." [42] He expressed similar sentiments regarding the years following his settling in Northampton: "my mind has been much entertained and delighted with the scripture promises and prophecies, which relate to the future glorious advancement of Christ's kingdom upon earth." [43] Whether or not Edwards then related the 1734-1735 revival to these promises cannot be proved from A Faithful Narrative.

The preface written by Isaac Watts and John Guyse, leading Independent ministers in Old England, is another matter. Attached to the printed version of Edwards' letter, it directed followers of Christ "to take notice of such astonishing exercises of his power and mercy, and give him the glory which is due, when he begins to accomplish any of his promises concerning the latter days." [44] The Northampton awakening proves how easily Christ can accomplish the predictions of his kingdom, they continued. Then he will spread salvation "through all the tribes and ranks of mankind," and his followers will "become as numerous as the spires of grass in a meadow newly mown." [45] While the writers did not identify the Northampton revival with those days, they did associate the two. Anticipating Edwards' later thought, they cited the awakening as an inducement to pray for those days and as a source of encouragement of faith and hope for their accomplishment. [46]

Less than two years later Edwards launched a project destined to become in his opinion "the great work of his life and his most significant contribution to theology." [47] It was a series of thirty-nine sermons first delivered to his congregation in 1739. Entitled A History of the Work of Redemption, the series was the seminal form of his projected theology or divinity and was developed historically rather than in traditional fashion. Using secular and

---

I, 28.) D.A.B., VI, 31, dates it "about 1740." While this sketch proves with reasonable certainty—the possibility that Edwards projected his later thought back on his earlier life cannot be ignored—Edwards' early engagement with millennial thought, it does not establish that he saw the 1734-1735 revival in those categories.

41   Edwards, III, 34.
42   Ibid., 35.
43   Ibid., 38. Also see Rooy, 287.
44   Edwards, III, iv.
45   Ibid., v.
46   Ibid., vii.
47   Ola E. Winslow, Jonathan Edwards..., 309.

sacred history, Edwards intended to recount God's past, present, and future dealings with creation, particularly the progressive unfolding of his plan of salvation. Edwards labored on the project sporadically throughout his career and emphasized its importance in his letter accepting his appointment as President of the College of New Jersey.[48] It never reached completion, however, and only after Jonathan Edwards, Jr., co-operated with John Erskine in its publication in 1774, could the public appraise it in its unfinished form.

The sermons are of particular significance since they pointedly link revival with the promised latter-day glory. What specifically caused Edwards to make this association at this time is probably not traceable. A combination of forces was operative, however, and may have contributed to the character of the work. Edwards undoubtedly noted the association Watts and Guyse had made in their preface to his earlier work. In 1737 Lowman's commentary appeared, and Edwards relied upon it in articulating his own eschatology in *The History of the Work of Redemption*.[49] Not to be deprecated is the New England tradition represented and defined by Cotton Mather, which associated reform and revival with the millennium. A desire "to re-arouse his congregation"[50] may have led Edwards to portray to his flock the felicities of the consummate revival. In any case in 1739 Edwards proclaimed that a revival would come which would end all revivals and that it would be spread by the natural means of preaching.[51]

Edwards begins this series of sermons by asserting that the church can be comforted in her afflictions by knowing that God will complete her deliverance already begun. Redemption was planned in the divine covenant of redemption prior to creation, he continues, and will culminate in final deliverance at the last judgment. History may be divided into three periods or stages of redemption: the fall of man to Christ's incarnation, the incarnation to the resurrection, and the resurrection to the consummation of all things. As harvest is to first fruits and day-time is to sunrise, so is the third

48 Rooy, 294. Rooy centers his analysis of Edwards' theology of missions on *The History of the Work of Redemption*. (294-309)

49 See Edwards, V, 214.

50 Rooy, 286.

51 On the relationship of preaching to revival in Edwards' thought see Peter Kawerau, *Amerika und die orientalischen Kirchen* (Berlin: 1958), "Das Predigtamt," 18-31. Kawerau also explains the relationship of revivals to the millennium and Edwards' use of the term "kingdom of God" for both: "Jedes Revival bedeutet ja einen Schritt zur Verwirklichung des Reiches Gottes, und da die Heilige Schrift mit dem Ausdruck 'Reich Gottes' nicht nur den in der dritten Weltperiode schrittweise sich verwirklichenden geistlichen Zustand der Dinge in seinem Werden meint, sondern ihn auch für den herrlichen Endzustand selbst verwendet, ... so muss sich bei einer genauen Prüfung der bisherigen Entwicklung des Reiches Gottes näher bestimmen lassen, an welchem Punkt diese Entwicklung in der Gegenwart angekommen und wie nahe das Reich Gottes als Endzustand herangerückt ist." (55)

period to the first two,[52] for during it the full effect of Christ's completed work will be felt. It is to this era that various Scriptural terms apply: " 'the latter days,' " or " 'the last days,' " " 'a new heaven and a new earth,' " and " 'the kingdom of heaven' " or " 'the kingdom of God.' " [53] Step by step the kingdom of Christ is displacing the kingdom of Satan. The Reformation was a great blow to the forces of Antichrist. Since then there has been a marked reform of doctrine and worship, preaching of the gospel to heathen, and revival of religion.[54] Regarding initial contact with the Indians Edwards notes that the discovery of a continent so long in the grip of Satan is "one thing by which divine providence is preparing the way for the future glorious times of the church, when Satan's kingdom shall be overthrown throughout the whole habitable globe." [55] Men everywhere shall become Christ's subjects. Even the discovery of the compass is a divine "preparation" for facilitating the spread of the gospel in "the glorious times of the church." [56] Do not the recent successes of Christianity in Russia and India and the revival of piety and benevolence in Germany and New England bespeak progress in the history of redemption?

To this point in his series of sermons Edwards has been able to trace the course of redemption by relying both upon "prophecy" and upon "the accomplishment of it in providence" or past events to guide him,[57] a methodology strongly reminiscent of Robert Fleming, Sr.[58] In the consideration of the future course of redemption we have only prophecy, explains Edwards. He urges caution in interpreting it.

The fall of Antichrist is his first topic of discussion. Two vials remain to be poured out against her, he indicates.[59] In general it can be said that a very bleak time for the interests of true religion will precede the completion of her fall. Such is the present age. Furthermore, God will accomplish this work gradually, through the use of such means as preaching.

> Some shall be converted, and be the means of others conversion. God's spirit shall be poured out first to raise up instruments, and then those instruments shall be used with success. And doubtless one nation shall be enlightened and converted, and one false religion and false way of worship exploded, after another.[60]

52 Edwards, V, 167-168.
53 *Ibid.*, 169-171.
54 *Ibid.*, 221.
55 *Ibid.*, 222.
56 *Ibid.*
57 *Ibid.*, 236-237.
58 Edwards openly acknowledged his debt to *The Fulfilling of the Scripture* in *Some Thoughts Concerning the Present Revival of Religion in New England* several years later. (VI, 17-19 and 205-206) The structure and content of Edward's sermons on redemption suggest that he had also used Fleming's work in preparing them.
59 Edwards, V, 237.
60 *Ibid.*, 238.

But ultimately how is this fall of Antichrist being achieved? Not by the power of rulers nor by the wisdom of the learned, but "by God's Holy Spirit" as predicted in Zechariah 4:6-7 and Ezekiel 39:29. Edwards acknowledges that he does not know when or where this will first occur or whether earlier revivals have in fact been the beginning of this work. When it does arrive, "vice and wickedness" will be curbed and conversion and zeal for the kingdom will reign.[61] Clear, powerful preaching and sound doctrine will prevail and reach all nations before the fall of Antichrist. Although a coalition of "the forces of Antichrist, and Mahometanism, and Heathenism" will desperately mount a mighty offensive against Christ's forces,[62] the latter will achieve absolute victory. The victory will mark the flowing of the seventh vial. Subsequent destruction of the residue of the forces of Satan's kingdom is assured, for, "when once the stone cut out of the mountain without hands had broken the image in pieces, it was easy to abolish all the remains of it."[63] Heresy, infidelity — especially Deism — and superstitious forms of worship will be abolished. The Roman Catholic establishment will be stripped of her wealth, trappings, power, and the homage rendered her by princes. Mohammedanism will fall. The obstinacy and blindness of the Jews will be dispersed.

> They shall flow together to the blessed Jesus, penitently, humbly, and joyfully owning him as their glorious king and only Saviour, and shall with all their hearts, as with one heart and voice, declare his praises unto other nations.[64]

The conversion of both the ten and the two tribes, prolifically preached by the prophets, will occur before the full glory of the Gentile segment of the church appears. Furthermore, the heathen will be converted.

> There will be a wonderful spirit of pity towards them, and zeal for their instruction and conversion put into multitudes, and many shall go forth and carry the gospel unto them. Then shall the joyful sound be heard among them, and the Sun of righteousness shall arise with his glorious light shining on those vast regions of the earth that have been covered with Heathenish darkness for many thousand years.[65]

The global character of Christ's undisputed rule is guaranteed by "many passages of scripture that can be understood in no other sense."[66] Its realization will mark the arrival of the new heavens and the new earth.

---

61 *Ibid.*, 239.
62 *Ibid.*, 241.
63 *Ibid.*, 243.
64 *Ibid.*, 245.
65 *Ibid.*, 246.
66 *Ibid.*, 247. Edwards cited Gen. 12:3; Haggai 2:7; Isa. 11:9, 65:22; and Dan. 7:27.

Edwards goes into greater than usual detail in describing the character of the latter days. He does not hesitate to depict them as "the principal time of the kingdom of heaven upon earth." [67] Although the prophecies of the glory of that era have had preliminary fulfillments throughout history, those days will be the time of "principal fulfilment." [68] Knowledge will thrive everywhere; hopefully "Negroes and Indians will be divines" and worthwhile books will be published in Africa and Asia.[69] Holiness will be so common that wickedness will be the exception rather than the rule. Rulers will foster true devotion. "There shall then be universal peace and a good understanding among the nations of the world, instead of confusion, wars, and bloodshed"; the nations shall form "one amiable society" and the various parts of the church be of mutual service.[70] The church will be well-ordered and disciplined, and hence, *beautiful and glorious.*" [71] Material prosperity will surpass that of the days of Solomon. Joy and happiness will be world-wide. Only the widespread apostacy at the close of the latter days will mar their glory. But that will be of short duration, for Christ will soon come in judgment.

For Jonathan Edwards in *A History of the Work of Redemption*, therefore, the millennium, or as he preferred to call it, the latter days, was the apex of God's work of redemption. It was essentially the age of the Spirit, who brought revival and quickened instruments to disperse the new age and to overthrow the forces of Satan. Here Edwards articulated the three-way relationship of revival, the dissemination of Christianity, and the new age. Although he hinted that past revivals might have marked the beginning of that age, he produced a basically dispassionate, theoretical study.

When the Great Awakening inundated New England the following year, however, its pervasiveness and intensity gave Northampton church-goers reason to believe that the era which their pastor had been describing had burst upon them. His sermons have aptly been described as "the blueprint for the millennial age in the years after the Awakening." [72]

In the crucible of the revival Edwards himself came to the conviction that the latter days or otherwise something bafflingly similar to them had arrived. In his contributions to the bitter debate on the legitimacy of revival and the sundry practices associated with it Edwards demonstrated this conviction.[73] In 1741 he defended the awakening as the fulfillment of

---

67   *Ibid.,* 250.
68   *Ibid.*
69   *Ibid.,* 251.
70   *Ibid.,* 253-254.
71   *Ibid.,* 254.
72   Heimert, 98.
73   In 1741 Edwards criticized the excesses of the awakening in *Distinguishing Marks of a Work of the Spirit of God. Some Thoughts Concerning the Present Revival of Religion in New England,* 1742, also steered a middle course on the subject.

prophecy and the first evidence of an even greater work. It excited him to think that America might be the scene of the inception of the new age.[74] A year later he asserted that the New Jerusalem had "begun to come down from heaven, and perhaps never were more of the prelibations of heaven's glory given upon earth." [75] In encouraging support for the revival he warned that if it was dangerous for God's people to refuse to assist and support any awakening, how much more so when the Spirit introduces "that happy day of God's power and salvation, so often spoken of" in Scripture.[76] The scale of the current operation of the Spirit indicated to Edwards that the revival was the precursor of "something vastly great." [77] It was the time of the new creation.[78] That the latter-day glory would begin in America, as he attempted to demonstrate in an extended section of *Some Thoughts Concerning the Present Revival*,[79] prompted high anticipations in Edwards for the significance of the Great Awakening. Was not "the sun of righteousness, the sun of the new heavens and new earth," to rise in the West? Did not this mean America? Of all the American colonies was not New England by virtue of her heritage the most likely spot for the rise of this work? Are not the present stirrings there "the dawn of that glorious day?" he asked.[80]

Edwards utilized his newly-certified conviction regarding the awakening by soliciting support for it. Making a fresh application of Psalm 2 : 8, he demonstrated to civil magistrates their responsibility to promote the cause.[81] It behooved ministers and parishioners alike to stand behind the movement. The wealthy should "devise some notable things" by which they could aid the advance of Christ's kingdom "at this time of such extraordinary advantage for it." [82] Everyone can fast and pray! [83] While he made no appeal specifically for missions, Edwards rejoiced that Indians and Negroes were also being converted during the awakening.[84] This augured the universal spread of the knowledge of God.

His most significant appeal was for the formation of prayer groups to

---

Both works, while condemning excesses, were in hearty support of the "vital religion" produced by the movement. His sermons on religious affections, originally preached in 1742-1743 and published in 1746, are a further attempt to explain the essence of true piety.

74 See Rooy, 289.
75 Edwards, VI, 49.
76 *Ibid.,* 59.
77 *Ibid.* See also 29 and 54.
78 *Ibid.,* 17.
79 *Ibid.,* 54-59.
80 *Ibid.,* 58-59.
81 *Ibid.,* 70-73.
82 *Ibid.,* 192.
83 *Ibid.,* 194.
84 *Ibid.,* 34-35.

intercede for continuing revival. As recent scholars have indicated, in *Some Thoughts on the Present Revival* Edwards anticipated the Scottish proposal for a concert for prayer.[85] Edwards suggested,

> I have often thought it would be very desirable, and very likely to be followed with a great blessing, if there could be some contrivance for an agreement of all God's people in *America,* who are well-affected to this work, to keep a day of fasting and prayer; ... and together with thanksgivings to God for so glorious and wonderful a display of his power and grace in the late out-pourings of his Spirit, to address the Father of mercies, with prayers and supplications, and earnest cries, that he would continue and still carry on this work, and more abundantly and extensively pour out his Spirit, and particularly upon ministers; and that he would bow the heavens and come down, and erect his glorious kingdom through the earth.[86]

It would be advisable for ministers to meet and settle upon a date for such gatherings.[87] It would also be advantageous to begin a monthly newsletter on the progress of revival. Perhaps some Boston minister, situated near the publishing houses, could oversee such a project.[88] No immediate action appears to have been taken by New Englanders, however.

After the awakening had lost momentum in 1743, Edwards wrote William McCulloch, under whose preaching the Cambuslang revival had occurred the previous year. To his Scottish counterpart Edwards expressed the assurance that God would soon revive his work and that it would not die out until it had "subdued the whole earth." [89] What had occurred in Scotland and New England was but the harbinger "of something vastly greater, more pure, more extensive." [90]

During the next several years that greater day tarried. In fact, antipathy and schism were the aftermath of the Great Awakening. Between 1744 and 1748, furthermore, there were no conversions to report in Northampton, and enmity against their pastor flared in many members of the congregation. It seemed as though New England had inherited all the tribulations of revival and none of its glory. Edwards did not lay the blame upon God

85 Kawerau shows that this piece, "bereits im folgenden Jahre 1743 in Edinburgh nachgedruckt," found an "alsbald lebhaften Widerhall" in the Scottish concerts for prayer. (68) Also see Rooy, 292, and Heimert, 80. This observation gives a more complete picture than that of Beaver in "The Concert...," 421, where he, technically correct, indicates the Scottish origin of the concert. In speaking of the Scottish origins of *An Humble Attempt,* Foster also fails to see the earlier influence of Edwards on the Scots. (375)

86 Edwards, VI, 198.

87 *Ibid.,* 199.

88 *Ibid.,* 206.

89 As quoted by Foster, "The Bicentenary...," 380.

90 *Ibid.*

for withholding his Spirit, however, but upon man for not moving him to pour it out.

When five hundred copies of a circular urging a renewal of the Scottish concert for prayer were distributed in 1746, therefore, Edwards supported this bid by writing *An Humble Attempt to Promote Explicit Agreement and Visible Union of God's People in Extraordinary Prayer*.[91] A two-year trial run of the movement had proved its redeeming merit. It was a program comparable to what Edwards himself had pleaded for several years earlier. Some concerted effort was needed to overcome the lethargy that had set in after the awakening.

In his tract Edwards said little theologically that had not appeared in his earlier works. New, however, was the central place given communal prayer in perpetuating revival. He divided the work into three parts. In the first he explained his text and gave an account of the work in Scotland. Zechariah 7 : 20-22 reads,

> Thus saith the LORD of hosts, It shall yet come to pass, that there shall come people, and the inhabitants of many cities; and the inhabitant of one city shall go unto another, saying, Let us go speedily to pray before the LORD, and to seek the LORD of hosts. I will go also. Yea, many people and strong nations shall come to seek the LORD of hosts in Jerusalem, and to pray before the LORD.[92]

Edwards felt that by jointly contracting to assemble in intercession for God's presence Christians would fulfill this text and move God to introduce the era of glory promised for the church. "This disposition to prayer" would grow gradually, eventually encompassing men of all stations in life and all nations in a revival of religion.[93] It was natural and logical, therefore, that the Scottish proposal should be supported. Edwards gave an historical account of the concert and included the full text of the proposal. Part II cited motives for compliance with the request and was replete with substantiating material from the prophetic portions of Scripture. The glory of the last days had not yet been accomplished. Its greatness was unspeakable. Had not Christ worked and prayed and suffered for that day? All creation was groaning for its arrival. Furthermore, Scripture is full of examples, incentives, and commands to pray for it. Without using the term, Edwards reminded his readers of the many "signs of the times" which made such prayer an urgent requirement. Such unity in prayer has beauty and good effects even apart from the end for which it is being proposed, he concluded. In the last part he answered objections to the proposal, a particularly

91 For résumés of the work see Rooy, 290; *V.R.G.*, V, 142-143; and Foster, "The Bicentenary . . . ," 376-380.

92 As given by Edwards, II, 431.

93 *Ibid.*, 437.

vicious one being the argument that since Antichrist's fall was still a long way off, serious efforts to promote Christ's kingdom were futile. On the basis of Revelation 11 Edwards proved that her fall was in process. Even though the concert might be practiced for several years without any remarkable results, he said in the closing paragraphs, it would be a mark of little faith if believers would "begin to be disheartened, and grow dull and slack in seeking of God so great a mercy." [94]

The impact of Edwards' tract was great. Early in 1748 five prominent New England ministers endorsed it in a preface to the American edition, which, showing the more apocalyptic eschatology of a man like Prince, left to the readers' discretion judgment on the correctness of Edwards' exegesis of the more controversial passages.[95] It undoubtedly promoted revival and hopes for the millennium for years after the Great Awakening. In 1757 awakening occurred at the College of New Jersey and in 1763-1764 more widely throughout the colonies.[96] Although the piece did not mention missions,[97] the long-range impact it had on that cause has been axiomatically asserted by historians. Foster says that it harbingered and contributed to exciting changes in the Anglo-American church world, especially to the modern missionary movement.[98] Van den Berg judges that its impact "almost equalled" that of Brainerd's diary.[99] Rooy shares Beaver's opinion that it became " 'the most potent means of missionary education and support' " in both the old and new world.[100] In a more recent publication Beaver asserts,

> The more spiritual consequences were the stimulation of the world-wide vision, the focusing of attention on salvation history in time, the linking of mission with the eschaton, and giving the Christian disciple a share in God's own mission as his co-worker in some sense.[101]

It must be emphasized, however, that these effects of the work did not all occur simultaneously or immediately. The vision of the nations it fostered

94 *Ibid.,* 540.

95 *Ibid.,* 430. The signers were Joseph Sewall, Thomas Prince, John Webb, Thomas Foxcroft, and Joshua Gee.

96 Heimert, 81.

97 Speaking of an early history of the concert for prayer movement, Kawerau says, "Und wir möchte dem Historical Statement glauben, wenn es S. 120 sagt, das Concert of Prayer habe zunächst, auch in Edwards' Humble Attempt, keine besondere Beziehung auf Foreign Missions gehabt." (69, n. 230)

98 Foster, "The Bicentenary . . . ," 375.

99 Van den Berg, 92.

100 Rooy, 290, quoting Beaver, *Ecumenical Beginnings in Protestant World Mission* (New York: 1962), 19.

101 Beaver, *Pioneers in Mission,* 24. He expresses much the same in "The Concert . . . ," 424.

and the attention which it drew to God's work of redemption in history — themes, indeed, which Anglo-American eschatology had been emphasizing for well over a century, and which had been quickened by Edwards' earlier writings and by those of his contemporaries — were the more immediate fruits of the book. But only at the end of the century did it make a widespread impact on organized missions and only then was the concert for prayer harnessed to the rebirth of mission effort.

After a decade of engagement with eschatological thought and what he had come to regard as eschatological events, Edwards was ready to move personally into the arena of missions. His own theology had indicated that widespread involvement with the nations was to be the wave of the church's future. The point was not lost on the Northampton pastor and his associates.

Edwards' first tangible contribution to missions came in 1749 with the appearance of *An Account of the Life of the Late Reverend Mr. David Brainerd,* which Edwards edited. Edwards' interest in the labors of his prospective son-in-law, who had been influenced by Edwards already during the Great Awakening and during his trouble at Yale, undoubtedly predated the appearance of this work, however. Late in 1742 Brainerd had been appointed by the commissioners of the S.S.P.C.K. in the middle colonies to minister to the Indians. For five short years he had worked among Indians in eastern New York — twenty miles from Stockbridge across Massachusetts' western border — in the forks of the Delaware region, and in central New Jersey. An awakening among his audience at the latter location in August, 1745 had marked the high spot of his brief career. Twice the S.S.P.C.K. had published installments of his journal, but it was the name of Edwards on the title page of the 1749 work that won "the book its initial hearing" [102] and assured Brainerd wider fame. The account also publicly associated Edwards with the missionary movement.

An Account was Edwards' edited version of Brainerd's diary, which the latter, when on his deathbed, had left to the disposal of his would-be father-in-law. Edwards' chief motive in publishing the diary was to recommend true piety to his readers.[103] Brainerd's self-sacrificial ministry was an inspiring example of such piety. Though less pronounced than Brainerd's morbid spiritual struggles, his aspiration for the kingdom of God among the Indians was a theme in his diary which did not pass unnoticed by Edwards. By 1749, therefore, both Edwards as editor and Brainerd as author had related concrete missionary efforts to the millennial or kingdom expectations inherent in the revival movement, and Edwards' own contribution to missions had found its inception.[104]

102   Ola E. Winslow, *Jonathan Edwards . . . ,* 240.
103   Edwards, III, 75.
104   For many of the facts in these paragraphs we are indebted to Beaver's biographical sketch of Brainerd, *Pioneers in Mission,* 105-110.

Just as Edwards' fervor for the expansion of the kingdom of God had developed during the revival so also did Brainerd's feeling intensify. Brainerd had been converted during the Great Awakening while a student at Yale, and his dedication to that cause provoked his expulsion from that institution.[105] From that time pleas for "the kingdom of Christ in the world" were a frequent part of his intercession,[106] engaging his attention even on his deathbed.[107] The thought of the kingdom's arrival cheered him.[108] He considered it as the time of the outpouring of the Spirit,[109] when such Messianic prophecies as that of the stone cut from the mountain [110] and of the coming of all nations to Christ [111] would be fulfilled. The Indians, with whom he conversed daily, assumed a dominant place in his reflections on the kingdom. His diary entry for Sunday, July 22, 1744 expressed complete acceptance of "all hardships he [i.e., God] should call me to among the Heathen." It continued,

> I had a strong hope, that God would 'bow the heavens and come down,' and do some marvellous work among the Heathen. And when I was riding to the Indians, three miles, my heart was continually going up to God for his presence and assistance; and hoping, and almost expecting, that God would make this the day of his power and grace amongst the poor Indians.[112]

Almost a year to the day later and a month before the big stirrings among the Indians at Crossweeksung Brainerd poured out his heart "for the enlargement of Christ's kingdom and for the conversion of my poor people." [113] He regarded the tender responses of his people to his preaching later that autumn as genuine "an appearance of the New Jerusalem" as there had ever been among them.[114] His hopes continued to rise. The following spring he prayed, "Oh that the kingdom of the dear Lord might come. Oh that the poor Indians might quickly be gathered in, in great numbers." [115] During the advanced stages of his tuberculosis he meditated on the same theme: "the Redeemer's kingdom is all that is valuable in the earth, and I could not but long for the promotion of it in the world." [116]

---

105 Edwards, III, 76 and 96-99.
106 *Ibid.*, 113-114.
107 *Ibid.*, 309.
108 *Ibid.*, 158, 238, 243-244, 246-247.
109 *Ibid.*, 209, 264.
110 *Ibid.*, 238.
111 *Ibid.*, 264.
112 *Ibid.*, 193-194.
113 *Ibid.*, 228.
114 *Ibid.*, 353.
115 *Ibid.*, 247.
116 *Ibid.*, 289.

As he lay dying in Edwards' Northampton parsonage, he hoped that "the time was at hand, when Babylon the great would *fall,* and *rise no more."*[117] Less than two weeks before his death Brainerd confided to Edwards that he had been reflecting much on " 'the old dear theme' " of the prosperity and glory of the kingdom, which he hoped "was *near* at hand." [118]

The missionary character of Brainerd's ardent longings for the kingdom did not fail to make a deep impression on Edwards. Time and again he alluded to them in his editorial comments on the diary. Edwards noted that Brainerd "often expresses great longings for the enlargement of Christ's kingdom, especially by the conversion of the Heathen to God; and speaks of this hope as all his delight and joy." [119] By his own admission, Edwards was moved by the prominent place Brainerd gave "the prosperity of Zion, the advancement of Christ's kingdom in the world, and the flourishing and propagation of religion among the Indians" in the family prayers offered in his host's home.[120] In a paragraph which demonstrates that Brainerd's readiness to sacrifice was subservient to the realization of the kingdom as his main missionary motive, Edwards showed the impact which Brainerd's desires made on him:

> After he came hither, as long as he lived, he spoke much of that future prosperity of Zion which is so often foretold and promised in the scripture. It was a theme he delighted to dwell upon; and his mind seemed to be carried forth with earnest concern about it, and intense desires, that religion might speedily and abundantly revive and flourish. Though he had not the least expectation of recovery, yea, the nearer death advanced, and the more the symptoms of its approach increased, still the more did his mind seem to be taken up with this subject. He told me, when near his end, that 'he never in all his life had his mind so led forth in desires and earnest prayers for the flourishing of *Christ's kingdom* on earth, as since he was brought so exceeding low at Boston.' He seemed much to wonder, that there appeared no more of a disposition in ministers and people to pray for the flourishing of religion through the world; that so little a part of their *prayers* was generally taken up about it, in their families, and elsewhere; and particularly, he several times expressed his wonder, that there appeared no more forwardness to comply with the *proposal* lately made, in a memorial from a number of ministers in Scotland, and sent over into America, for *united extraordinary prayer,* among Christ's ministers and people, for the *coming of Christ's kingdom:* and he sent it as dying advice to *his own congregation,* that they should practice agreeably to that proposal.[121]

117 *Ibid.,* 299.
118 *Ibid.,* 306.
119 *Ibid.,* 195.
120 *Ibid.,* 288.
121 *Ibid.,* 298.

Brainerd's congregation soon followed his advice. They supported the Scottish proposal, as did many Presbyterians in the middle colonies.[122]

The piety of the young missionary and his passion for the conversion of the Indians must have strengthened and even encouraged Edwards when the time came for his removal to Stockbridge. Resisting suggestions to locate in Scotland, Edwards chose the rigors of the Massachusetts frontier. This decision marked another step in his personal involvement in missions. His own theology, particularly his eschatology, abetted by Brainerd's example, had prepared him for this move. Although he was ill-equipped in a number of ways for his new role, and although his short ministry among whites and Indians was not marked by success, his presence at that remote outpost reinforced for succeeding generations the missionary implications of his widely-acclaimed writings.

It is disconcerting to speculate on the effect it might have had on the awakening of the modern missionary movement had Edwards never heard of Brainerd and never been driven into the wilderness. Had that been true, it is doubtful that the missionary awareness and force of Edwards' authoritative Calvinistic eschatology would have been made as explicit and credible as it subsequently was to his readers. But we need not engage in such speculation. The circumstances in Edwards' life co-operated to forge a coalition of millennial thought and missionary enterprise that was a major force in the origin of the modern missionary movement in the 1790's. Beaver has gone so far as to say that "basically due to the writings of Jonathan Edwards" the cause of "missions became wedded to eschatology for the next century and a half." [123] Although she was a more promiscuous spouse than this generalization would indicate, missions did enter a strong and enduring bond with millennial thought. If the two major forces behind nineteenth century Anglo-American missions could be isolated, a convincing case could be constructed for their being the theology of Jonathan Edwards and the example of David Brainerd.

2. Old Lights and New Lights co-operate

In the intensity of the Great Awakening issues arose which divided New England ministers into two camps. Old Lights opposed the revival and its associated practices, such as itinerating, opening pulpits to visiting evangelists, lay exhorting, and the physical effects generated by the high pitch of emotions. New Lights endorsed the movement as a mighty out-pouring of the Spirit and cited the increase in sanctified living in its defense. The awakening was hardly more than a complicating factor in the breach that

---

122 *Ibid.* See Beaver, "The Concert...," 424.
123 Beaver, "Eschatology...," 65.

had begun to open in Congregational theology prior to the revival years, however.[124] For when the revival's power had been spent, men's alignment according to deeper theological issues became apparent. Old Light-New Light differences faded with the passing of the events and practices which had originally caused them. Nathaniel Appleton, to cite but one instance, had barred Whitefield from his Cambridge pulpit in the early 1740's, but welcomed the English orator in 1754. This was as it should have been among those with a common theological viewpoint. This commonness explains the appearance of Old Light as well as New Light names on missionary rolls. Both parties drew water from common eschatological wells. Both parties sensed the missionary impulse in the prophecies upon which their thought rested. The only difference was that New Lights associated the distractions of the day with the kingdom of Christ, while the Old Lights, seeing the excesses, were moved to evangelize more vigorously for the new age. Considered on the eschatological plane, therefore, Heimert's generalization that "the missionary enterprise . . . betrayed the antagonisms of the age" is dubious.[125]

Some impressive contributions to missions in New England during this period were made through the efforts of men who were not participants in the awakening. Anticipation of the promised kingdom was a large factor in their drive.

John Sergeant left a Yale tutorship and turned his back on the enticements of the regular ministry by accepting the offer tendered by the commissioners of the New England Company to serve as a missionary to the Mohegans. From 1735 until 1749 he labored diligently at Stockbridge among the Indians of western Massachusetts. A day-school and later a boarding school became important projects in the mission and through Captain Thomas Coram, who had visited the settlement, were brought to the attention of the king's chaplain, the Reverend Doctor Ayscough. In response to Ayscough's subscription of twenty guineas to the boarding school, Sergeant expressed his thanks and linked the churchman's support to the promises of Christ's kingdom.

> May his Kingdom be enlarged, and *the Fulness of the Gentiles brought* into his holy Church. I have had large Experience of the Truth of his gracious Promises, and esteem your kind and condescending Notice of me, as an Instance of the Fulfilment of his Promise

---

124 Sweet, 134-137, discusses doctrinal developments in New England subsequent to the Great Awakening. The Old Light-New Light parties of New England should not be confused with the Auld Licht-New Licht divisions in 1799 in the Burgher (Associate Synod) and in 1806 in the Anti-Burgher (General Associate Synod) communions in Scotland. The latter divisions were based on differences of opinion regarding the role of civil officials in ecclesiastical matters. See Burleigh, 323-324.

125 Heimert, 91.

to them that deny themselves for his, and the Gospel's Sake.[126]

These promises sustained an interest in missions that had ripened long before the revival harvests, however.

"For my self, I am not ashamed to own, I am one of those who look . . . for a far more glorious state of things; both among *Jews* and *Gentiles,* than has ever yet been seen," spoke Charles Chauncy at the height of the Great Awakening.[127] It appears to be a curt, ironic disavowal of the New Light explanation of the revival. He continued by asserting that only the Father knows when and by what instruments the promised state will begin. Like a careful spiritual physician Chauncy diagnosed the wounds of the awakening and prescribed prayer for the outpouring of the Holy Spirit in large doses.[128] He was one of the most active and visionary sponsors of missions in New England. Not only did he serve on the Boston board of correspondents of the S.S.P.C.K., but he was an instigator of the unsuccessful attempt to form an indigenous American society in 1762.[129] In the former capacity he had extensive dealings with Eleazer Wheelock. Far ahead of his time in missionary anthropology, Chauncy had a deeper appreciation for Indian culture than his contemporaries.[130] Choosing Genesis 22 : 18 as his text for Joseph Bowman's ordination sermon, Chauncy explained that the growth of Christ's gospel kingdom has been promised, and that that kingdom will spread to all nations of the earth.[131]

At Sergeant's ordination Appleton preached on the necessity of being a consecrated minister. His officiation demonstrates the preacher's interest in missions. At Stephen Badger's ordination twenty-eight years later he testified that "the Knowledge of the Truth shall spread, and fill the Earth, as the Waters do the Seas." [132] Missionaries would be the agents of this growth.

Among New Lights millennial hopes took on historical immediacy in the revivals. The benefits to missions outlasted the passing peaks of religious fervency, however.

Joseph Bellamy and Samuel Hopkins, friends and colleagues of Edwards who were frequent visitors at Stockbridge, perpetuated Edwards' theology. Both men published important works on the millennium.[133] Especially

126 As quoted by Samuel Hopkins [of Springfield], *Historical Memoirs Relating to the Housatunnuk Indians* (Boston: 1753), 125. The letter is dated May 20, 1746.

127 Charles Chauncy, *The Out-Pouring of the Holy Ghost* (Boston: 1742), 32.

128 *Ibid.,* 43-44.

129 *vide infra,* 141.

130 These facts are based on Beaver, *Pioneers in Mission,* 190. See also *D.A.B.,* IV, 42-43.

131 Beaver, *Pioneers in Mission,* 190-209.

132 *Ibid.,* 145.

133 Bellamy's famous sermon, "The Millennium," appeared in his *Sermons Upon*

Hopkins retained interest in missions over the years. It may have originally been stimulated by his uncle, also Samuel Hopkins, who wrote an account of the Sergeant years of the Stockbridge mission. Edwards A. Park, Hopkins' biographer and editor of his works, feels that his uncle "seems to have had considerable influence in directing the sympathies of his nephew towards our aboriginal tribes." [134] The nephew preached to the Indians of Stockbridge, frequently entertained Brainerd in his home, and corresponded with Gideon Hawley and Eleazer Wheelock on missionary matters. After moving to Newport, Rhode Island, Hopkins proposed a mission to Africa and denounced the slave trade, which was a chief source of income to the wealthy shippers in his congregation. He was one of the first Americans to call for a halt to traffic in slaves.[135]

Joseph Sewall, minister of the Old South Church in Boston, inherited the interest in missions of his father, Samuel. Already in 1726 he was appointed commissioner of the New England Company, a post his father had laid aside shortly before. Several years later he began serving the S.S.P.C.K. in the same capacity and in 1733 delivered the ordination sermon for the first three American missionaries supported by that body. Psalm 2 : 8 appeared on the title page of the printed address; Sewall used prophecies of the conversion of the Gentiles to encourage his hearers and linked the S.S.P.C.K. efforts with the overthrow of Satan, the fall of Antichrist, the pouring out of the Spirit on all flesh, and Christ's reign over all nations.[136] His associate minister, Thomas Prince, also participated in the service. The two men saw eye to eye on missions, the revivals, and eschatology. When the annual convention of pastors in Massachusetts Bay met in Boston in May, 1740, Prince addressed it on "The Endless Increase of Christ's Government." He traced the westward march of the gospel from Canaan to New England, expected that in time all America would "be full of pure and pious churches," and predicted that the gospel would continue its advance and conquer Asia, India, Persia, and Africa before returning to Zion, where it had begun its course.[137] A conflagration and 360,000 years — a millennium of prophetic years — of glory will follow for the saints, he said, and suggested several ways, one of them being missions, by which the millennium could be promoted. Several years later he defended the revivals in a series of sermons [138] and began *Christian History*, his periodical defend-

the following Subjects (Boston: 1758), 43-70. For Hopkins' much later work *vide supra*, 119, n. 18.

134 Edwards A. Park, (ed.), *The Works of Samuel Hopkins, D.D. With a Memoir of his Life and Character*, 3 vols. (Boston; 1852), I, 10.

135 *vide infra*, 205f. for Hopkins' mission efforts and millennial views during and after the Revolutionary War.

136 Beaver, *Pioneers in Mission*, 58, 61, 64.

137 Prince, *Six Sermons*, 27-28.

138 *Ibid.*, sermons II-IV.

ing the Great Awakening.[139]

The millennial basis of the missionary support contributed by many other New Lights could be indicated. Several significant examples are Samuel Buell, Eleazer Wheelock, and Ebenezer Pemberton. Like so many other missionary sermons on diverse themes, Pemberton's speech at David Brainerd's ordination included for the listeners' encouragement a reminder of the prophecies regarding the latter days.[140] This Presbyterian minister from New York was chairman of the S.S.P.C.K.'s correspondents in the middle colonies. As a young graduate from Yale during the Great Awakening Samuel Buell became a close follower of Edwards, was a friend of Brainerd, and began sustained contact with the Indian pastor, Samson Occum. Having helped Occum on several occasions, Buell appropriately delivered his ordination sermon, in which he advised the Indian, "Often Refresh your Heart, with a believing Remembrance of the many ample Promises, which have Respect to the magnificent Enlargement, Light, Purity, Glory and Felicity, of the Divine Redeemer's Kingdom, in these last Days." [141] Wheelock was also influenced by Edwards during the Awakening. Taking Occum into his home for training in 1743, he built up an educational project for Indian youth which received support from a number of sources in England and America. In 1762 he preached at the ordination of one of his students, Jeffry Smith, and explained how the church of Christ would be enlarged in the latter days.[142]

Those who had chosen the New Light position and those who had represented the Old Light viewpoint pooled their efforts in founding the Society for Propagating Christian Knowledge among the Indians of North America. The Massachusetts legislature granted a charter in 1762, and enthusiasm for the project ran high until the king, acting on the advice of the fearful Archbishop of Canterbury, refused to endorse it. Sewall had been elected vice president, and Appleton, Wheelock, and Chauncy all had been moving forces behind the new body. The society is a monument to New England's unified missionary effort and vision.

3. Balm in Scotland

By the middle of the eighteenth century it became apparent that three religious emphases existed in the Church of Scotland: moderatism, high Calvinism, and evangelicalism. The former had its "roots in the spirit of inquiry and criticism" of the Enlightenment and reacted against the heresy-

---

139 See Beaver, *Pioneers in Mission,* 38-41, for facts on Sewall and Prince.
140 *Ibid.,* 122-123.
141 *Ibid.,* 178.
142 *Ibid.,* 218f.

hunting mood stirred up by the Simpson cases in the teens and twenties.[143] It eventually became the dominating spirit of the church until the evangelical awakenings at the end of the century. The evangelicals opposed patronage and defended a vital piety. Evangelicals reprinted *The Marrow of Modern Divinity* at the time of the first Simpson heresy trial late in the second decade of the seventeenth century. Evangelicals rejoiced in revival, and the evangelical temper predominated in the established church even after the first secession was finalized in 1740. Until the middle of the century the majority of ministers, "the mass of the common people," and a number of leading synods and presbyteries were evangelical.[144]

Revival produced affinity among evangelicals. Already in May, 1739, Ralph Erskine and his brother Ebenezer had sent separate letters to Whitefield regarding their field preaching in Scotland. "Oh, that all who were truly zealous knew one another!" yearned Whitefield upon receiving Ralph's correspondence.[145] Eight days later he rejoiced when a letter from Ebenezer informed him of "his preaching last week to fourteen thousand people." [146] Similarly the Cambuslang revival became a rallying point for Scottish evangelicals and stimulated international contact. Whitefield toured the northern country to fan the blaze. Edwards, whose influence among the leading evangelicals would be difficult to exaggerate,[147] and Thomas Prince inquired about its progress from New England. Evangelical leaders such as John Willison of Dundee, "whose writings remained for long, together with Boston's *Fourfold State,* the favourite religious literature among the people of Scotland," [148] Alexander Webster of Edinburgh, John Maclaurin of Glasgow, John Robe of Kilsyth, and John Erskine of Greyfriars, Edinburgh were among the keenest sponsors of revival. Along with Thomas Gillespie of Carnoch, "we may be sure" that Willison, Maclaurin, Robe, and Erskine were among the anonymous sponsors of the 1744 Scottish proposal to continue the concert for prayer for revival.[149] Another was undoubtedly McCulloch of Cambuslang. Robe had estimated the dimensions of the movement in a letter to Prince the previous autumn.[150]

143 Burleigh, 295.
144 *Ibid.,* 291. Henderson, 139, says that evangelicals predominated during the first part and at the end of the century. On the theological emphases and their relation to the *Marrow* controversy see Stewart Mechie, "The Marrow Controversy Reviewed," *The Evangelical Quarterly,* XXII, 1950, 20-31.
145 George Whitefield, *George Whitefield's Journals* (London: 1960), 266.
146 *Ibid.,* 275.
147 See Van den Berg, 118; Foster, "The Bicentenary...," 377; Henderson, Chapter X; and E. A. Payne, "The Evangelical Revival and the Beginnings of the Modern Missionary Movement," *The Congregational Quarterly,* XXI, 1943, 229-230.
148 Burleigh, 291.
149 Foster, "The Bicentenary...," 377.
150 Edwards, II, 443.

Gillespie was later deposed in an unfortunate controversy surrounding the patronage issue and became the father of the Relief Church.[151]

Like the earlier works of Edwards, the writings of the evangelicals linked revival with the millennium and defended an eschatology with built-in incentives for missions. It is little wonder, therefore, that many of these men and their published works eventually provided powerful support for that cause. A survey of several of their pertinent works reveals the heartbeat of Scottish missions during this period.

When the Synod of Angus and Mearns convened in 1733, Willison bewailed the sinful conditions of the day in the opening sermon to his colleagues. He exhorted them to do all in their power to effect a renewal of reformed religion by praying for an outpouring of the Spirit and by grounding their churches in truth.[152]

Before the occurrence of the Cambuslang revival Willison published a series of sermons which was probably the most widely read divinity in Scotland during the latter half of the eighteenth century. By 1786 they had passed through no fewer than eight editions. Appearing early in 1742 — the preface is dated "Dundee, Jan. 20, 1742"[153] — the twelve sermons were delivered with Scotland in mind. However, "they are composed in such a strain, as to be useful and applicable to any church under the like distempers."[154]

Preaching the same forthright Calvinistic message of sin, repentance, and reconciliation as Edwards and the Mathers, Willison catalogued Scotland's sins in the first eight sermons, which were based on texts from Jeremiah. Scotland's "folly and obstinancy" are the cause of her present plight, said the preacher.[155] She can be cured of her maladies and be restored, however. He pointed the people to Christ and his atoning blood as the only balm capable of healing the country.

The ninth and tenth sermons were based on II Corinthians 3 : 8. In them Willison emphasized that "the effusion of the Spirit with a preached gospel makes a very glorious dispensation."[156] His ministrations or "gracious influences upon the hearers of the gospel"[157] have a number of glorious effects on people and on the church in general. He stressed that Christians owe thanks and praise to Christ for earning and making possible these

151   Burleigh, 283-284.

152   See the published form of his sermon, *The Church's Danger and the Minister's Duty* (Edinburgh: 1733).

153   John Willison, *The Balm of Gilead, for Healing a Diseased Land; with the Glory of the Ministration of the Spirit: And A Scripture Prophecy of the Increase of Christ's Kingdom, and the Destruction of Antichrist* (8th ed.; Falkirk: 1786), A2v.

154   *Ibid.,* A2r.

155   *Ibid.,* 3.

156   *Ibid.,* 97.

157   *Ibid.,* 107.

effusions of the Spirit and that they should pray earnestly for them.[158] Taking cognizance of such outpourings in the awakenings in other parts of the world, in his preface Willison laid a large share of the responsibility for revival in Scotland on his colleagues. All ministers must preach the gospel of grace and "exert themselves for removing out of the way all letts and hindrances of the kingdom of Christ, that so his dominion may spread from sea to sea, thro' all nations of the earth."[159]

The last two sermons, destined to become the most famous, treated the crescendo of Christ's kingdom.

> The increase of Christ's kingdom and glory in the world is absolutely certain and necessary. It must infallibly be, for God hath said it, Jer. xxiii.5. 'A king shall reign and prosper in the earth.' Psal. lxxii.8. 'He shall have dominion from sea to sea.' Psal. cxxxii.18. 'Upon himself shall his crown flourish.'[160]

Willison understood the kingdom virtually as Edwards did. The kingdom is not restricted to a period at the end of history, though it will reach its fulness then, he said. But it can and has suffered "decay and diminution" at times.[161] It is not marked by "outward splendor and greatness" but by glory "of a spiritual and heavenly nature."[162] Gradually, surely, "Christ's mediative kingdom" and "his manifestative glory" will spread. This will occur in a geographical sense:

> In the increase and spreading of gospel light thro' the world, so that the dark places of the earth shall be enlightened with the knowledge of Christ; and those places which had but twilight discoveries of him, shall attain to brighter views of his excellency and usefulness, and to a clearer insight into the gospel mysteries, and the way of salvation thro' Christ and his righteousness imputed to the sons of Adam. . . . Then is it that Christ shall increase, and his kingdom be enlarged, when 'the earth shall be filled with the knowledge of the glory of the Lord, as the waters cover the sea,' according to the prophecy of Habakkuk, Hab. ii.14.[163]

Seen in a more ecclesiastical dimension, the kingdom will be characterized by Christ's supplying the church with ministers equal to the task at hand. They "shall be men of large hearts, fluent tongues, and public spirits."[164] It almost seems as though Willison were personally and intimately ac-

---

158 *Ibid.,* 113-114.
159 *Ibid.,* A2v.
160 *Ibid.,* 120.
161 *Ibid.,* 121.
162 *Ibid.*
163 *Ibid.,* 121-122.
164 *Ibid.,* 122.

quainted with the army of pioneer missionaries of two and three generations later when he described the ministers of the latter days as

> willing to run all hazards by sea and land; to venture all that is dear to them in the world, their reputation, life, and all the comforts of it, for Jesus Christ; and chearfully content to spend and to be spent for the increase of his kingdom and glory, and the gathering of souls to him.[165]

The similarity should not strike one as startling, however, for these pioneers were molded by the ideals of Willison and his contemporaries. If Christ will raise up such ministers at the end of the ages, he will also bless their labors with a great growth in "the number of Christ's subjects and followers," continued the Scot.[166] All "kingdoms of the earth shall become the kingdoms of the Lord"; it will include the return of the Jews to Christ and the fulness of the Gentiles.[167] Truth in doctrine and worship will triumph over error and superstition.[168] Christ's enemies, Mohammedanism and the Roman Catholic Antichrist, will topple, and Satan will be bound.[169] True piety and holiness will permeate all men's dealings with one another and with God.[170] When speaking about Christ, Christians will manifest joyful openness rather than shame and fear.[171]

When will these days occur? This "is greatly connected with the destruction of Antichrist."[172] About the time of the fall of Rome Scripture "is more particular" than about any of the other latter-day events, said Willison.[173] The signs which indicate the nearness of that time are formality of religion, false doctrine, heavenly portents, war, earthquakes, confidence among the church's enemies, and the fall of the tenth kingdom, by which many understand France.[174] As had countless other students of prophecy before him, Willison tried to determine the boundaries of the 1260-year reign of Antichrist. He rejected various combinations: 456-1716, 476-1736, and 713-1973.[175] He conceded, however, that Antichrist had received blows in both 1716, when the Protestant Hanovers were guaranteed the English throne, and 1736, when the Moravians, Oxford Methodists, and Whitefield

---

165 *Ibid.*
166 *Ibid.*
167 *Ibid.,* 123. Willison cites relevant prophecies: Isa. 2 : 2; Micah 4 : 1-2; Isa. 60 : 8; Rev. 2 : 15; Rom. 11 : 25-26; Psal. 102 : 15-16, 22.
168 *Ibid.*
169 *Ibid.,* 124.
170 *Ibid.*
171 *Ibid.,* 125.
172 *Ibid.,* A2v.
173 *Ibid.,* 128.
174 *Ibid.,* 128-129.
175 *Ibid.,* 132-134.

became recognized spiritual forces. The most likely date for the rise of Antichrist was 606, when Boniface III was declared the universal bishop.[176] The *terminus ad quem* which Willison established, 1866, was accepted widely for many years in both Britain and America.

After making a number of applications in his sermons, none of which explicitly recommended missions, he concluded, "If you can do no more ..., pour out earnest prayers to God for fulfilling his promises...."[177]

We may be sure that Willison himself prayed and worked for revival in Scotland and that he exulted when it did come later that year.[178] It appeared to other evangelicals that God had favored their homeland with outpourings of the Spirit as he had America and England before her. John Erskine "published an anonymous pamphlet" intimating that the revivals in the Scottish west-country "might be the beginning of the latter-day glory."[179] He saw them as evident signs or indications of the new age. Although his biographer judged that Erskine carried "his ideas farther than the subject required, or the circumstances warranted" and that all the twenty-one year old's views were sanguine,[180] Erskine was not alone in hoping that the current awakenings were only the beginning of a movement that would fill the earth with the knowledge of Christ.

Those hopes motivated a number of older and more mature men than Erskine to engage with him in a concert for prayer for the spread of the kingdom through continued outpouring of the Spirit. The concert was planned and popularized for two years by personal conversation and correspondence, not via a published appeal. By the time the two years designated for the project had expired, however, the plan had been put into practice in England and North America as well as in Scotland.[181] Edwards, who by virtue of his contact with the Scots was in a position to know, described their motives as the desire to beseech God

> that he would *appear in his glory*, and favour Zion, and manifest his compassion to the world of mankind, by an abundant effusion of his *Holy Spirit* on all the churches, and the whole habitable earth, to revive true religion in all parts of *Christendom*, and to deliver *all*

176 *Ibid.*, 134.

177 *Ibid.*, 142.

178 He journeyed to Cambuslang to observe the outbreak personally, and, stopping long enough to preach a sermon on his return trip, he sparked a revival in Kilsyth. *D.N.B.*, LXXII, 28.

179 Payne, "The Evangelical Revival ...," 229. The full title of Erskine's tract is a complete indication of its content: *The Signs of the Times Considered; or, the High probability, that the present appearances in New England, and the West of Scotland, are a prelude of the glorious things promised to the Church in the latter ages* ([n. p.]: 1742).

180 Wellwood, 125-126.

181 Edwards, II, 442-443.

nations from their great and manifold spiritual calamities and miseries, and bless them with the unspeakable benefits of the kingdom of our glorious Redeemer, and *fill the whole earth with his glory*.[182]

Although the published *Memorial* of 1746 was concerned with the mechanics of prolonging the successful endeavor, it did cite as the "chief scope" of the concert the promotion of *"prayer that our Lord's kingdom may come."* [183]

The anticipation of Christ's kingdom was certainly partially responsible for the appearance of six strongly anti-Roman Catholic sermons preached by Willison in reaction to the Jacobite uprising of 1745. Believing that the fall of Antichrist would be one of the initial events in the spread of that kingdom, the Dundee pastor warned Britain of the Roman error, defended current policy against the Jacobians, and elaborated a number of ways by which his readers could combat Catholicism.[184]

In a volume of sermons dedicated to the Countess of Huntingdon, Lady Selina, Robe of Kilsyth drew a clear and direct line from the revivals through the concert for prayer for the kingdom to explicit mission effort. Praying the third petition of the Lord's Prayer is tantamount to asking "that God may everywhere revive his work, by pouring down abundantly his Spirit on all flesh, according to the promises of his word, particularly these relating to the last days," said Robe.[185] The last chapters of Isaiah portray and promise the glory of Zion's revivals. Referring to an earlier article in which he had argued the point more fully, he urged support for the concert for prayer.[186] He reinforced his plea by reprinting the *Memorial* and by citing from Edwards' *An Humble Attempt*. He appealed particularly to those who had not joined the concert and to those who had given it up. It is their duty to pray for that kingdom; the thought of Jews, Moslems, and heathens perishing in ignorance of Christ should stir men to pray for the coming of Christ's kingdom among those peoples.[187] "Enter into this agreement, and you'll have a hand in all that conversion-work thro' the whole earth, which shall be the fruit of the Lord's hearing these united prayers." [188] On the day of judgment men will be confronted with those converted through their intercession. In the same vein Robe commended the work of the S.S.P.C.K. to his readers. The efforts of that body are

---

182 *Ibid.,* 440. Also see Beaver, "The Concert . . . ," 421.

183 Edwards, II, 444.

184 The title of his work was *Popery another Gospel* (Edinburgh: 1746).

185 James Robe, *A Second Volume of Sermons in, Three Parts* (Edinburgh: 1750), iv.

186 The article appeared in the April, 1745 issue of *Christian Monthly History* and is probably the earliest public appeal on behalf of the concert for prayer. It could have been the model for Edwards' *An Humble Attempt* the following year.

187 Robe, xvi-xvii.

188 *Ibid.,* xx.

"directly subservient to the advancement of his [*i.e.*, Christ's] kingdom," [189] he asserted. Without doubt the zealous missionaries and faithful correspondents of the society have furthered the work of Christ's kingdom. Robe's book appeared almost simultaneously with Edwards' edition of Brainerd's life and diary. Both pieces consciously linked the work of revival, regarded as the first victories in the church's latter-day glory, with mission efforts.

Throughout the remainder of this period the leading Scottish evangelicals continued to proclaim similar hopes for the end of history. An essay of John Gillies, controversial Glasgow minister who opened his pulpit to Wesley and introduced the singing of hymns into his congregation,[190] is evidence of the consistency with which evangelicals viewed these matters. Many prophecies foretell the gradual growth of Christianity among the Gentiles while the Jews remain obdurate, explained Gillies. Others, "complex predictions," were partially fulfilled by initial Gentile conversions and will be completely fulfilled when all nations acknowledge Christ.[191] After the fall of the fourth or Roman monarchy Daniel predicts the rise of several "seducing powers," noted for their opposition to God. Their opposition will continue for centuries, until "the time frequently called by this prophet the 'time of the end,' and characterized as the time of the universal conversion of nations, Jews and Gentiles, to the true religion."[192] Gillies portrayed the kingdom of Christ which will arise at that time as the stone cut from the mountain. (Daniel 2 : 42)[193] He went on to demonstrate the harmony of Daniel and Revelation. More cautious than some of his colleagues, Gillies did not suggest a possible date for the fall of Antichrist.

Scottish evangelicals were agreed, therefore, in awaiting the prophesied spread of Christianity in the latter days.

These evangelicals have been called "the driving power behind" the S.S.P.C.K.[194] An assessment of their role and of the place of their eschatological expectations in the contemporary missionary movement must take several factors into consideration, however.[195] The society itself was begun by an episcopalian minister in the "Leighton tradition." [196] Irenic, the body incorporated many of the ideals of her sister societies to the south. The

---

189 *Ibid.*, xxiv.
190 Burleigh, 294 and 304.
191 John Gillies, *An Essay on the Prophecies Relating to the Messiah* (Edinburgh: 1773), 141.
192 *Ibid.*, 175.
193 *Ibid.*, 176.
194 Rooy, 292.
195 Our understanding of the S.S.P.C.K. has been hindered by the lack of a thorough study of that organization such as the Anglican societies and the New England Company have been given.
196 Maclean, 5.

humanitarian emphasis always loomed large in the society's sermons. After 1750 Moderates took an active part in her affairs, as the appearance of the name of William Robertson, historian and principal of Edinburgh University, on society records indicates. On the other hand, evangelicals like John Witherspoon, who later immigrated to the colonies to assume the presidency of the College of New Jersey and who led in the struggle for independence, gave only incidental attention to eschatological themes in their addresses to the annual gatherings. To suggest, therefore, either that evangelicals were the sole advocates of missions in Scotland or that their eschatology was the only consideration in their support of missions would be gross exaggeration.

Against the background of these qualifications, however, it may safely be concluded that the eschatology of the evangelicals was the chief "driving power" behind Scottish missionary activity at this time. Is it accidental that the S.S.P.C.K. broadened her overseas efforts among the Indians during the revivals, when missions were linked to the eschatological understanding of those events? It is beyond dispute that virtually all of her correspondents and missionaries in America were evangelicals, sons of revival. Furthermore, the expectations which became so pronounced during the awakenings can be found in the publications of the S.S.P.C.K.

Alexander Webster proclaimed that though the gospel had not been preached in China and America by Jesus' twelve disciples, "the 'Sun of Righteousness' has gone on *gradually* enlightening those 'dark Places of the Earth'; and... 'the Fulness of Time' is fast approaching" when Isaiah 11 : 9 will be fulfilled and Jews and Gentiles shall be united in the church of Christ.[197] He closed on the same note.[198]

The preface to Brainerd's published journal was written by the society's correspondents in the middle colonies. They gave as "the design of this publication" the giving of glory to God and the gratification of "the pious curiosity" of those anticipating the coming of the heathen to Christ in the latter days.[199]

> When we see such numbers of the most ignorant and barbarous of mankind, in the space of a few months, 'turned from darkness to light, and from the power of sin and Satan unto God,' it gives us encouragement to wait and pray for that blessed time, when our victorious Redeemer shall, in a more signal manner than he has yet done, display the 'banner of his cross,' march on from 'conquering to conquer, till the kingdoms of this world are become the kingdoms of our Lord and of his Christ.' Yea, we cannot but lift up our heads with joy, and hope that it may be the dawn of that bright and

197 Alexander Webster, *Supernatural Revelation the Only Sure Hope of Sinners* (Edinburgh: 1741), 29.

198 *Ibid.,* 49.

199 Edwards, III, 317.

illustrious day, when the Sun of Righteousness shall 'arise and shine from one end of the earth to the other;' when, to use the language of the inspired prophets, 'the Gentiles shall come to his light, and kings to the brightness of his rising;' in consequence of which, 'the wilderness and solitary places shall be glad, and the desert rejoice and blossom as the rose.'

It is doubtless the duty of all, in their different stations, and according to their respective capacities, to use their utmost endeavours to bring forward this promised, this desired day. There is a great want of *schoolmasters* among these Christianized Indians, to instruct their youth in the *English language,* and the principles of the *Christian faith:* for this, as yet, there is no certain provision made; if any are inclined to contribute to so good a design, we are persuaded they will do an acceptable service to the 'kingdom of the Redeemer.' And we earnestly desire the most indigent to join at least, in their wishes and prayers, that *this work* may *prosper* more and more, till the 'whole earth is filled with the glory of the Lord.' [200]

Even the Moderate Robertson interpreted past missionary spirit and effort in terms of the prophesied spread of "the knowledge of Christ to nations 'far off.' " [201] He saw past success as encouragement for further success. In his 1768 sermon John Gibson described the prophecies still awaiting accomplishment: the flight of the angel preaching the everlasting gospel to all nations (Revelation 14 : 6), the reign of Christ as the one and only Lord of the earth (Zechariah 14 : 9), the triumph of peace over destruction and righteousness over judgment (Isaiah 32 : 16), the universality of joy and productivity (Isaiah 35 : 1), and world-wide fear of the Lord (Isaiah 59 : 19).[202]

The humanitarian and the eschatological emphases converged in the golden anniversary sermon of the society. The text, Isaiah 11 : 9, describes the effects of the gospel in "harmonizing the minds and manners of mankind," said the preacher.[203] Men will be changed into docile and courteous citizens. "This happy transformation shall extend wide as the gospel extends, and keep pace with that knowledge of the Lord by which it is produced." [204] The promises of the spread of this knowledge are numerous.[205] Genuine worship, moral virtue, peace, happiness, enlightenment, comfort for the present and glory in the hereafter are effects of this knowledge. True

200 *Ibid.,* 318.

201 William Robertson, *The Situation of the World at the Time of Christ's Appearance* (Edinburgh: 1755), 43.

202 John Gibson, *The Unlimited Extent and Final Blessedness of God's Spiritual Kingdom* (Edinburgh: 1768), 10-11.

203 James Brown, *The Extensive Influence of Religious Knowledge* (Edinburgh: 1769), 3.

204 *Ibid.,* 3-4.

205 Brown cites Ps. 72 : 8, 11, 17; Zach. 14 : 9; Mal. 1 : 11; Matt. 24 : 14; Rev. 11 : 15. (*Ibid.,* 40-41).

knowledge will be fostered by faithful preaching, by obedient attending to the gospel, by sending Christian merchants and missionaries among the heathen, and by educating youth in sound doctrine. Therefore, "ye servants of Jesus, proceed in your pious and benevolent work," urged the preacher.[206] The time of fulfillment "is nearer than you imagine." Opportunities are opening in America, Africa, and Asia. A war has begun which may overthrow the Turks; the Jesuits are in disrepute.[207] But "laying aside speculations," the preacher reminded his hearers of the society's extant efforts: foreign missions and one hundred fifty-three schools attended by over seven thousand students. "Watered by the dew of heaven, the seed which was as a grain of mustard, hath shot up into a tree, whose branches have spread far, and whose fruit is healthful and rich." [208]

The awareness of the nations and of their imminent conversion was expressed in a burst of Scottish foreign mission interest. For the first twenty-five years of her existence the S.S.P.C.K. had confined her work to Scotland's borders. But in fulfillment of the conditions of a bequest by Dr. Daniel Williams, in 1731 that society requested a number of prominent New Englanders to serve as her board of correspondents in America and the following year contributed toward the support of three missionaries.[209] A second board of correspondents for the middle colonies was established several years later and employed Azariah Horton to work among the Long Island Indians and David Brainerd to evangelize natives on the western frontier. The society engaged the services of Brainerd's brother John to replace him in 1748. During the 1760's the society broadened its work by creating a third board of commissioners — for Connecticut — by aiding the Indian minister Samson Occum, by underwriting some of Eleazer Wheelock's expenses, and by ordaining Joseph Bowman through its Boston board. Among other missionaries supported by the board Samuel Kirkland, who worked among the Oneidas, was the best known. The S.S.P.C.K. contributed toward educating Bristol Yama and John Quamine as missionaries for their native Africa, a project for which the Newport,[210] Rhode Island pastors Samuel Hopkins and Ezra Stiles made repeated appeals. These efforts were forerunners of the great wave of foreign missions which began at the end of the century.

206 *Ibid.*, 42.
207 The power of the Jesuit order was sharply curtailed in 1767, and the order was dissolved in 1773.
208 Brown, 43.
209 See Beaver, *Pioneers in Mission*, 33-34.
210 Maclean, 6.

4. "Not a little dry morality" — English contributions

Simple chiliasm also became widespread throughout the major English churches, where in many cases it was quickened by revivals. Independents, Anglicans, and Baptists all accepted this position. The posthumous appearance of Isaac Newton's *Observations upon the Prophecies of Daniel and the Apocalypse* in 1733, the investigation of prophecy by leading bishops, the writings of the Whitby school, and Edwards' publications enlivened anticipation of the glory of the church at the end of time. Few new mission endeavors were undertaken, however. For English Protestants this was a time for sowing. They sowed their eschatological seed thickly, and in the next period their sons reaped a big harvest of new missionary undertakings.

As early as 1719 Isaac Watts had predicted that "Jesus shall reign where'er the sun Does his successive journeys run." [211] As we have seen from his preface to Edwards' *A Faithful Narrative*, eighteen years later the nonconformist hymn writer dared to hope that the Northampton awakening was the inauguration of the latter days.[212] Both his famous hymn and his preface to Edwards' report were "associated, in the mind of the author, with the approach of this 'latter-day glory.' " [213] Several years later Watts also sponsored Edwards' *The Distinguishing Marks*. His hopes for the end of history were similar to those of John Owen, whom he succeeded in London's Mark Lane pulpit. Watts in turn influenced a wide circle of nonconformists, which included Philip Doddridge.

Ernest A. Payne considers 1737 a crucial year for the development of Doddridge's mission interest. That year Doddridge read the Watts-Guyse edition of *A Faithful Narrative*, he began corresponding with Count von Zinzendorf regarding Moravian missions, and he was informed of Moravian and Methodist interest in the Indians of Georgia.[214] In 1741 he drew up a list of five proposals regarding missions and presented them to "three different assemblies of ministers." [215] Possibly at Zinzendorf's instigation, Doddridge suggested 1) daily prayer for missions, 2) quarterly prayer meetings for missions at mutually agreed upon times and places, 3) study of Biblical promises of the spread of Christ's kingdom, 4) dissemination of information on missions, and 5) contributions for missions. Stated more fully, the third read,

We do hereby express our desire, that some time may be then

---

211 As given in *Psalter Hymnal* (Centennial edition; Grand Rapids: 1959), 463.
212 *vide supra*, 124-125.
213 Foster, "The Bicentenary . . . , 380.
214 Payne, "Doddridge and the Missionary Enterprise," 83-84. Many of the facts in this paragraph on Doddridge are based on Payne's chapter.
215 *D.N.B.*, XV, 162.

spent, if God give an opportunity, in reviewing those promises of Scripture, which relate to the establishment of our Redeemer's kingdom in the world; that our faith may be supported, and our prayers quickened, by the contemplation of them.[216]

Tokens of Doddridge's faith and prayers were his corresponding membership in the S.S.P.C.K., his preface to an abbreviated edition of Brainerd's life and diary, and his desire that his only son would become a missionary to the Indians of New York. Many of the two hundred students in his academy must have been stimulated by his interest. What missionary concern existed in nonconformist circles, however, had no outlet in independent societies.

The record of Anglican revivalists is little better. It has correctly been observed that John Wesley is by no means "the chief name" on missionary roles of the period.[217] His attenuated service in Georgia was not motivated by millennial expectations.[218] Although he accepted the mild millennialism current in his day, and although he even preached a sermon on Isaiah 11 : 9,[219] he did not associate his missionary labor with the latter days. In spite of Edwards' influence on him, Whitefield, in his evangelization, was likewise driven by soteriological motives, though he too adopted simple chiliasm. Only rarely did he speak of conversion in association with the end of history. During a visit to Gibraltar he attended a synagogue and later recorded his longing for the day when all Israel would be saved.[220] When a converted Indian, whom the editors of his journals suggest may have been Samson Occum, attended his service, Whitefield prayed, "Fulfil Thy ancient promises, and let Thy Son have the heathen for His inheritance, and the uttermost parts of the earth for His possession." [221] These and other references to the latter days occur only incidentally in his journals, however.

More fruitful and recently-discovered missionary enterprises are found in the college and mission established and supported through the Countess of Huntingdon, Whitefield's most devoted and illustrious disciple. Much like the school of Eleazer Wheelock, to whose envoys campaigning for

216 As quoted by Payne, "Doddridge and the Missionary Enterprise," 89.
217 Payne, "The Evangelical Revival . . . ," 226.
218 In two separate works Martin Schmidt uses the same words to express Wesley's understanding of missions: "Schlüssel zum Ursinn des Evangeliums, . . . Wiedererweckung der Urchristentums, . . . existenziellen Weg zum eigenen Heil." *John Wesley,* 2 vols. (Zurich & Frankfurt a. M.: 1953, 1966), I, 118; and "Der Missionsgedanke des jungen Wesley auf dem Hintergrunde seines Zeitalters," *Theologia Viatorum,* I, 1949, 95.
219 John Wesley, *The Works of the Rev. John Wesley, A.M.,* 14 vols. (3rd. ed.; London: 1829), VI, 277-288.
220 Whitefield, 135-136.
221 *Ibid.,* 419. Also see 428.

funds in England she extended support, the Countess' school in the middle colonies was designed to train evangelists to work among colonists and Indians. Although the project folded at the outbreak of the Revolutionary War, it has been concluded on the basis of a recent investigation of the correspondence between the Countess and her laborers in America that millennial expectations of the Edwardean type were the spiritual foundation upon which her effort rested.[222] She and her agents believed that they were involved in establishing the coming kingdom of Christ on earth in the latter days.

If both the Wesleyan and the Calvinistic Methodists eventually moved outside the Church of England, a third group of evangelicals remained within her walls.[223] Later known as the Evangelicals, these sons of the church shared the concern for vital, spiritual Christianity centered on personal conversion and a life of benevolent service. Theirs was also an unswerving optimism for the future of Christ's kingdom. It is best exemplified by a series of fifty sermons delivered by John Newton of St. Mary Woolnoth, London, in 1786. Based on texts used by George F. Handel in his majestic "Messiah," the addresses manifest the mild chiliasm of the Evangelicals, the founders of the Church Missionary Society.[224] But once again, there is no record of eschatologically grounded mission efforts by this group prior to the 1790's.

The more scholarly apocalypticism of the bishops was manifested in the annual sermons of the S.P.G. Like the evangelical eschatology it was based on the prophesies of the Old and New Testaments. Such favorites as Psalm 2 : 8,[225] Isaiah 11 : 9,[226] Malachi 1 : 11,[227] and Revelation 14 : 6-7 [228]

---

222 This information regarding the Countess of Huntingdon's American mission and its eschatological basis is based on Orchard, Chapter II, section 3, "The Countess of Huntingdon." The correspondence, discovered within the last few years, is currently undergoing classification at Westminster and Cheshunt Colleges, Cambridge.

223 Walsh, 137, defends the thesis that the Evangelical Party did not owe its rise to Wesley or Whitefield. In so doing he attempts to refute those scholars—he lists them (136-137, n. 4)—who adopt the contrary opinion. In his engrossment with the position he has previously so ably and so correctly developed (vide supra, 116f.), does not Walsh perhaps overlook the frustrating complexity which the evangelical awakenings share with every widespread and sustained historical movement? John Newton, to cite but one example, did after all fall under the influence of Whitefield for a time. See O.D.C.C., 951. The influence of Wesley and Whitefield did contribute in part to the rise of the party, therefore.

224 Newton's series was published as The Messiah in 1786. Handel's oratorio, coincidentally, was written in the throes of the Evangelical Revival in 1741. However, we have been unable to find any evidence that Handel was influenced by the awakenings in composing The Messiah.

225 Shute [Barrington], S.P.G. (a.s.) (London: 1775). Though not strictly an S.P.G. annual sermon, William Smith's A Discourse Concerning the Conversion of The Heathen Americans (Philadelphia: 1760) was delivered before a convention of

154

were selected to emphasize the missionary imperative. The preachers repeatedly expressed their conviction that there was a "beautiful harmony" among all the prophets in anticipating the future glory of the church.[229] Prophecy would be fulfilled when the fulness of the Gentiles would be gathered into the church.[230] The distinct identity of the Jewish people was read as an assurance of their prophesied national conversion.[231] The advance of the gospel in the course of history was seen as the progressive fulfillment of prophecy.[232] Steadily the gospel has been moving westward, it was pointed out: from Palestine, to continental Europe, to Britain. In "a *second* remarkable period" it would flourish in America.[233] For this reason the S.P.G. had to sustain and increase her effort in the new world. The wealth and civilization of England will be used effectively to spread civilization to all the Indians of North America, asserted a preacher on the authority of "Old *Hakluyt*." [234]

The bishops confessed ignorance on the date of the universal triumph of Christianity and cautioned against speculation. In fact, anyone who compares Biblical promises with "the present extent" of Christianity in so small a portion of the world must conclude that the era of glory is still one of "the secret things" which belong only to God, it was asserted.[235]

> And as there are general declarations in Scripture concerning the state and condition of the universal Church in the future and latter ages of the world; it becomes not us to be too curious and inquisitive after the particular 'times or the seasons which the Father hath put in his own power': But to contribute our endeavours towards introducing that happy system and constitution of things, which is the accomplishment of these prophecies; by diffusing the knowledge of God and his Christ, and advancing the cause of truth, virtue and righteousness amongst men.[236]

Other sermons also linked the inability to determine times and seasons with

episcopal clergymen and before the College and Academy of Philadelphia and was dedicated to the S.P.G. and Archbishop Thomas. Representing the same theology and tradition as the annual sermons, it too was based on Psalm 2 : 8.

226 Richard Terrick, S.P.G. (a.s.) (London: 1764); and Smith, 24.

227 Martin [Benson], S.P.G. (a.s.) (London: 1740).

228 Thomas Hayter, S.P.G. (a.s.) (London: 1755); and John [Thomas], S.P.G. (a.s.) (London: 1747), 9.

229 Smith, 2-3; also see Robert Drummond, S.P.G. (a.s.) (London: 1754), 6-7; and William George, S.P.G. (a.s.) (London: 1749), 10.

230 George, 10.

231 Edward Cresset, S.P.G. (a.s.) (London: 1753), 11-12.

232 Richard Osbaldiston, S.P.G. (a.s.) (London: 1752), *passim*.

233 Smith, 15; also see [Benson], 3.

234 Smith, 20-21.

235 Drummond, 4.

236 *Ibid.*, 6.

the imperative to strive for the realization of the prophecies by means of missions.[237]

The certainty that Jews and Gentiles, men of all nations, would one day acknowledge Christ, therefore, was cited as a chief reason for S.P.G. activity. But without the evangelical commitment to the awakenings little fervency or urgency was attached to eschatological passages in that society's documents. That emphasis was not important in the sermons of the second Anglican-dominated society, the S.P.C.K.

Before concluding our survey of millennial expectations in English missions of this period, we do well to pause and consider the leading representative of the Particular or Calvinistic Baptists, John Gill. We do this for two reasons. First, while the logical deductions made from the doctrine of election by representatives of high Calvinism — such as Gill — have frequently been judged as impediments to evangelism,[238] little recognition has been taken of the strongly evangelistic note in Gill's eschatology. Our second reason for discussing Gill is that the Particular Baptists were the pioneers in foreign missions in the 1790's. Gill's eschatology undoubtedly contributed to that rebirth of missions.

Gill's doctrine of the latter days appeared in a sermon delivered in 1753. There will be a "spiritual" and a "personal" reign of Christ in the latter days, he said. These terms apply to two distinct and consecutive periods of time, which are "too often huddled and jumbled together" by writers on the subject, he continued.[239] Both are still future. The spiritual reign, which is a more perfect version of Christ's current method of ruling, will be introduced by a blast from the seventh trumpet marking the fall of Antichrist.[240] His fall will be achieved through Christ's "gospel attended by his spirit and power."[241] Faithful ministers preaching this gospel will move seven angels, signifying seven Protestant rulers, to pour out the seven vials of divine wrath against Antichrist. When they are empty and Antichrist's downfall is complete, there will be no obstacles remaining to prevent the spread of the gospel to all nations.

> This will be, when the 'angel,' not any particular minister, as *Luther,* or any other, but a sett of gospel-ministers in the latter day, so called from their office, 'shall flee in the midst of heaven'; discharge their office with great readiness and swiftness, and in the most public manner in the church of God; 'having the everlasting gospel,' not a little dry morality, but the gospel of the grace of God, the good news

---

237 [Benson], 31; [Thomas], 9; Richard [Trevor], S.P.G. (a.s.) (London: 1750), 15.

238 See Geoffrey F. Nuttall, "Northamptonshire and *The Modern Question,"* *Journal of Theological Studies,* New Series, XVI, 1965, 102.

239 John Gill, *The Glory of the Church in the Latter Day* (London: 1753), 7.

240 *Ibid.,* 11.

241 *Ibid.,* 12.

of life and salvation by Jesus Christ; ... These will be very diligent and industrious, spare no pains, be indefatigable in their work; they will be 'many,' and 'will run to and fro'; and by this means 'knowledge' will be 'increased': this will be the time, even in the *Philadelphian* state, when there will be an 'open door set,' which 'no man can shut'; an opportunity of preaching the gospel every where, and which will be taken and used.[242]

This preaching will be blest by "very large conversions every where." [243] Roman Catholics, Moslems, and pagans will all be converted. The Jews can only be converted as Paul was, "by the immediate power, and grace of God." [244] Finally, the spiritual reign of Christ will be marked by a great outpouring of the Spirit, the full accomplishment of Joel's prophecy associated with Pentecost in Acts 2 : 17-20. The Spirit will assure truth or gospel light, purity of liturgy and church government, brotherly love, holiness, and peace with prosperity.[245] Only toward the close of the spiritual reign will Christ appear visibly in his human nature to begin his personal reign.

Gill did not speculate on the date of Antichrist's fall. He and other high Calvinists waited patiently, trusting God to make plain when his corps of elite ministers should go into action. And when the impetuous William Carey tried to force the divinely-determined pace for history in his famous sermon to the Northamptonshire Association, he was dutifully reminded of this truth. But with the outbreak of the French Revolution it appeared to many that God had begun that decisive battle against Antichrist for which they had been waiting.

5. Summary

In Anglo-American eschatology the latter days had always been associated with the universal knowledge of Christ. When the revivals of this period were linked with the latter days, therefore, every prayer for revival or for the kingdom assumed an immediate missionary dimension. This was made even more explicit by men who saw that Christian knowledge would be spread by preaching. Consequently, throughout this period many gave themselves for work among the American Indians, and others raised appeals for sending men to nations even more remote.

To Jonathan Edwards the Great Awakening appeared to be the beginning of the latter days. This conviction evolved gradually. It was based on

---

242   *Ibid.,* 19-20. Gill's doctrine of the everlasting gospel was reinforced in his *An Exposition of the Revelation of S. John the Divine* (London: 1776), 164-165.
243   Gill, *The Glory . . . ,* 21.
244   *Ibid.,* 24. This was essentially Mede's position.
245   *Ibid.,* 26-29.

such sources as New England's anticipation of the outpouring of the Spirit, the simple chiliasm recast by Whitby, his own prior writing, and his experience with revival. He spoke of the awakening primarily in the categories of the outpoured Spirit and the kingdom of Christ. The kingdom, he felt, would become world-wide through organized prayer and through preaching. Missions assumed an increasing role in his thought, writings, and life as the implications of his eschatological explanation of the revivals became increasingly clear to him. During the awakenings other New Lights similarly became aware of their missionary obligation and supported missions with a new vigor.

Old Lights, sharing the eschatology of the New Lights but loath to apply it to the Great Awakening, defined and supported missions in eschatological terms. Both groups unitedly worked for the new age through common missionary endeavors.

In Scotland John Willison's writings portrayed the universal spread of Christian faith in the latter days. The Cambuslang revival promoted hopes that those days had arrived, and James Robe used that conviction to solicit united prayer and support for missions.

The English bishops' dispassionate analyses of prophecies regarding the end of time were reflected in S.P.G. annual sermons, but they did not produce the urgency for missions generated by the evangelicals. Among Baptists John Gill's writings on the latter days contained missionary implications, but, except for the Countess of Huntingdon's American mission, no nonconformist mission projects were produced or sustained by millennial incentives.

Several new eschatological emphases — and they were only emphases — were significant for Anglo-American missions in this period. The outpouring of the Spirit and the kingdom of Christ were applied to local revivals as the first ripples of a movement that would engulf the earth. The notion of the westward course of the gospel was still prominent in this era. As men increasingly recognized their obligation to pray and preach the new age into reality, the notion of the everlasing gospel received more emphasis. It was during this time when men thought themselves to be entering the latter days that more interest was shown in defining the nature of those days. Ultimately, however, it was the total impact of a fresh interpretation of many Biblical promises to meet new situations that contributed new life to the missionary movement.

Chapter V

The fall of Antichrist
(1776-1810, Britain)

A. General Background

England was faced with new problems in the late eighteenth century. Her American colonies, grieved over heavy taxation and English indifference to their complaints, declared their independence in 1776 and waged an eight year war with their mother country. The industrialization, just beginning in the earlier period, gained momentum. With it came the squalor of urban slums and the injustices perpetrated on an unprotected labor force. Britain's economy profited from the slave trade, which supplied the fettered armies to produce the raw cotton to feed her textile mills. If humanity was cheap in urbanized England and in the holds of her slavers, it was romanticized by Captain Cook's discoveries and reports on the South Sea Islands. In general, the British rejected the humanism of the Continental philosophers, preaching their gospel of democratization. In their propriety and conservatism most Englishmen did not succumb to the excesses of foreign thought and example, and various religious segments on the British scene reacted in horror to the threatening new monster they saw in the atheistic and deistic systems of their day, commonly lumped together as "Infidelity."

English Christians, particularly the evangelicals among them, challenged the evils of those days. Zachary Macaulay and William Wilberforce led the struggle against the slave trade. Robert Raikes through his Sunday schools and Hannah More through the Religious Tract Society spread secular and religious knowledge to combat the ignorance and evils of the industrial areas. The danger of Infidelity was constantly held before the people.[1]

But no new development so aroused British anticipations or anxieties — depending upon whom one has in mind — as did the French Revolution.[2] To the traditional Anglican and to the Church of England's establishment

---

1 Leading Baptists Andrew Fuller and John Ryland, Jr., sponsored an English edition of *The Nature and Danger of Infidel Philosophy* (Bristol: 1799), a series of lectures by Timothy Dwight, Jonathan Edwards' grandson and President of Yale.

2 See Moorman, 294-295; Van den Berg, 121-122; and, for contemporary dissenters' position, David Bogue and James Bennett, *History of Dissenters from the Revolution in 1688, to the Year 1808*, 4 vols. (London: 1808-1812), IV, 189f.

as a whole it was a terrifying example of what could happen if republican forces were ever unleashed on their side of the Channel. Politically progressive and historically conditioned to suspect any Erastian coalition, dissenters generally welcomed the Revolution as the birth of a new age. Their hopes were dampened by the regicide of 1793 and the ensuing excesses and were virtually extinguished by the Napoleonic wars. Dissent's initial reaction was largely an expression of her antipathy toward Roman Catholicism. Only a decade earlier a bill according privileges to Catholics had provoked large-scale riots in London, Edinburgh, and Glasgow.[3] The powerful Moderate William Robertson, himself in favor of the bill, conceded that he had completely misread public opinion on the issue. The anti-Catholic theology of Willison and Edwards had molded a generation of evangelical opinion.

On the ecclesiastical scene many Scottish Moderates and the upper echelons of English clergy cultivated higher social contacts. Consequently accusations of their consorting with Infidelity and neglecting the common man were frequent. Needed reform in the English church was not forthcoming. Nevertheless, the majority of the clergy on both sides of the border undoubtedly performed their duties faithfully. Among evangelicals of all denominations the leavening power of the gospel was particularly pronounced. Revivals stirred throughout Scotland, Wales, and England. In the Church of England groups clustered in Cambridge around Charles Simeon, in Sommerset around Hannah More, and in Chapham around Rector John Venn.[4] A new vitality and an address to social issues also was found among Presbyterians in Scotland and Independents in England. The modern missionary movement was not the least significant product of the evangelical spirit.

B. *Millennial Expectations*

As had the political upheavals of the Civil Wars and the Commonwealth period, the French Revolution produced a flood of eschatological thought and activity. A small percentage was bizarre, such as Richard Brother's fancy that he was " 'God Almighty's Nephew' " who would lead the Jews back to Palestine and rebuild the temple and Joanna Southcott's willingness to seal a "believer" as one of the 144,000 for a minuscule fee varying from twelve to twenty-one shillings.[5] The vast majority was not based on such subjective illumination, however, but on scholarly attempts to determine the meaning of Biblical prophecy.

Much of the literature produced on millennial expectations was in the

3 Moorman, 312; Burleigh, 306.
4 Moorman, 315-319.
5 P. G. Rogers, *The Sixth Trumpeter*, 3-7; *O.D.C.C.*, 1276.

form of reprints of previous works on the subject. A striking example is a publication by Henry Hunter. On February 3, 1793, he addressed his Scottish Church of London Wall on the occasion of the trial, condemnation, and execution of Louis XVI. Although Englishmen differed in their evaluation of the Revolution, Hunter vouched for their unanimity on the king's execution as "an act of complicated inhumanity and injustice." [6] By simultaneously weakening Rome's power, however, God was bringing good out of evil, indicated Hunter. Louis XVI's death was but one of many signs of the nearness of the latter days, when righteousness and peace would flourish. Because his predecessor at London Wall, Robert Fleming, Jr., had predicted current happenings with uncanny accuracy in a long-forgotten study, Hunter republished Fleming's full work with the printed version of his own sermon.[7] Two years later Hunter reprinted the combination, this time with an abridgment of Fleming's work, in a collection of his own sermons. The Fleming reprint was so well received that it appeared again in 1809 in both London and Edinburgh editions.[8]

The search for the key to the secrets of history led to the reprinting of other works. Excerpts from Thomas Goodwin's commentary on Revelation were printed under the title *The French Revolution Foreseen, in 1639*. It was given this title since "the events which have lately taken place in France, so exactly correspond with what he conceived to be the design of this part of the Prophetic writings." [9] If men do not agree with Goodwin's interpretation, continued the editor, perhaps those competent in Biblical exposition will be challenged to take a new look at that book in the light of contemporary events. A third reprint which appeared in conjunction with the French Revolution was the last two sermons of John Willison's *The Balm of Gilead*, published as *A Prophecy of the French Revolution, and the Downfall of Antichrist*. Appearing in 1793, it too was edited anonymously.

After 1800 attempts to associate the French Revolution with the fall of Antichrist on the authority of reputable British commentators became more ambitious. Anthologies of eschatological observations began appearing with reprinted works on prophecy. The 1803 edition of Bishop Thomas Newton's *Dissertation on the Prophecies* and the two 1809 editions of Fleming's work contained basically the same collection of citations, which were slightly reworked and rearranged in each source. From such illustrious

6 Henry Hunter, *Sermons*, 2 vols. (London: 1795), II, 231.

7 *vide supra*, 111f., for Fleming's study.

8 They are entitled respectively *Apocalyptical Key* (London: 1809), and *A Discourse on the Rise and Fall of Papacy* (Edinburgh: 1809). The prefaces of both editions indicated the work's relevance as an accurate application of prophecy to current affairs in France.

9 Thomas Goodwin, *The French Revolution Foreseen, in 1639* (London: [n. d.]), 5. The editor chose to remain anonymous.

divines as John Owen, Thomas Goodwin, James Ussher, Isaac Newton, Henry More, Christopher Love, John Gill, Robert Fleming, Jr., and John Willison it was "proven" that the best expositors between 1550 and 1800 from all denominations had in one manner or another anticipated the momentous days of the French Revolution and the tumbling of Antichrist. Sometimes the application of the citations was forced, as when Archbishop Brown's 1551 evaluation of Jesuit casuistry and John Knox's 1572 condemnation of French Catholic intrigues in the Huguenot wars were deemed relevant to the 1790's.[10] The various entries demonstrated much diversity. Not every quotation dealt with the same issue. Love and Fleming were cited for the accuracy of their dating. Owen and More were quoted on political upheaval. Isaac Newton and Pierre Jurieu became authorities on the French dissipation of Antichrist. It mattered little to the editors that these men often differed sharply with one another's eschatology, and the contexts from which the citations came were of little consequence to them. It was believed that the men and their works illuminated the later age, and for the editors that was the crucial factor!

A number of works on the latter days and related subjects were not directly motivated by the events in France. Appearing before 1790, they reinforced the eschatological understanding of the Revolution when it occurred, however. Notable among these are the various editions of Willison's sermons, John Erskine's editions of Prince's sermons and of Edwards' *A History of the Work of Redemption,* and John Sutcliff's 1789 edition of Edwards' *An Humble Attempt.* Gill's commentary on Revelation also was much consulted during the turbulence of the 1790's.[11]

During the closing years of the eighteenth century an intensification in the interpretation of prophecy occurred through a number of new studies. Some of them were a direct attempt to explain the events in France. Others were part of a general resurgence of interest in eschatological themes. While not strictly belonging to either category, the Evangelical Thomas Scott's commentary on the entire Bible, produced in weekly installments between 1788 and 1792, had "an enormous circulation." [12] His mild chiliasm unwittingly aided Anglicans in giving an eschatological explanation to current events.[13] Dissenters Hunter, David Bogue, and Andrew Fuller, all among the most dedicated missionary leaders of the period, wrote on eschatological themes and will be discussed in the course of this chapter. Especially the views of Bogue and Fuller are exempt from the strong

10 See Fleming, Jr., *Apocalyptical Key,* 111-112.
11 *vide supra,* 157.
12 *O.D.C.C.,* 1233.
13 See Scott's *The Holy Bible, Containing the Old and New Testaments; with Original Notes, and Practical Observations,* 4 vols. (London: 1792), comments on Isa. 65 : 16-25; Dan. 12 : 7, 11; and Rev. 11 : 2.

162

orientation to political events which marked the writings of James Bicheno, a nonconformist minister.

In 1793 Bicheno queried his readers on the French Revolution, "Is it one of those commotions produced by the conflicting passions of men, that rise and sink, and are soon forgotten? or is is one of those events which mark the great eras of time, and from which originate new orders of things?" [14] He elected the latter, identified Louis XIV as the beast of Revelation 13 : 11, and interpreted the fall of the French royal house as a remarkable advance in the fall of Antichrist and toward the inception of the millennium in 1864. In 1794 a second, enlarged edition of his speculations appeared, and in 1797 he was obliged to justify England's gruelling war with the French constitutional regime, which he had earlier identified as God's appointed instrument for the overthrow of Babylon.[15] Bicheno anticipated the conversion of the Jews, the spread of the gospel to all nations, and the coming of the millennium — all by "a mixture of natural and supernatural causes." [16] He became the spokesman for many dissenters, and in the light of developing tensions between France and Britain they looked to him, among others, to reconcile their earlier hopes regarding France with their British patriotism.

Anglican expositors, expressing Tory sentiments, generally rejected dissenters' initial optimism regarding the Revolution. Samuel Horsley, a protégé of William Lowth and eventual Bishop of St. Asaph, propagated millennial sentiments but condemned the Revolution for undermining religion and morality and linked the Republic with one of the apocalyptic beasts, Voltaire with the mystery of iniquity, and Napoleon Bonaparte with Antichrist.[17] George S. Faber, Vicar of Stockton upon Tees, was in turn a follower of Horsley and Bishop Newton. In 1805 his successful exposition of the prophecy of the seventy weeks (Daniel 9 : 24-27) appeared, and the following year *A Dissertation on the Prophecies* was cordially received by Evangelicals.[18] Between 1806 and 1810 Faber's eschatological observations and debates were prominent in *The Christian Observer*, the Evangelical

---

14 James Bicheno, *The Signs of the Times* (London: [1793]), "Advertisement."

15 James Bicheno, *The Probable Progress and Issue of the Commotions Which Have Agitated Europe Since the French Revolution* (London: 1797). The full title of the second edition of the 1793 work was *The Signs of the Times: or the Overthrow of the Papal Tyranny in France, the Prelude of Destruction to Popery and Despotism; But of Peace to Mankind.*

16 James Bicheno, *The Restoration of the Jews, the Crisis of all Nations* (London: 1800), 95.

17 Orchard's manuscript, Chapter I.

18 The full title of Faber's work is *A Dissertation on the Prophecies, that have been fulfilled, are now fulfilling, or will hereafter be fulfilled, relative to the great Period of 1260 Years; the Papal and Mohammedan Apostasies; the tyrannical Reign of Antichrist, or the Infidel Power; and the Restoration of the Jews.*

forum. The reviewer of *A Dissertation on the Prophecies* evaluated the writer's place among contemporary expositors:

> The extraordinary events which have taken place in the world, and more particularly in Europe, during the last fifteen or twenty years, have naturally directed the attention of thoughtful and inquisitive men to some of the Scripture prophecies in a more particular manner: and though many erroneous interpretations and crude conjectures have been advanced by some writers, knowledge has undoubtedly been increased by this consideration of 'the signs of the times.' It is with much satisfaction that we are called upon to notice the researches of Mr. Faber in this department of sacred literature.[19]

Faber's success may be gauged by the rapidity with which a second edition of this work appeared — in 1807.

In spite of their differences the commentators mentioned so far all anticipated a gradual approach of the latter-day glory of the church through natural, though God-ordained, means. In this period other expositors articulated and disseminated a more complex chiliasm or premillennialism. Such were Hatley Frere, English experimenter in education and printing as well as expositor whose writings influenced the Irvingites, and, of earlier vintage, Elhanan Winchester, American Universalist and clergyman. The latter, defending the personal appearance and reign of Christ with his saints during the millennium, explicitly rejected the missionary dimension of Gill's eschatology.[20] Prior to 1810, however, complex chiliasm was defended by only a minority of British expositors.

Simple chiliasm, with its strong emphasis on the gradual arrival of the promised kingdom through preaching and conversion, was in vogue. As it had fifty years earlier, this eschatology gave heavy accent to concerts for prayer for revival and reform in religion. As the world's ranking sea power, England figured prominently in discussions on the spread of the kingdom. Whether they approved or disapproved of the French Revolution, evangelicals all saw the sign of the latter days in the humbling of the Roman Catholic establishment. Her fall meant the removal of the major impediment to that kingdom. Seen against this background, the resurgence in missions becomes understandable. That this eschatology permeated the new missionary societies to their cores will be demonstrated in this chapter.

C. *Mission Efforts*

The vitality of the new period made little impression upon the established

---

19 "Review of Faber's Dissertation on the Prophecies," *The Christian Observer*, V, 1806, 614.

20 Elhanan Winchester, *A Course of Lectures, on the Prophecies that Remain to be Fulfilled*, 4 vols. (London: 1789), II, 15-16.

societies. Where they could, they continued their work faithfully. Unfortunately, the American Revolutionary War disrupted some of their best efforts. The New England Company discontinued funds to subjects who were " 'levying War against Great Britain & their lawful Sovereign.' " [21] Such veteran missionaries as Gideon Hawley and John Sergeant, Jr., found themselves without support as their benefactors opened new fields in Canada. S.P.G. evangelism in the colonies collapsed when practically all of her priests fled home. The once vibrant work of the S.P.C.K. in India had grown languid, and the East India Company used her control in that sub-continent, given her by Robert Clive's victory, to avert any new missionary initiatives. Although Scottish Presbyterian sympathy with the colonial cause sustained their support of American missions, that support had always been token in comparison with her work on the home front. By 1809 she had more than a hundred centers for training Highland girls in homemaking and employed more than three hundred teachers "besides missionary ministers, catechists, and pensionary students of divinity." [22]

Since her major theater of missions was either closed to her or capable of being served by new and indigenous American organizations, Britain naturally sought new outlets for the new mission fervor of the 1790's. The birth of missions to Africa and Asia at this time is by no means a surprising development but a logical and even necessary consequence of existing circumstances. The incompatibility of the new life with the vested theological and ecclesiastical interest of extant missionary structures forced the creation of new societies. In 1792 Baptists formed the Baptist Missionary Society and sent William Carey to India. Deeply impressed by Carey's example and letters, a handful of Anglicans and nonconformists banded together three years later in an ecumenical enterprise called the London Missionary Society. When Evangelicals developed qualms about the advisability of such co-operation, they founded the Society for Missions in Africa and the East — in 1799. It soon became known as the Church Missionary Society, the name which we shall use.[23] In the Church of Scotland new initiatives for missions were taken in 1796 with the organization of the Glasgow Missionary Society and the Scottish Missionary Society. They were founded by evangelicals, who that same year saw their proposal for a foreign missionary society for the Church of Scotland defeated by a small margin by the Moderate bloc at the General Assembly. The British and Foreign Bible Society, founded in 1804, arose out of the evangelical milieu and society spirit and became a vital auxiliary to the missionary

21 Kellaway, 277.
22 *A Short Account of the Society in Scotland for Propagating Christian Knowledge in the Highlands and Islands* ([Edinburgh]: 1809), 8-9.
23 These new societies will hereafter be abbreviated B.M.S., L.M.S., and C.M.S. respectively.

organizations. The formation in 1809 of the London Society for Promoting Christianity amongst the Jews was the result of renewed faith in the approaching conversion of Israel.

Evangelicals spearheaded the organization of new mission efforts in this period, therefore, and sent missionaries to new fields in Africa, Asia, the Americas, and the Pacific. Their vision of the promised univeral spread of the gospel and their faith that God would make good those promises were to change the map of the Christian church in the nineteenth century.

D. Missions and Millennial Expectations

Although simple chiliasm had become universal in Anglo-American churches by this period, we can nevertheless discern a line of development in the missionary impact of this eschatology after 1776. In a sense, like the revivals, the eschatological missionary impulses were natural and independent reactions to common stimuli by Christians with a common theological background. This background included a common hermeneutical approach to prophecy, a common understanding of history, and the theological pre-suppositions on which these first two rested. In this case the major stimuli were the French Revolution with the events surrounding it and the interest in the ends of the earth which had been produced by recent geographical discoveries. Thanks to cheap editions of sermons and rising literacy, this eschatology had filtered from theologian to preacher to parishioner in a generation and a half. The result of the combination of factors just mentioned was a missionary interest and fervor of incalculable proportions. It appeared everywhere in a few short years, from the London metropolis to outlying Scottish shires. Nevertheless, the eschatological missionary impulses passed on an overgrown but distinguishable path leading from Scotland to Scottish circles in London and to the Baptist Midlands and from all three to the Independents and evangelicals more generally. There were perhaps parallel and dissecting routes, but this was the most pronounced and the one we shall follow.

1. A lengthy dawn — the Scottish societies

The paradigm of Scottish evangelical missionary interest through the last half of the eighteenth century was John Erskine. Delivering the sermon to his synod in 1750, he urged the Scottish church to emulate Paul, who was constrained by Jesus' love to " 'fly like a flaming seraph from pole to pole, to proclaim the ineffable glories of his lovely Jesus.' " [24] Six years later he

24 Letter to the editor, *The Missionary Magazine*, I, 1796, 152-153.

addressed the annual gathering of the S.S.P.C.K., and he served as a director of "uncommon diligence and exertion" of that society for many years.[25] Even when physical incapacitation forced his absence from that body's proceedings, she consulted him as her authority on her American affairs. From the time he had written his work on signs of the times Erskine had been interested in the fulfillment of prophecy. That interest came to its most significant fruition when in 1773 he edited and published Edwards' sermons on the work of redemption. His conviction that these sermons would be of uncommon interest was not a misjudgment, for the work went through many editions.[26] It was essential in preparing the British mind for the missionary awakening.

Erskine contributed directly to that awakening by sending a bundle of books to his Baptist friends in the Midlands, who, upon reading the enclosed copy of Edwards' *An Humble Attempt,* started concerts for prayer for the spread of Christ's kingdom. From these concerts Baptist missions developed. Edwards' observation that Scripture was the only source of information regarding "what God designs by that series of revolutions and events that are brought to pass in the world" were poignant in 1793, when Erskine gave them to the British reader in yet another reprint.[27] During the unsettled mid-nineties Erskine anticipated the latter days and in a sharp debate with Moderates during the 1796 General Assembly opposed the idea that history was not ripe for foreign missions since a number of preliminary prophecies still awaited fulfillment.[28] The Moderates differed from the evangelicals by maintaining that " 'philosophy and learning' " must precede evangelization and in suspecting evangelical mission enthusiasm — manifested in the two Scottish societies formed two months before — as "seditious" and a dangerous manifestation of current political disruption.[29] The charge is understandable in terms of the welcome which Erskine and the evangelicals had given the French Revolution as a portent of the gospel age. In the same year that the synod was held, Erskine's devotion to the spread of Christ's kingdom moved him to edit a supplement to John Gillies' account of the success of the gospel. It concentrated on revivals and missions.[30] For more than fifty years John Erskine hoped, prayed, and worked for the reign of

25 Memorial by Jedidiah Morse, *The Massachusetts Missionary Magazine,* I, 1803, 38.
26 The British Museum possesses editions from 1774, 1786, 1788, 1799, 1812, and 1816.
27 Jonathan Edwards, *Miscellaneous Observations on Important Theological Subjects,* John Erskine (ed.) (Edinburgh: 1793), 28.
28 Van den Berg, 160, and 160-161, n. 313.
29 Elizabeth G. K. Hewat, *Vision and Achievement, 1796-1956* (London: 1960), 5-6.
30 John Gillies, *A Supplement to Two Volumes (Published in 1754) of Historical Collections,* John Erskine (ed.) (Edinburgh: 1796).

Christ, and the cause he had come to represent gradually gained strength in Scottish circles.

It was represented in London by many of the men who served on the S.S.P.C.K.'s corresponding board there and who delivered her annual sermons in Salters Hall. While the Baptist contribution to missions in this period is well known and has rightly been stressed by scholars, it has overshadowed this nursery of later L.M.S. leaders.[31] Many of these leaders were of Scottish descent and served either Scottish congregations or English dissenting churches in the southern country. Henry Hunter, David Bogue, and John Love, all Scottish ministers in southern England, addressed the board.[32] In 1790 Hunter was made its secretary. The names of Hunter and other members of his immediate family appear on early L.M.S. subscription lists as generous donors. Bogue and Love were among the founders of the new society. After her establishment the L.M.S. was supported by much the same constituency and made use of many of the same leaders as the Scottish board. Roland Hill, William Jay, and T. Young preached before both bodies.[33] Hill served on the first L.M.S. Board of Directors — one of twenty ministers in that capacity.[34] James Steven, Scottish minister at Covent Garden who had participated with David Bogue in preliminary discussions on the need for a dissenting foreign missionary society and who was also one of the original directors,[35] spoke before the S.S.P.C.K. board in London in 1798. It becomes clear, therefore, that Scottish influences stood behind the formation and work of the L.M.S. through the London board of the S.S.P.C.K. and that amicable relations between the two bodies persisted after 1795.

The attention given to the latter days by those associated with the Scottish board may be gauged by the example of Hunter, who shouldered much of her work and in 1795 wrote a history of the S.S.P.C.K.[36] Already in 1780 he addressed her in a sermon anticipating the universal spread of Christianity and victory over wickedness and religious indifference. He puzzled about the lengthy delay in the arrival of the millennium.[37] Hunter's

---

31 On Baptist missions see especially the contributions of E. A. Payne in our bibliography. Payne, "The Evangelical Revival...," 233, recognizes the "distinguished part" played by Scottish ministers in London.

32 Hunter addressed her in 1780 and 1789, Bogue in 1792, Love in 1794.

33 They preached before the L.M.S. in 1795, 1797, and 1805, and before the board in 1796, 1803, and 1807, respectively.

34 See Richard Lovett, *The History of the London Missionary Society, 1795-1895*, 2 vols. (London: 1899), I, 39-40, for a full list of directors, including some half dozen Scottish ministers.

35 *Ibid.,* 5.

36 Hunter's history was entitled *A Brief History of the Society in Scotland for Propagating Christian Knowledge.* See *D.N.B.,* XXVIII, 286-287, on Hunter.

37 Henry Hunter, "The Universal Extent, and Everlasting Duration of the Redeemer's Kingdom," in *Sermons,* I, 209.

excitement during the French Revolution over the nearness of the latter days and his republication of Fleming's study have already been noted.

A decade later Hunter's study on the conversion of the Jews contributed to the swelling interst in that event. He gave a general historical survey of that people and devoted particular attention to them at the time of Christ's birth, in English history, in France and Germany in his day, and in their various sects. His final section surveyed the views of Christian theologians concerning the future conversion and restoration of the Jews to their homeland.[38] An appendix consisting of six sermons addressed to the Jews by Hunter and prominent men in the L.M.S. was prefaced with an irenic appeal for *rapprochement* between Jews and Christians.

> Animated, we trust, by a spirit of philanthropy, and real faith in the Scriptures of Truth, we have not beheld the state of our Jewish Brethren with careless indifference or infidel contempt. We have judged it our duty to endeavour to excite renewed and solemn investigation of those Sacred Oracles which we profess alike to receive, whether Jews or Christians. We feel it of the last importance to our own souls to know the true Jehovah, and the Messiah, who is the sum and substance of all the Prophecies and Promises, and in whom alone *all the nations of the earth shall be blessed.*[39]

In his early interest in the fulness of Christ's kingdom, in his anticipations during the French Revolution, and in his efforts to convert the Jews Hunter typifies the burning eschatological issues of his day, both for fellow-travellers on the London board and for evangelicals in general.

When we consider the board sermons, we are struck by the intensity and frequency with which the preachers discoursed on eschatology. A simple chiliasm with no radically new developments, the doctrine of the latter days lies at the heart of the understanding of missions in these sermons. The preachers felt that missions belonged to the eschaton, which was impinging upon them.

Often millennial hopes were occasioned in the sermons by the major events and issues of this period, just as significant events had occasioned hopes in Anglo-American theology and sermons in previous generations. In 1779 the American Revolution was seen as an obstruction to the coming of the kingdom through the S.S.P.C.K., although the preacher quickly speculated that God might soon turn chaos into order in the interests of mankind and of "the enlargement of the Redeemer's kingdom."[40] Another

38 He quoted Witsius, Gill, Edwards, Doddridge, and Whitby, among others. Henry Hunter, *The Rise, Fall, and Future Restoration of the Jews* (London: 1806), 64-72.

39 *Ibid.,* iii..

40 Thomas Toller, *The Coming and Enlargement of the Kingdom of God* (London: 1779), 17.

preacher generalized that he rejoiced "in every object" which portended the fulness of Christ's kingdom.[41] David Bogue found his world "big with great events," not the least of which was the overthrow of the tyrannical, papal-supporting government of Louis XVI.[42] He considered "the present zeal for liberty" as a God-given, "preparatory step" for the spread of Christ's millennial kingdom.[43] For him it was part of what he had earlier called — using language reminiscent of the Eliot tracts — "a dawn of considerable length," which would precede "the clearer rays" of extended mission efforts and the noon of the latter days.[44] Likewise the Infidelity raging in England was regarded as preliminary to the triumph of the gospel, which would be sown and carefully nurtured until the "abundant harvest" promised in Psalms, Isaiah, and Romans was reaped.[45]

This eschatology was grounded in the gamut of Biblical prophecy. The favorite missionary texts of previous generations occurred most frequently in the board sermons: Psalm 2 : 8, 72 : 17; Isaiah 11 : 9; Daniel 2 : 44, 7 : 14; Matthew 6 : 10, 13 : 31-32. Bogue captured the sheer inspirational effect of these passages with the words of Revelation 19 : 6, which had also been used by Handel, " 'Hallelujah, for the Lord God omnipotent reigneth' "; The verse was similarly employed by another Scottish minister several years later in a sermon preached to the Paisley Missionary Society.[46] The prophecies of the fulness of the kingdom pointed to the fruition of God's redemptive work in history, and by the manner in which they employed these passages the preachers expressed their debt to Edwards. Particularly Thomas Toller's sermon showed the relationship of prophecy to prayer and human agency, of which preaching in general and the S.S.P.C.K. in particular were given as examples.[47]

In investigating prophecy the S.S.P.C.K. board preachers found many exciting dimensions of the latter days. These characteristics became principles for guiding the society's concrete missionary policy. In this way the spread of knowledge became the major objective of both her Moderate and evangelical members. Practically this meant the maintenance and broadening of the society's educational program in the Highlands, for ignorance bred superstition and unbelief. Knowledge, however, brought enlightenment and

41 Robert Winter, *The Happy Tendency and Extensive Influence of the Christian Dispensation* (London: 1788), 29.

42 David Bogue, *A Sermon Preached at Salters-Hall, March 30th, 1792* (London: 1792), 46-48.

43 *Ibid.,* 49.

44 *Ibid.,* 19.

45 George Hay Drummond, *On Religious Indifference* (London: 1795), 21.

46 Bogue, 52. See also the review of John Snodgrass' *Prospects of Providence respecting the Conversion of the World to Christ* in *The Missionary Magazine*, I, 1796, 186.

47 Toller, 14-17. Also see Nathaniel Jennings, *Divine Tuition* (London: 1782), 6-7.

enlightenment made the acceptance of Christ and his kingdom easier. This line of reasoning was driven to its logical limits by Moderates at the General Assembly of 1796. For Moderates it was important to bring men to a higher cultural and intellectual plateau which was capable of sustaining a viable Christianity. More often the connotation of "knowledge" as the saving knowledge of faith in Christ was emphasized in the sermons, however. This was the patently evangelical emphasis, in which the cultural benefits brought by Christian knowledge were always seen as stemming from penitence and belief. In spite of their different emphases, however, both parties believed that the knowledge of Christ would eventually engulf all nations, Jews and Gentiles, and would bring the sweet effects of benevolence and love. Among these effects would be a general "abhorrence of war" and compassion for the oppressed Africans.[48] Quoting the opening verses of Isaiah 35, John Love declared that by acts of benevolence "the words of ancient prophecy" would be fulfilled.[49] But the preachers did not make bare acts of benevolence the substance of their proclamation. Benevolence was always integrated with living faith in Christ. Such fully-orbed Christianity would dominate the millennium. Preaching on the second petition of the Lord's Prayer, Bogue summarized, "The words do so evidently relate to the planting of the Christian religion, and to the propagation of it among the nations which were sitting in darkness, that nothing is necessary by way of explanation." [50] The dissemination of this knowledge among Highlanders had always been the primary objective of the S.S.P.C.K. To this Robert Winter recommended "a second object." [51] The indigent dwellers in other remote areas of Great Britain should be trained for productive agriculture and industry, he indicated. This would render them not only "industrious and useful" but also "happy." Winter regarded the society's comprehensive approach to the whole man as consistent with the character of the latter days.

Surveying the global state of religion much as Carey did that same year, Bogue asserted that the widespread ignorance of Christ was due to the "negligence and indifference" of Christians in propagating their faith.[52] He lauded previous Protestant missionary undertakings, rejected the excuses of those who said the time was not ripe as "the language of pusillanimity and sloth," [53] and pleaded not only for preaching and prayer for the latter days but especially that the S.S.P.C.K. would "extend its views to the

---

48 Bogue, 50-51. Years later Bogue's peace ideal was expressed in *On Universal Peace*, Tract no. VI of the Society for the Promotion of Permanent and Universal Peace (London: 1819).

49 John Love, *Benevolence Inspired and Exalted by the Presence of Jesus Christ* (London: 1794), 23.

50 Bogue, 2.

51 Winter, 29.

52 Bogue, 17.

53 *Ibid.*, 20.

remote corners of the world." [54] The preachers of the board sermons increasingly realized that British Christians and the S.S.P.C.K. should "be numbered among the instruments used by Providence for spreading the Redeemer's kingdom among men." [55]

In summary we see, therefore, that the eschatological dimension was present in the S.S.P.C.K. understanding of missions prior to and simultaneously with the general missionary awakening. Through her corresponding board that society passed the kingdom ideal of missions to the new societies, primarily the L.M.S. This ideal was quickened by current events, grounded in prophecy, and determinative for the program and urgency of mission work.

Missionary fervor was by no means restricted to Scottish circles in London but also took Scotland itself by storm, the hesitancy of Moderates notwithstanding. In April, 1796, a month before the historic General Assembly debate, Erskine preached the first sermon before the Scottish Missionary Society "to a very crowded congregation in St. Andrew's Church." [56] This society and those formed in Glasgow, Dundee, Greenock, Kelso, Paisley, Perth, and Stirling were not only fore-runners of church-related missions, but are a measure of the pervasive mission interest in Scotland at this time. By 1797 auxiliary prayer societies for missions could be found "'all over the north.'" [57] Through their widely read missionary forum, *The Missionary Magazine,* which was also begun in 1796 and was under the auspices of no one society, Scottish evangelicals kept abreast of such significant events as the initial gospel approaches to English Jews by William Cooper.[58] Missionary enthusiasm intensified when recognized missionary leaders like Andrew Fuller visited Scotland, preaching in support of the fledgling movement.[59] Missions also received official sanction and support from the Burghers (Associate Synod), and a Relief Church synod commissioned Neil Douglas' Gaelic mission.[60] But it was the independent societies which expressed the breadth of Scottish mission support as Scots from all denominations banded together to express their faith that through the arm of the missionary movement God would give Christ the nations as his inheritance.

---

54 *Ibid.,* 35.

55 Winter, 33. Also see Toller, 16-17.

56 Hewat, 5.

57 *Ibid.,* 9.

58 *The Missionary Magazine,* I, 1796, 186-188.

59 *Ibid.,* IV, 546-551, for a review of Fuller's sermon on Ps. 22 : 27, "'All the ends of the world shall remember, and turn unto the Lord: and all the kindreds of the nations shall worship before thee.'" (546) While his evening sermon was published, this sermon delivered on Sunday morning, October 13, 1799 in the Circus in Edinburgh apparently never appeared in print and was reviewed here by a hearer.

60 Hewat, 12, mentions the Burghers as the only Scottish denomination to give official support to missions in the last decade of the eighteenth century.

The leadership of the local missionary societies was generally in the hands of local clergy. These men in turn were most deeply motivated by eschatological expectancy, which they communicated in their missionary propaganda. In Edinburgh John Erskine led the way, as has already been shown. John Snodgrass of Paisley, Robert Balfour of Glasgow, and Neil Douglas of Dundee assumed much responsibility for the societies in their areas and deserve brief treatment.

From the time that Robert Millar had written his history of the spread of Christianity, Paisley had been the center of mission interest. Before immigrating to America, John Witherspoon, Paisley minister, had been a strong supporter of the S.S.P.C.K. Early in the nineteenth century a Paisley area Scot, Claudius Buchanan, undoubtedly molded by his Paisley heritage and having fallen under the influence of Charles Simeon of Cambridge, served as an East India Company chaplain in India and stirred Evangelical interest in missions, particularly in the conversion of the Jews.[61] But it was John Snodgrass, Witherpoon's successor, who guided Paisley into the missionary awakening.

In 1794 Snodgrass encouraged the S.S.P.C.K. by saying that although the society's missionaries did not see immediate results on their work, they were " 'sowing seed which [might] be fruitful in another age.' "[62] His interest in apocalyptic matters is confirmed by four years of lectures on Revelation delivered between 1792 and 1796.[63] His 1796 address to the Paisley society, which was allied with the L.M.S., interpreted the present " 'extraordinary appearances' " in politics and religion as encouragements for missionary support.

> 'By the general consent of prophecy, the reign of Antichrist is now hastening to an end. The aspect of providence, for some time past, has quickened our expectation of his fall. This will pave the way for the overthrow of every system by which the empire of iniquity and error has been maintained; and this again will be succeeded by the age of righteousness and truth.'[64]

He found it particularly comforting that missions were taking such impressive new strides in an age of widespread Infidelity. God's "absolute sovereignty" will be fully demonstrated in the "grand" events of "the latter times of the church on earth," he said.[65] Sovereignty did not preclude but presupposed

61 vide infra, 195-196.

62 Review of Snodgrass' 1794 annual sermon to the S.S.P.C.K., *The Missionary Magazine*, I, 1796, 157.

63 They were eventually published as *A Commentary, with Notes, on Part of the Book of the Revelation of John* (Paisley: 1799).

64 Review in *The Missionary Magazine*, I, 1796, 185.

65 John Snodgrass, *Prospects of Providence Respecting the Conversion of the World to Christ* (Paisley: 1796), 4.

"the use of human activity and exertion," for "the first preparatory step" for that age will be the divine provision of "men *full of faith, and of the Holy Ghost*" to preach it into existence.[66] With the debates of the General Assembly still sharply etched in his memory — the sermon was delivered on June 10, scarcely a month later — Snodgrass rejected "that favourite maxim with many" that missions will succeed only among previously civilized nations.[67]

Since the sermon was largely devoted to the prophecies of the universal conversion of the world and the effects of that great accomplishment, it is questionable whether it was as "original" as the reviewer suggested.[68] Many readers undoubtedly concurred, however, that it was "among the most masterly" recent missionary sermons.[69]

Like many evangelicals Robert Balfour of Glasgow expressed his early interest in missions in a sermon to the S.S.P.C.K.[70] On April 14, 1796, he addressed the Glasgow Missionary Society on the "dry bones" passage, Ezekiel 37 : 1-10, which he interpreted as predicting the conversion of Jews and Gentiles. To skeptics who said that the time for missions to all men had not arrived, Balfour recommended David Bogue's "clear, and full, and conclusive" rejoinder.[71] Balfour's devotion to the missionary cause carried him to London in 1798, where he delivered an annual sermon before the L.M.S.

Neil Douglas of the Relief Church in Dundee showed himself to be "a social reformer" — although not as "far in advance of his day" as has been asserted — in his appeal for banning the slave trade.[72] Not only did he address the local missionary society on different occasions, but his best known sermon, "Messiah's Glorious Rest in the Latter Days," placed social reform in an millennialist context. The list of some thirty amenities, many of a social nature, to be enjoyed by the saints during that period sounds suspiciously like those given by Samuel Hopkins in *The System of Doctrines,* which deepened the influence of Edwardean eschatology in Scotland.[73] Douglas did not conceive of the millennium in terms of a

---

66 *Ibid.,* 5-6.

67 *Ibid.,* 14.

68 *The Missionary Magazine,* I, 1796, 182.

69 *Ibid.,* 185.

70 Entitled "Liberal Charity Stated and Recommended on the Principles of the Gospel," it was delivered on June 5, 1789, and appeared under the uninteresting title *Sermons on Interesting Subjects,* a collection of Balfour's sermons, (Glasgow: 1819).

71 *Ibid.,* "The Salvation of the Heathen Necessary and Certain," 129. On Bogue's 1795 sermon, to which Balfour had reference, *vide infra,* 187-188.

72 *D.N.B.,* XV, 343. His appeal was *A Monitory Address to Great Britain* (1792).

73 Hopkins' influence on Scottish evangelicals was great, as was that of Edwards his teacher. The list of subscribers to his published theology includes a number of Scots who must have read his appendix on the millennium with great

"personal and visible" return and reign of Christ with those "literally raised from the dead." [74] In defining it as the conversion of the nations by normal "steps of providence" and their extended happiness, he echoed the views of his Scottish contemporaries. The "steps" included prayer, the provision of missionaries for the work, financial support, the overthrow of idolatry and other opposition, the power to work miracles, the preliminary spread of Infidelity, and judgments on guilty nations.[75] Douglas delivered the address twice, on successive days in May, and he spent the summer months on a mission to the Gaelic-speaking region of Argyllshire. The published account of his work expressed the idea that current mission undertakings were in "perfect unison" with Biblical predictions of many running to and fro throughout the earth with the knowledge of God.[76] His proposal for publishing an edition of the Psalms and the New Testament in Gaelic was consistent with his vision of the global spread of Christian knowledge.

These examples from Scottish circles could be expanded and many others added. These sufficiently portray the pervasiveness of Scottish missionary interest, however, and to depict the characteristics of its eschatological dimension. In the simple chiliasm of earlier theologians brought to new life by the events of their times, the Scots found the vision and the motive to contribute to the birth of a new, global era in Protestant missions.

2. *Promises in travail — the B.M.S.*

Among John Erskine's many correspondents in Europe and America were the Northamptonshire Baptists Andrew Fuller and John Ryland, Jr., to whom he habitually forwarded "any interesting publications" received from America or printed in Scotland.[77] In April, 1784, he sent Ryland a parcel containing Edwards' *An Humble Attempt,* which Ryland handed to John Sutcliff, a Baptist colleague. Several weeks later, at the latter's initiative, the Northamptonshire association resolved to devote the first Monday of the month to concerts for prayer for revival and the spread of Christ's kingdom.[78] In soliciting support for the meetings, the association circulated a letter which advised the participants to extend their horizon beyond their local church and association: " 'let the whole interest of the Redeemer be

interest. John Erskine alone subscribed to twelve sets, and in England John Ryland, Jr., applied for six. Hopkins, *The System of Doctrines,* I, xv.

74 N[ei]l Douglas, *Messiah's Glorious Rest in the Latter Days* (Dundee: 1797), 9.

75 *Ibid.,* 56-63.

76 N[ei]l Douglas, *Journal of a Mission* (Edinburgh: 1799), 4.

77 John Ryland, *Life and Death of the Reverend Andrew Fuller* (London: 1816), 240.

78 Payne, "The Evangelical Revival...," 229.

affectionately remembered, and the spread of the gospel to the distant parts of the habitable globe be the object of your most fervent requests.'"[79] Fuller created early sympathy for the concert idea in a 1784 sermon appendix entitled "A Few Persuasives to a General Union in Prayer for the Revival of Religion."[80] By 1786 the Baptist Association of the Midlands had begun participation in the movement, and other nonconformist churches followed suit.[81] Sutcliff listed the participants in 1789 in his preface to a new edition of Edwards' book, which he recommended as a guideline for all Christians interested in the advancement of the kingdom.

This resumption of concerts for prayer coincided with important shifts in theological emphasis among the Particular Baptists. The high Calvinism of John Gill and John Brine had predominated in these circles. Gill had taught that an army of ministers would preach the new age into existence after dramatic changes in the political and ecclesiastical situations.[82] In many Baptists this fostered a complacency regarding their responsibility in influencing the course of history. In its effect on Baptists' sense of responsibility for their neighbor, high Calvinist supralapsarianism stifled a widespread call to repentance and conversion.[83] The leaders in Baptist missions opposed this spirit of resignation to both the course of history and the destiny of individual men. The basis of their opposition was in part the new manner in which Jonathan Edwards had reconciled divine sovereignty and human responsibility in his study on the freedom of the will. His writings had been studied by Fuller since 1777 and subsequently made a deep impression on Ryland, Sutcliff, and Carey. Fuller had also been studying an earlier Baptist controversy revolving around the free offer of the gospel and the duty of the unconverted to believe. In the 1730's and 1740's Gill had opposed advocates of a more evangelical Calvinism on these issues.[84] Fuller sympathized with Gill's opponents and also forsook his high Calvinism for a more evangelical faith, which was expressed in his *The gospel worthy of all acceptation*.[85] This little book swayed many Baptists to what became known as "strict Calvinism," and the older position was defended by a diminishing following.[86] In 1813 Fuller indicated that of the twenty-

79 As quoted by Foster, "The Bicentenary...," 381.
80 *D.N.B.*, XX, 310.
81 Beaver, "The Concert...," 425.
82 *vide supra*, 156-157.
83 Payne, "The Evangelical Revival...," 227.
84 Matthias Maurice, *A modern question modestly answer'd* (1737), and Abraham Taylor, *The modern question* (1742). Nuttall has made a thorough study of the controversy and its influence on Fuller in "Northamptonshire and *The Modern Question*."
85 Nuttall dates its appearance 1785, "Northamptonshire and *The Modern Question*," 101. Payne, "The Evangelical Revival...," 227, says it was written in 1781 and published in 1784. *D.N.B.*, XX, 310, does not date it.
86 Years later, refuting charges of over-reliance upon Edwards, Fuller distin-

three Baptist congregations in the county three or four were still "what are called high Calvinists."[87] The strict Calvinists increasingly gained strength and became the vanguard of the foreign missionary movement.

Before long the concerts for the spread of the kingdom and the new theological emphases assumed a distinct foreign missionary dimension for Northamptonshire Baptists. Ryland's esteem for the kingdom theology of Edwards and for Brainerd's sacrificial example in spreading the kingdom motivated him to name his sons Jonathan Edwards Ryland and David Brainerd Ryland! But William Carey is the acknowledged father of Baptist foreign missions. "His heart appears to have been set upon the conversion of the heathen before he came to Moulton in 1786."[88] More than any of his colleagues Carey desired to translate the global character of the kingdom ideal into reality. In spite of its morbid, almost depressing character, Edwards' life and diary of Brainerd became, as Ryland put it, virtually a "second Bible" for Carey.[89] For a number of years he served as school-master, cobbler, and minister at Moulton, near Kettering, where Fuller was minister. There he participated in the concerts for prayer. There he developed his skills in linguistics and horticulture, which would later serve him so well in India, and related to his missionary vision the statistics and other knowledge being assembled by such explorers as Captain James Cook. His vision took shape at Moulton, where "his conversations, prayers, and sermons" usually assumed a missionary dimension.[90]

In what could have been a pre-planned appeal in the spring of 1791, Sutcliff and Fuller delivered two missionary sermons, "Jealousy for the Lord of Hosts" and "The Pernicious Influence of Delay," before the Clipstone meeting of the Northamptonshire association. Carey then rose and asked if " '... it were not practicable, and our bounden duty, to attempt somewhat toward spreading the gospel in the heathen world?' "[91] The ensuing discussion was marked by much "serious and earnest concern ... for the enlargement of the kingdom of our Lord," and Carey was asked to formulate and publish his thoughts on the matter. At the association meeting at Oakham on June 16 Sutcliff and Fuller were asked to publish

guished three types of Calvinism: high, moderate (Baxterian), and strict (his own position). The latter he felt to be closest to Calvin. Payne, "The Evangelical Revival...," 227-228, n. 10.

87 Andrew Fuller, *Miscellaneous Pieces on Various Religious Subjects*, collected and arranged with notes by J. W. Morris (London: 1826), 82.

88 *Periodical Accounts Relative to the Baptist Missionary Society*, 6 vols. (Clipstone: 1800-1817), I, 1.

89 Payne, "The Evangelical Revival...," 228. In "Doddridge and the Missionary Enterprise," 98. Payne suggests that Carey may have used Doddridge's abridged edition.

90 *Periodical Accounts*, I, 2.

91 *Ibid.*

their sermons. Carey's thoughts were published early the following year, after he had moved to Leicester.[92] It was at the association's annual meeting in Nottingham on May 31, 1792, that Carey preached a stirring sermon on Isaiah 54:2-3, urging his hearers to "expect great things from God" and "attempt great things for God." Seen against the background of the Edwardean understanding of the prayer concerts and of the term "kingdom," the nature of the eschatology conjured by this sermon becomes obvious. Carey was telling his hearers that they could expect the latter-day glory of the church but that their efforts were required for realizing that day. In Carey's Nottingham sermon the vision of the renewed concerts and the potential of the new theological emphases converged in a powerful appeal for a missionary society. After the sermon had been delivered, the delegates resolved " 'that a plan be prepared against the next ministers' meeting at Kettering, for forming a society among the Baptists for propagating the gospel among the heathen.' "[93] At Kettering, on October 2, 1792, the B.M.S. became a reality.[94]

An Enquiry became the charter of the missionary movement. Its defense of the binding character of the Great Commission is well known. What is less obvious to the casual reader but certainly more basic to Carey's theology of missions is the framework of his discussion, namely the belief that, as promised in the prophets, history is moving toward its culmination in the kingdom of Christ. This framework of *An Enquiry* is laid bare in the introduction. Already in the first sentence Carey stressed prayer and work for the kingdom. In short strokes he sketched the essence of history. Adam's fall and the universality of its effects through the times of the flood, of Abraham, of the nation of Israel, and of Carey's own Infidelity-ridden generation were traced and were contrasted with the opposing forces of God.

> Yet God repeatedly made known his intention to prevail finally over all the power of the Devil, and to destroy all his works, and set up his own kingdom and interest among men, and extend it as universally as Satan had extended his.[95]

To that end he sent Christ, and Christ in turn commissioned his disciples to preach to all creatures. Since their time the gospel has met with considerable success, concluded Carey.

This brought Carey to his own day, and he faced its missionary problems

---

92 They appeared as *An Enquiry into the Obligations of Christians to Use Means for the Conversion of the Heathens* (Leicester: 1792).

93 *Periodical Accounts*, I, 3.

94 The original name was The Particular Baptist Society for Propagating the Gospel amongst the Heathen.

95 Carey, 5.

squarely, logically, and forcefully. In Section I he refuted those — chiefly high Calvinists — who believed that the missionary obligation was no longer binding or that the time was not ripe for implementing it. He gave a brief history of missions in Section II, and Section III constitutes his famous survey of the world's religions. Practical objections to missions were raised, discussed, and dismissed in the next section. "If the prophecies concerning the increase of Christ's kingdom be true," concluded Carey in Section V, Christians should "concur with God" in promoting his work.[96] Under such concurrence he included concerted prayer for the Spirit's effectual blessing of all human efforts, the establishment of a missionary society, and liberal contributing. Since "Christians are a body whose truest interest lies in the exaltation of the Messiah's kingdom," they should overcome all fears and obstacles and sacrifice all lesser gain in supporting its growth.[97] For William Carey "exalting the Messiah's kingdom" meant total dedication to spreading the gospel to the ends of the earth as promised in Scripture and commanded by Christ.

Promises of Christ's world-wide dominion motivated men to enter mission work and sustained them through its difficulties. John Thomas, who accompanied Carey to India in 1792, found "the divine predictions we have of the latter day" and the divine injunction to preach God's glory to the heathen "reason enough to go and preach to them."[98] After having spent more than a year in India without gaining a convert, Carey wrote, "Yet this is our encouragement, the power of God is sufficient to accomplish every thing which he has promised, and his promises are exceedingly great and precious respecting the conversion of the heathens."[99] Two years later he confided to Fuller that among other motives "above all, the increase of the Redeemer's kingdom" rendered him content "to die in the work" he had begun.[100] When John Fountain joined Thomas and Carey, he extolled the progress of the kingdom, particularly since 1744, but admitted that it had been small "when contrasted" with what was still to come:

> 'All the promises do travail
> With a glorious day of grace.'[101]

The missionaries joined in concerts for prayer with English Christians, held their own concerts, and rejoiced over news of revival in England.[102] Jubilant, Fountain linked the completion of the Bengali translation of the New

96 *Ibid.,* 77.
97 *Ibid.,* 82.
98 *Periodical Accounts,* I, 19.
99 *Ibid.,* 69-70.
100 *Ibid.,* 300.
101 *Ibid.,* 322.
102 *Ibid.,* 185, 294, 299, 341.

Testament with the fall of India "before the Universal Conqueror." [103] Carey shared his exhilaration at a time "when every thing portends the downfall, the speedy downfall of all that oppose the dear Redeemer's reign." [104] Sensing its significance for his work, he watched European politics with deep interest, although his perspective was of necessity from newspapers and periodicals yellowed with six or eight months of age. From the *Evangelical Magazine* he received "much encouragement" and hope that his next letters would announce "that Babylon the Great is fallen indeed." For then Mohammedanism would fall, "at which time I expect that the missionary spirit will greatly increase, and hosts go forth with the banner of the cross flying; not to subdue kingdoms with instruments of death, but with the words of everlasting life." [105] He interpreted the missionary spirit, which by 1798 had swollen to a considerable movement, as "a prelude to the universal spread of the gospel!" [106] In the face of disappointment he consoled himself with the knowledge that he was sowing the harvest that would be reaped by his successors. [107]

Just as did the men in India, the directors and the society's constituency in England envisioned their work and support as contributions toward the eventual realization of Christ's promised universal dominion. At her second meeting the B.M.S. resolved that an address to English Christians be drafted to publicize the society and solicit support for her. The address adduced "arguments of the most powerful nature," namely,

> That the sacred scriptures assure us of the univeral conquests of the Redeemer, that 'his dominion shall extend from sea to sea, even to the ends of the earth;' that 'the kingdoms of this world shall become the kingdoms of our Lord and of his Christ;' and that 'the isles shall wait for his law.' [108]

A member of Carey's Leicester congregation expressed the church's sentiments regarding the loss of their pastor to foreign missions: " 'We have been praying . . . for the spread of Christ's kingdom amongst the heathen; and now God requires *us* to make the first sacrifice to accomplish it.' " [109] About the time when Carey and Thomas sailed for India — on June 13, 1793 — the Northampton association expressed faith in Christ's on-going conquest, urged the churches to pray and sacrifice for the mission, and indicated that with almost two-thirds of the world population pagan and

---

103 *Ibid.,* 316.
104 *Ibid.,* 328.
105 *Ibid.,* 375.
106 *Ibid.,* 403. Also see 490.
107 *Ibid.,* 489-490.
108 *Ibid.,* 12.
109 *Ibid.,* 35.

millions more under "the eastern and western antichrist" Christ had only inherited a fraction of his dominion.[110] In 1795 the society sent missionaries to the freed-slave colony in Sierra Leone. The B.M.S. letter to the church there suggested that it had been placed in Africa "for such a time as this" and that "by the *little leaven* at *Sierra Leone*" the entire continent might eventually "be leavened." [111] The Bristol Baptist Church encouraged a young Indian congregation by reminding it of the promise of the out-poured Spirit.[112] And when four new missionaries volunteered for service in India in 1799, Sutcliff and Samuel Pearce encouraged them with the Biblical promises of success.[113]

During the early years of the society's existence the B.M.S. circle demonstrated only a very mild chiliasm linking missions to the universal reign of Christ. Carey's hopes — already noted — surrounding political events in Europe are the nearest thing to Baptist speculation on dates. Toward the end of the old and during the first ten years of the new century Baptist leaders became bolder. Fuller speculated on apocalyptic images in a missionary address to an Edinburgh audience in 1799. "The last branch of the last of the four beasts is now in its dying agonies. No sooner will it be proclaimed, Babylon is fallen! than the marriage of the Lamb [*i.e.*, recognition of Christ as Lord by men everywhere] will come." [114] Through Dr. Charles Stuart, prominent Edinburgh minister and son-in-law of John Erskine, Fuller's attention was drawn to Faber's discussions about the Apocalypse which were appearing in *The Christian Observer*. In 1809 and 1810 Fuller lectured and wrote on the subject.[115] Simultaneously it was reported that "we who live in these latter days" see the signs that the time of the kingdom has arrived.[116] Successes in the flourishing mission at Serampore had strengthened the eschatological forces that had originally called the B.M.S. into being.

110 *Ibid.,* 50.
111 *Ibid.,* 102.
112 *Ibid.,* 507.
113 *Ibid.,* 511 and 519.
114 *The Missionary Magazine,* IV, 551. These are the reviewer's words and should not be weighed as heavily as Fuller's own. However, it was customary for the speaker to read reports of his address before their publication, and this review certainly gives the gist of Fuller's sermon.
115 See Fuller, *Miscellaneous Pieces . . . ,* 274-276 and 298-300. Also see J. W. Morris, *Memoirs of the Life and Writings of the Rev. Andrew Fuller* (London: 1816), 249-261, for a survey of Fuller's *Expository Discourses on the Apocalypse* (London: 1815). In 1815 his *Prophecies relating to the Millennium* also appeared. See Van den Berg, 120.
116 *Periodical Accounts,* V, 114.

3. *Calls and motives — the L.M.S.*

The roots of no other missionary society formed during the period under study are as tangled and as diffuse as those of the L.M.S. When they are isolated and analyzed, however, it becomes apparent that each one — Evangelical, Methodist, Independent, and Scottish Presbyterian — drew its main missionary sustenance from a hopeful, millennial eschatology. The contributions of the Scots have already been demonstrated in detail and will be bypassed here. The Baptists, who had their own society, did not share in the ecumenical enterprise of the L.M.S., although their early missionary example, including its eschatological dimension, shaped and inspired the contributions of other groups to the new society.

Wedged between the western boundaries of Leicestershire and Northamptonshire, Warwickshire was soon kindled by the spark struck by her Baptist neighbors to the east. A group of Independent ministers led by George Burder of Coventry and Dr. E. Williams of Birmingham met to explore the missionary obligation of all Christians as early as the summer of 1793.[117] They soon resolved that missions were the obligation of all Christians, that the use of means was mandatory, and that they would circulate a recommendation for the establishment of a missionary fund. They joined the Baptists in concerts for prayer on the first Monday of the month.[118] These concerts for the spread of the kingdom affected Independents as they had Baptists. They resulted in the formation of a missionary society — in this case the L.M.S.[119] After the formation of the society the practice was sustained, and in London the response became so "enthusiastic" that the city was eventually quartered and four meetings conducted simultaneously.[120] Her debt to Edwards was acknowledged in 1814, when the L.M.S. sponsored an abridged edition of his *An Humble Attempt.*

Prayer for the coming kingdom was not the only eschatological contribution of Warwickshire Independents, however. When the society was in the throes of formation, Burder made a powerful appeal for support which "was very widely circulated."[121] It contained a strong politico-eschatological argument for the feasibility of the immediate establishment and support of a new society.

> May we not indulge a hope that the happy period is approaching, when the Redeemer shall take unto him his great power and reign? ...And is there not a general apprehension, that the Lord is about to produce some great event? Already have we witnessed the most

117 Lovett, 12; and Payne, "The Evangelical Revival...," 233.
118 Foster, "The Bicentenary...," 381.
119 Bogue and Bennett, IV, 383f., traces this development.
120 Beaver, "The Concert...," 425-426.
121 Lovett, 18.

astonishing transactions; and is it not probable that the great Disposer of all is now about, by shaking terribly the nations, to establish that spiritual and extensive kingdom which cannot be shaken? Let us then, utterly and sincerely disclaiming all political views and party designs; abhorring all attempts to disturb order and government in this, or any other country; vigorously unite, in the fear of God, and in the love of Christ, to establish a Missionary Society upon a large and liberal plan, for sending ministers of Christ to preach the Gospel among the Heathen.[122]

The measure of the Warwickshire influence is the appointment of Burder and Williams to the original Board of Directors.

What may be called the Trevecca tradition constitutes another source of influence in the founding of the L.M.S. In a perceptive study of Trevecca, the Countess of Huntingdon's seminary for training Calvinistic Methodists, Geoffrey Nuttall has demonstrated the pervasive influence of the school through its students and on other colleges and academies.[123] He finds that Trevecca names "are prominent" among the society's first subscribers, signers of the first circular letter, and those elected to her first committee.[124] John Eyre, a Trevecca alumnus, was among those directly responsible for organizing the society. In 1792 he began the widely circulated *Evangelical Magazine*, which in October, 1793, ran an article entitled "Remarks on the Prophecies and promises relating to the Glory of the Latter Day."[125] It suggested that concerts for prayer be linked with the missionary movement and posited a gradual introduction of the latter days, hopefully not far off. The article, stressing what had become common doctrine, underlined the belief that in answer to prayer the Spirit would remove faction and contention among Christians and would Christianize the heathen.

Thomas Haweis, who as early as 1757 had been barred from Anglican orders for his evangelical sympathies, was quickened in his "zeal" and "missionary interest" by Whitefield and Samson Occum.[126] He eventually became Rector of Aldwinkle, Northamptonshire, and chaplain to Lady Selina, with whom he often discussed missions in America and the prospects for beginning additional missionary projects in other parts of the world.[127] In the November, 1794, issue of the *Evangelical Magazine* Haweis reviewed Melville Horne's *Letters on Missions*, which had appeared earlier that year

---

122 George Burder, "An Address to the serious and zealous Professors of the Gospel," *Sermons Preached in London at the Formation of the Missionary Society* (London: 1795), xvii. Lovett, 18-24, gives extensive citations from this address.

123 Geoffrey F. Nuttall, "The Significance of Trevecca College, 1768-91," Cheshunt College, Cambridge Bicentenary Lecture delivered at Westminster and Cheshunt Colleges, 18 May 1968 (London: 1969).

124 *Ibid.*, 19.

125 Orchard, 40.

126 Payne, "The Evangelical Revival...," 233.

127 *vide supra*, 153-154, for the Countess' work in America.

and which further stimulated Haweis' missionary contributions.

The impact of Horne's book on the founders of the L.M.S. was akin to that of Carey's book on the Baptists. While not strictly of the Trevecca tradition, Horne was an Anglican of evangelical sympathies. He had spent fourteen months in Sierra Leone, where he had hoped to engage in missionary activity in conjunction with his chaplaincy. His hope frustrated, he returned to England, where he published this appeal "to the Protestant Ministers of the British Churches" for an ecumenical missionary organization. His second letter began by noting the "prophecies and promises" which assure that in "this last and most perfect dispensation of the everlasting gospel" Christianity will become "the religion of every tribe, and kindred, and tongue." [128] Christ's peace, righteousness, truth, and mercy will spread to all nations, he continued, and these prospects should cause us to "exert all our strength in disseminating the gospel." [129] He sketched the work of the apostles and called for, if possible, "more than apostolick labours." [130] For "the latter ends of the world are fallen upon us, and we have many considerations to excite us." [131] Among these "considerations" Horne included the continuing dominance of crescent over cross in the Middle East, the progress of divine vengeance against "the Roman Antichrist," the mockery of atheism and godless philosophy, natural "prodigies," and the influence of French atheism in southern Europe.[132] Warning England of the dangers of the age, he urged her to heed the "signs" and to "put forth those exertions to which they call us." [133] In a later letter he used what was basically Carey's argument to refute the excuse that the time for missions was not eschatologically opportune.[134]

Horne's book exercised simultaneous but independent influence on Haweis and Samuel Greatheed prior to the appearance of Haweis' review. Greatheed was tutor at Newport Pagnell Academy, an institution influenced by Trevecca, and he, like Haweis, served on the first Board of Directors of the L.M.S. On the basis of a marginal note in Greatheed's copy of the first volume of L.M.S. annual sermons, Stephen Orchard proves that in response to Horne's appeal Haweis and Greatheed made donations of £ 500 and £ 100 respectively to the proposed society and that these donations, also reported in the November, 1794, issue of the *Evangelical Magazine,* were an added stimulus in the founding of the society.[135] The review and the book so gripped Eyre that he and several friends discussed missions at bi-weekly

128 Melville Horne, *Letters on Missions* (Bristol: 1794), 11.
129 *Ibid.,* 12.
130 *Ibid.,* 20.
131 *Ibid.*
132 *Ibid.,* 20-21.
133 *Ibid.,* 21.
134 *Ibid.,* 97-100.
135 Orchard, 41 and 57, n. 30.

meetings at Castle and Falcon, out of which the L.M.S. developed the following summer.[136] The book influenced another L.M.S. leader, for Burder, in his address referred to above, also acknowledged his debt to Horne. It becomes apparent, therefore, that evangelical Anglican and Methodist influences, interacting and often traceable to the Countess and the Trevecca tradition, were another source of L.M.S. vitality and that they in turn drew their missionary life from a sense of eschatological immediacy.

Before turning to the formation of the L.M.S. and her annual sermons, we must consider another root of the society. It centered in Bristol, home of John Ryland. Upon receiving a letter from Carey in July, 1794, Ryland summoned David Bogue, Independent minister in Gosport, and James Steven, Church of Scotland minister at Covent Garden in London, both of whom were in Bristol at the time, to his home to share Carey's letter with them.[137] Bogue, it will be remembered, had addressed the S.S.P.C.K. board in London in compelling eschatological terms only two years before,[138] and as a Scottish minister in London Steven was at the focal point of that board's work. It was logical that Ryland should presuppose their interest, therefore. Upon leaving Ryland's home, the pair met with John Hey, Independent minister in Bristol, to discuss methods of arousing public interest in missions. All three eventually became founders of the L.M.S., but more immediately, Bogue published an appeal to non-Baptist dissenters in the September issue of the *Evangelical Magazine*. He noted a number of reasons for engaging in mission work. He found "greatest encouragement" for the cause in the many promises of the universal knowledge of Christ; "and every promise is a call and a motive to enter on the service without delay." [139] Missions were "the cause of God" and therefore could not fail.

During the autumn of 1794 the Castle and Falcon prayer and discussion sessions for missions developed out of the informal, Tuesday-morning gatherings of London ministers at Baker's Coffee House, Change Alley. Bogue's appeal, Horne's book, and Burder's circular all acted as a leaven for the movement. A corresponding committee was appointed, and John Love, Church of Scotland minister in London who had been appointed secretary, issued a notice to London ministers calling an organizational meeting for the following summer and urging support and prayer meanwhile. Three days at the end of September were devoted to the organization of the society and to sermons. Ministers and laymen assembled from all parts

136 Lovett, 12.
137 *Ibid.*, 5.
138 *vide supra*, 170-172.
139 David Bogue, "Address to Professors of the Gospel," in *Sermons Preached in London, at the Formation of the Missionary Society* (London: 1795), v. Also see Lovett, 6-10.

of the country. Hesitancy and remaining opposition to missions were swept aside by constant references to the overwhelming evidence of divine prophecy and to the auspiciousness of the hour. The years of yearnings and pleadings for the kingdom in nation-wide concerted prayer climaxed in the London gatherings. The effect was overpowering. Bogue spoke of the forming of "an history in the epoch of man," the beginning of the spread of the kingdom at home and abroad which would not stop " 'till the knowledge of God cover[ed] the earth as the waters cover the sea.' " [140] One reporter recorded that the impact on the crowds compelled them to confess, " 'This is a new Pentecost.' " [141]

During the London organizational meetings it was decided, largely upon Haweis' suggestion, that Otaheite or Tahiti would be the society's first venture, though she considered the entire non-Christian world as her potential field. In 1796 thirty missionaries, most of them laymen, sailed on the *Duff*. Two years later a second expedition followed. Both voyages were dismal failures, since piracy, severe passages, and inadequate preparation of the missionaries took their toll. Richard Lovett laments that during the first ten years of her existence the society realized only *"nine* effective workers"* out of sixty sent out.[142] Surprisingly, the society's resolve was not weakened, and we must conclude that it was largely the "encouragement" of the divine promises that sustained her in these early disappointments.

Although the intensity of the eschatological element abated somewhat after the London meetings, its centrality in the L.M.S. conception of missions was never questioned. It is highly probable that the thinking of no other Anglo-American society falling within the time period of our study was as completely dominated by mild millennial expectations as that of the L.M.S. Preaching on the "Advantages of Patience" — perhaps because he had toiled through the previous thirty-six annual sermons before drafting his own — Samuel Bottomley remarked on their predominance in the L.M.S. addresses. A great majority of the sermons was based on those "promises and predictions" most apt to promote the budding missionary movement. Speaking of the promises, he said, "Of these we must be reminded every time we meet; — without them, the Missionary wheel will clog: — they are as necessary for Missionaries, every day and every night, as their daily bread, or nightly rest...." [143] And the audience usually was reminded of them, though it was in the "pleasing variety" which Bottomley admired. There were sermons on the importance of prayer for the kingdom and

---

140 As quoted by Lovett, 36.
141 *Ibid.*, 38.
142 *Ibid.*, 65.
143 Samuel Bottomley, "Advantages of Patience," in *Four Sermons* (London: 1803), 37.

sermons on its universal extent. Some sermons emphasized the spread of
knowledge in the latter days and others the certainty of prophecy's fulfillment. In 1802 the preachers concentrated on "the Messiah" — his triumphs,
his glory, and his throne. Sometimes the ecclesiastical dimension of the
millennium was the theme, and at other times the wonders of that age were
described. The feebleness of missionary means was contrasted with the
grandeur of their effects. God's design for history, objections to missions,
discouragement in the work, and the destiny of the Jews were all themes
which were forthrightly proclaimed from the perspective of the *eschaton*.
Many of the sermons were based on texts long associated with the millennial
understanding of missions. It is of dubious value to analyze the sermons'
eschatology in detail, however, since it contains little, if anything, essentially
new to our study. Several incidental motifs and their significance do deserve
mention, however.

Although we have characterized millennial expectations in L.M.S. circles
as "intense" — especially during the organizational meetings — and as "central" to the understanding of missions, they by no means represent a chiliasm
that had lost touch with reality. They belonged to the simple or postmillennial tradition, and were best described by Bogue in his sermon during the
September, 1795, meetings. In response to the objection that the time for
the conversion of the nations had not yet arrived, Bogue repeated the same
principle which had long been the chief axiom of careful Anglo-American
interpretation of prophecy: "Till predictions be accomplished we cannot, in
most cases, define with certainty, the precise period of fulfillment." [144]
Therefore, to engage in the controversy on whether the millennium will begin
"at the distance of two hundred years," as "many" think, or "about the
middle of the next century," as "some suppose," is not the main issue.[145]
And to allow Christian action to be scheduled by chronological speculations
was preposterous to Bogue. "But I beg you to consider that in aiming to
propagate the gospel, we are to be guided by what God enjoins as a duty,
not by what he delivered as a prediction," he pleaded.[146] The duty is to
preach as commanded by Christ, he continued. Only through preaching
would the millennium be realized, and then only in God's time. For Bogue,
therefore, the essence of the mission was proclamation. Through proclamation the millennium, "that AEra when all the nations of the earth shall

144   David Bogue, "Objections Against a Mission to the Heathen," in *Sermons
Preached in London...*, 126. Balfour, "The Salvation of the Heathen...," 129,
recommended Bogue's argumentation on this point as "clear, and full, and conclusive."

145   *Ibid.* Fleming, Jr., was the chief authority for the later date, and Willison,
among others, leaned toward the nineteenth century date. *vide supra,* 112 and 145-146.
With both of these theologians, however, concern with dates was incidental and did
not eclipse an emphasis on proclamation.

146   Bogue, "Objections Against...," 126.

have received the gospel," would be gradually realized.[147] Two hundred years is hardly enough to accomplish this feat, and the gospel must then enjoy even "more rapid success" than during apostolic days, he added.[148] There was not a day to lose in establishing and pursuing missions.

If Bogue showed the centrality of preaching in missions, others defined its nature when they delivered sermons on the knowledge of the Lord to be spread in the latter days. The object of this knowledge is not nature nor the achievements of men, but "Jehovah as revealed in the Scripture," stressed John Findlay in a sermon on Isaiah 11 : 6-9.[149] This is the most valuable of all knowledge. It is not an intellectual, speculative, or cold knowledge, but "the saving practical knowledge" spread by preaching as applied by the Spirit.[150] It "is accompanied with faith and love, . . . deeply affects the heart, and influences all the conduct."[151] Only when this knowledge becomes universal will the millennium dawn, for it will act as a leaven on life and culture in general, said the preachers in making the same evangelical point as S.S.P.C.K. preachers.[152]

Against this background they discussed the amazing character of the millennium. One spoke of the gospel's ability "to make one nation a blessing to another," "to unite the hearts of men to one another," and "to promote mutual intercourse among nations" and "mutual communion in religious concerns."[153] Another saw the thousand-year reign of Jesus Christ as a time of unprecedented brotherly affection, but warned that its arrival was being hindered by the slave-trade, which would have to be abolished "before the sable sons of Africa can be expected to embrace Christianity."[154] Even the battles on the home front, therefore, were waged in part to facilitate the spread of the knowledge of God and the realization of the millennium.[155]

L.M.S. leaders gave wider expression to the relationship of missions and the millennium than appeared in the annual sermons. Several men were involved in the renewal of concern for the conversion of the Jews, as will become apparent later in this chapter. Joseph Hardcastle, later to become the society's treasurer, reasoned that events in France in 1797 might be

---

147 *Ibid.*

148 *Ibid.,* 127.

149 John Findlay, "The Universal Diffusion of Divine Knowledge; with Its Happy Effects," *Four Sermons* (London: 1799), 6.

150 *Ibid.,* 9.

151 *Ibid.*

152 *vide supra,* 170-171.

153 George Lambert, "The Greatest of Blessings, both in its Nature and Effects," in *Four Sermons* (London: 1796), 35-39.

154 Herbert Mends, "Dark Providence no just Reason of Discouragement in Missionary Exertions," *Four Sermons* (London: 1801), 34.

155 The slave trade was outlawed by Parliament in 1807.

"the third woe," a prelude to the seventh and final trumpet, which would herald the arrival of Christ's kingdom. He urged the society to distribute Bibles in France in preparation for that glorious day.[156] Since his eschatology was definitely not in the Bogue or in the general L.M.S. vein, his proposal was not accepted by the society. At the turn of the century Alexander Waugh, who had been involved in L.M.S. affairs from the society's inception, addressed the S.S.P.C.K. in a millennial address on "Messiah, the Sun of Righteousness." An L.M.S. address to religious Dutch citizens was translated by J. T. van der Kemp, her liaison with her affiliated society in the Netherlands, and contained millennial elements.[157] But David Bogue's interest in the subject was perhaps the most sustained of that of any L.M.S. leader. Like Andrew Fuller he addressed his congregation on eschatology in a series of lectures which were later published.[158] For more than twenty years he pleaded for and supported missions as the instrument for realizing the latter-day glory of the church, a definition which was the core of the society's self-understanding.

4. The "peaceful wars" of the establishment — the C.M.S.

Anglican contributions to the missionary awakening were initially made through the L.M.S. and through existing ecclesiastical channels. In addition to the Trevecca tradition's role in the L.M.S. the influence in missions of Charles Simeon and of the wealthy and prominent members of the Clapham Sect must be recognized. Simeon, influential in Cambridge University circles and as Vicar of Holy Trinity church, received his evangelical piety under the preaching of Henry Venn of Huddersfield and communicated it to several young men for whom he helped secure appointments as chaplains for the East India Company. David Brown arrived in India in 1787 and was followed by Claudius Buchanan and Henry Martyn. Although these chaplains were not strictly speaking missionaries, through their writings and personal contacts they roused Evangelical support for missions. Meanwhile via the *Periodical Accounts* Simeon had been following Baptist work and had fallen under the influence of John Erskine during a visit to Scotland.[159] When the Evangelical ministers of the Eclectic Society in

---

156 Orchard, 43-44.
157 *Adres van het Zendings Genootschap te London, aan de Godsdienstige Ingezetenen der Vereenigde Nederlanden* ([no place]: 1797). It spoke of "de beroering, waar mede God thans ter tijd der natiën schudt" (5) and of "de gunstige dag" (11) of the gospel. It suggested that the Netherlands' influence in and knowledge of South Africa and Southeast Asia qualified her as the instrument for realizing the dawn of that day in those areas.
158 *Discourses on the Millennium* (London: 1818).
159 Payne, "The Evangelical Revival...," 234.

London and of several similar groups elsewhere decided on the advisability of forming a missionary society based on church principles,[160] therefore, it was largely Simeon's influence that lay behind the framing of the C.M.S. in 1799. John Venn, Rector of Clapham and son of the former Vicar of Huddersfield, was elected president. Charles Grant, who had returned from a lucrative tenure in India and had settled in Clapham, used his influence to promote the Sierra Leone project for freed slaves and the appointments of Evangelical chaplains and was made a vice-president of the C.M.S.

The role of millennial expectations in the formation of the C.M.S. was weaker than it had been in the founding of the L.M.S. Although the names of Thomas Scott, John Newton, and George S. Faber appear on the initial list of subscribers, the eschatology which Scott and Newton had previously defended in print hardly assumed an explicit role in the initial years of the society's life. This was true even though a mild millennialism was accepted by such important C.M.S. figures as Simeon and John Venn.[161] It is virtually absent from the annual sermons of the first five years, however. It was mentioned in passing only in the 1803 sermon.[162] When the society sent Melchoir Renner and Peter Hartwig to Africa the following year, it was with only mild reminders that they were instruments in the coming of Christ's kingdom.[163] Although among the East India Company chaplains eschatological motivation was not unimportant,[164] its influence appears not to have been dominant but incidental before, roughly, 1805. In the C.M.S. we find, therefore, that unlike the other evangelical missionary societies founded during this period, millennial expectations played little part in calling the society into existence. In this she manifested her Anglican character and similarity to the S.P.G. and S.P.C.K. Politically conservative, her members generally failed to see the portents in political events that dissenters did. The strong allegiance to the church, upon which the C.M.S. was founded, may well have repressed a sense of the progress of history

---

160 The Anglican conceptions of the church and ecclesiastical office later became a source of tension between the C.M.S. and the German evangelicals whom she employed as missionaries. For a recent assessment of those tensions see John Pennington, "Church Principles in the Early Years of the Church Missionary Society: The Problem of the 'German' Missionaries," *The Journal of Theological Studies,* New Series, XX (Part 2), October, 1969, 523-532. On the origins of the C.M.S. see Michael M. Hennell, *John Venn and the Clapham Sect* (London: 1958), 216f. and especially 228-237.

161 See Simeon's comments on the second petition of the Lord's Prayer in *Horae Homileticae,* 21 vols. (4th ed.; London: 1841), XI, 185-187. On a sermon containing these mild expectations and preached by Venn in Clapham see Hennell, 246-247.

162 Van den Berg, 163, speaks of only "scanty allusions" to millennial expectations in C.M.S. sermons.

163 *Proceedings of the Church Missionary Society,* V, 1805, 355.

164 See Van den Berg, 162.

in her definition of missions — though the two are not necessarily incompatible.[165]

These restrictions on a millennial understanding of missions were not able to withstand two new developments in the middle of the first decade of the nineteenth century. The first was the discussion provoked among Anglicans by Faber's writings.[166] The second was the work begun among London's Jews, a venture whose ecumenical character and culmination in the London Society for Promoting Christianity amongst the Jews merits separate treatment in the following section.

Already in 1803 Faber broached millennial themes in a letter to the editor of *The Christian Observer*. He had been watching the exploits of Napoleon in the Middle East, and he suggested that the French general might be "the king of the north" (Daniel 11 : 40) whose rise was to coincide with the fall of the pope and who would invade Palestine, conquer Egypt, launch forays against Ethiopia and Libya, but bypass Edom, Moab, and Ammon.[167] Faber found it momentous that Napoleon had campaigned against the former countries but had been barred from the last three by the intervention of Sir Sydney Smith. According to Bishop Horsley, he continued, the ranking maritime power — in Faber's day, England — would probably defend the restored Jews against this "king's" aggression. The seeds of a political chiliasm similar to that of Bicheno were detected by the magazine's readers and did not go unchallenged.[168]

Faber continued to develop his thought throughout the next few years, however, and in 1806 his two volume *magnum opus* appeared and was given a fifteen page review for *Observer* readers. Interpreting Daniel, Faber conjectured that the apostate Church of Rome would be permitted to oppress the true church for 1260 years beginning in 606. Mohammedanism, "the eastern apostasy," was concurrent, and both, together with a third, short-lived enemy which would arise near the end of the period, would be overthrown simultaneously. Then the restoration of the Jews to Palestine would begin, and when God's controversy with the nations had been settled the millennium would commence. In separate chapters Faber, consulting former expositors such as Mede and Bishop Newton, wrestled with the interpretation of major prophecies and eschatological terms and symbols. He identified revolutionary France as the Antichrist, whose rise he dated from August, 1792, the month when the old civil order was abolished and atheism was openly avowed. The seven vials of divine wrath, several of which had already flowed, were all considered to be posterior to that date.

---

165 For an analysis of the interaction of the eschatological and ecclesiological motives for missions see Van den Berg, 182f.

166 *vide supra*, 163-164.

167 *The Christian Observer*, II, 1803, 589.

168 *Ibid.*, III, 1804, 9-11.

Eventually France, the third enemy, would be brought down with the apostate church and Mohammedanism. It was Faber's solid conviction that the events of his day, however traumatic, were all steps toward the kingdom of Christ. Consequently he urged Britain to maintain the pure Christian faith, to foster authentic rather than nominal piety, and to use every possible means to promote their religion at home and abroad.[169]

Faber's thorough, authoritative positions evoked a two-year avalanche of discussion in the columns of the magazine.[170] Not all Evangelicals agreed with his exposition, but after 1806 it became impossible for them to ignore millennial issues. The effect on Anglican missions was not long in coming. Anglican Evangelicals became the staunchest allies of missions to the Jews. Nor were they permitted to forget the conversion of the Gentiles, as is indicated by a series of articles on that topic "which has by no means received in these days that attention which it attracted in the age of the Apostles."[171] Claudius Buchanan's writings and sermons, which stressed the Jewish motif, popularized the emphases of simple chiliasm among Evangelicals.

By 1811 Melville Horne, addressing the annual gathering of the C.M.S., reckoned that these expectations "seem to have obtained a general prevalence," especially in England.[172] He cast the Bible and missionary societies in the role of forerunners of the millennium, chided the Church of England clergy for not responding to the missionary vision by giving their support, and reminded his audience that they had gathered to excite one another to fight the "peaceful wars" to be fought before Christ's millennial victory.[173]

> The trumpet of the Millennial jubilee is, at last, heard among the thousands of Israel, and will soon fill all the tents of Jacob. Serious Christians of all denominations are espousing the cause of missions, and anxious to 'prepare the way of the Lord.'[174]

What was required to nerve men for the "strenuous exertions" of missions? "We must be raised and fired, by near views of the glory of the latter day."[175]

Such language would have been foreign to the C.M.S. ten years earlier.

---

169 *Ibid.,* V, 1806, 614-621 and 686-695.

170 *Ibid.,* VI, 1807, 17, 148, 356, 430, 497, 565, 641, 701, 706; and VII, 1808, 1-4, 69-72, 141-147, 209-214, 281-285, 345-349, 417-422, 481-491, 685-688, 688-691. The number of references alone indicates Faber's impact on Evangelicals.

171 *Ibid.,* VII, 1808, 80.

172 Horne's sermon is appended to Claudius Buchanan's *Christian Researches in Asia* (Boston: 1811), 236.

173 *Ibid.*

174 *Ibid.,* 251.

175 *Ibid.,* 257.

Its usage indicates, however, that within a decade the society had come to rely on millennial expectations for her missionary vision and inspiration.

In the older Anglican societies eschatological themes achieved neither the intensity nor the consistent emphasis which they received in evangelical missions. Some half dozen sermons of both the S.P.C.K. and S.P.G. dealt with the gradual advance of Christianity as guaranteed by prophecy. This advance would encompass Gentiles and Jews, could not be dated, and would occur by the means of missions. Thus prophecy did function as a low-keyed source of encouragement for missions. One preacher gingerly suggested that current political turmoil might be a shaking of the nations in preparation for "some signal spiritual revolution."[176] But his sermon was exceptional, and even he warned against "men of speculative ingenuity, or of warm imaginations."[177] Nevertheless, though this mild chiliasm was not as fervent as evangelical expectancy, it functioned as a recurring source of strength and direction for the work of these societies.

5. *White Jews and black Jews — the London Society for Promoting Christianity amongst the Jews*

Not since the 1650's had the thought of the conversion of the Jews received as much attention in Anglo-American missions as during the period under study. Although the *Institutum Judaicum* had been established at Halle in 1728, little of the Pietist zeal for the conversion of Jews appears to have been communicated to England. Likewise, the new interest in the Jews seemingly owed little to seventeenth century English discussions. Revived interest had humble origins in the mid-nineties, but within twenty years it captivated even the most genteel Evangelicals.

In August, 1796 a London bookbinder's apprentice named William Cooper, whose master refused to release him for the first L.M.S. expedition to Tahiti, was preaching to crowds, it is reported, of over four thousand in the open air and at Lady Selina's chapel in Spa Fields.[178] He attracted many Jews to his services, and he addressed them on the Messiah. God has not rejected his ancient people, he preached, but for centuries has preserved them as a distinct race for the day when he will fulfill the Scriptures by saving all Israel. Cooper continued to address Jews, and his success in gaining an audience was reported as far away as Edinburgh as "certainly astonishing."[179] Men in evangelical circles began asking whether the time for the conversion of the Jews had arrived.

---

176 Henry [Bathurst], S.P.G. (a.s.) (London: 1810), 4.
177 *Ibid.*, 6.
178 *The Missionary Magazine*, I, 1796, 186-187.
179 *Ibid.*, 188.

Interest in the Jews among L.M.S. leaders may be dated from Cooper's sermons, though it was not until Joseph S.C.F. Frey enrolled at the L.M.S. Gosport academy in 1802 that their interest was pursued on an organized basis. A converted German Jew, Frey held prayer meetings for other converted Jews in his own home.[180] The following year, 1805, he began lecturing on the Old Testament and preaching to London Jews.[181] The L.M.S. directors sponsored an address in 1806 in which they urged Christians of all denominations to engage in prayer and support for Frey's work, which had met with several conversions. The editors of *The Christian Observer* suggested to the bishop of London that he sponsor an Anglican lecture for Jews and stimulate interest for their conversion among his clergy.[182] The same year several leading dissenters, most of them directors of the L.M.S., co-operated in the publication of a collection of addresses on the conversion of the Jews. Edited by Henry Hunter, it is an index of the interest which had arisen in the subject.[183]

Thomas Haweis, John Love, Samuel Greatheed, and a Rev. Nicol contributed sermons to the study, whose components are arranged for optimum psychological impact without compromising the uniqueness of Christian truth. Hunter's factual introduction is followed by an irenic address to Jewish leaders and Haweis' equally irenic first sermon. In the second sermon Love listed the differences keeping Jews and Christians apart and summarized, "We long to see that profound repentance, which shall take place when the ancient prediction shall be largely accomplished." [184] The following sermons by Nicol, Greatheed, and Haweis, once again, continued to stress the uniqueness of Christ as Messiah. The simultaneous conversion of the Jews and fulness of the Gentiles was the theme of Hunter's sermon on Romans 11 : 25-33. These "two co-eval and concurring events" are still to occur, he stressed, and they will "exert a mighty influence on the production of each other." [185] Many unfulfilled prophecies indicate the approach of a glorious time when Israel shall be received "into the pale of the Christian church." [186] Observing that only one-sixth of mankind was nominally Christian, Hunter thought that the world was "very far" from the readiness required to meet the new age, however.[187] He acknowledged that the work in London had been largely futile, but noted that "many Christian spirits" had been inspired and

---

180   *The Christian Observer*, III, 1804, 10.
181   Lovett, 96.
182   *The Christian Observer*, V, 1806, 254.
183   *vide supra*, 169, for Hunter's contributions to this symposium.
184   Hunter, *The Rise* . . . , 54.
185   *Ibid.*, 167.
186   *Ibid.*, 181.
187   *Ibid.*, 182.

instructed by the renewed interest in the Jews' conversion.[188] He urged Christians to show uncommon charity to a people too long abused in the name of Christ. His observation was well-taken, for the base of interest, prayer, and support being built in British churches as he wrote was to be the strength of the movement in succeeding decades.

The leading Anglican apologist for missions among Jews was Claudius Buchanan. His experiences in India added a new, romantic dimension to appeals for Jewish missions. During visits in southern India in 1806-1807 and in 1808 Buchanan gathered information regarding the Jewish communities in Cochin, which was a center for Jews in remote parts of Asia and therefore "a fountain of intelligence concerning that people in the East." [189] He researched their history, their opinions regarding their future, their social structure, and their social values. He also procured a number of worn, unused manuscripts from their synagogues for collation by Cambridge scholars.

Buchanan discovered two relatively independent Jewish communities and traditions in Cochin, "the white Jews" and "the black Jews." "The white Jews" supposedly immigrated to the Malabar coast at the time of the destruction of the second temple in Jerusalem. In 490 they reportedly obtained a charter from the local potentate. It granted them various privileges, including considerable jurisdiction and relative isolation in a separate community, Cranganor. From time to time they received groups of persecuted Jews from Judea, Spain, and other places. In Cranganor they flourished for a thousand years until the carnage rendered by a community power struggle greatly reduced the settlement. "The black Jews" dated their arrival in India much earlier. Having intermarried with Hindus and having assumed Indian racial and cultural characteristics, they were shunned as inferior by "the white Jews." Nevertheless, they enjoyed commercial contact with Jewish colonies as remote as Afghanistan, Chaldea, Tartary, and China. They were a source of important knowledge for Buchanan, and he was excited by their averred report that the ten tribes resided largely in Chaldea.

The historical veracity of the information imparted by Buchanan is not of concern to us. His account is significant for the fascination with Jewry which it generated — his "researches" passed rapidly through several British and American editions — and particularly for its millennial framework. According to Buchanan's understanding of prophecy three events were nearing: the dissipation of papal power, the waning of Islamic power, and the completion of God's anger against the Jews. The first two could well be "the means of awakening the Jews to consider the evidences of that religion which predicted the rise and fall of both." [190] The Jews' conversion

---

188 *Ibid.*, 184.
189 Claudius Buchanan, *The Works of the Rev. Claudius Buchanan, LL.D.* (New York: 1812), 133.
190 *Ibid.*, 131.

is guaranteed, continued Buchanan, and their presence in all countries and familiarity with all languages will afford Christ a ready army of ministers. He was impressed with the certainty and frequency with which the Jews with whom he spoke referred to their return to Palestine and the reconstruction of Jerusalem, though he doubted that all Jews would or could return. He was heartened to discover upon returning to England that the London Society for Promoting Christianity amongst the Jews (1809) had been established with Frey as its evangelist. Its work corresponded to his own convictions regarding the conversion of that people. Furthermore, the Hebrew translation of the New Testament undertaken by the society excited Buchanan because the gospels were scheduled to appear in 1811, "the very year which was calculated long ago" by Samuel Lee "as that in which 'the times of happiness to Israel' should begin."[191] Claudius Buchanan expected that in the days of the millennium the Jews would be the most effective evangelists in Asia.[192]

Buchanan's "researches" on the Jews of Asia were not only interpreted in terms of his inherited Anglo-American eschatology, therefore, but his new discoveries were used to embellish that tradition with romantic nuances which had wide popular appeal. It was a motif that appeared regularly in his subsequent sermons.[193]

It was during Buchanan's tenure in India that disagreements on policy matters between Frey and the L.M.S. directors reached the breaking point. Frey resigned his position with the L.M.S. and soon afterwards joined the newly founded London Society for Promoting Christianity amongst the Jews. These developments were a windfall for Anglicans. Stimulated by Buchanan's writings, they showed increasing interest in the conversion of Israel and eventually assumed sole responsibility for the new society. The cause became "the strongest evangelistic interest of Simeon's later life," and became a dominant theme in his correspondence after 1813.[194] This spokesman of Evangelicals joined the new society in 1810 and preached its annual sermon the following year.[195]

Once again, therefore, faith in the promised conversion of Israel led to

---

191 *Ibid.,* 149. On Lee *vide supra,* 93, n. 83. Lee's calculations appeared in *Israel Redux, or the Restauration of Israel* (London: 1677, 1678, 1679).

192 Buchanan, *The Works . . . ,* 155.

193 See "The Star in the East," *ibid.,* 291-318, especially 297-298; "The Light of the World," *ibid.,* 318-344; and his address to the London Society for Promoting Christianity amongst the Jews, *ibid.,* Appendix, 33-40.

194 Arthur Pollard, "The Influence and Significance of Simeon's Work," in *Charles Simeon, 1759-1836,* Arthur Pollard and Michael Hennell (eds.) (London: 1959), 180. Van den Berg, 118-119 and 122.

195 Charles Simeon, *The Jews Provoked to Jealousy* (London: 1811). An appended advertisement suggests titles by Andrew Fuller, John Ryland, Thomas Scott, and Buchanan, among others, for further reading on the conversion of the Jews.

the founding of an Anglo-American missionary society.[196] The differences between the London Society and the New England Company should not be minimized. The former was based in large measure on the hypothesis that New England's Indians were descendants of the ten tribes, while for the latter Palestine became the focal point. But both were born amid politically portentous events, and both were grounded in the Biblical hope that God would restore his chosen people to a position of glory in the latter days.

6. Summary

To trace the influence of millennial hopes on the awakening of the modern missionary movement in Britain is a complex task. The dominant trend can be traced from Scotland as represented by John Erskine to both the Baptists of the Midlands and the S.S.P.C.K. corresponding board in London. From both sources and from the Trevecca College tradition eschatological ideas influenced the formation of the L.M.S. The eschatology of these groups was the simple chiliasm articulated by Jonathan Edwards and John Willison. Its missionary dimension is evident from the centrality which concerts for prayer were given in Scottish, in B.M.S., and in L.M.S. circles. In the B.M.S. the missionary movement was abetted by shifts in theological emphasis. Representing the influences operative on the strict Baptists, William Carey drafted the authoritative appeal for foreign missions. The thrust of *An Enquiry* was toward the establishment of the kingdom of Christ through missions, current objections to which were convincingly answered. In Scotland millennial ideals as defended by local leaders sustained the new missionary societies in several cities. Henry Hunter was the chief spokesman on the eschatological hopes in which the S.S.P.C.K. corresponding board in London carried on her work. In the L.M.S., the thought of her major leaders, the appeals circulated for her formation, and her annual sermons were all dominated by the aspiration of the promised latter days.

In dissenting circles current events and trends kindled hope and, in turn, missions. The events in France were the major cause for optimism regarding the fall of Antichrist. It was believed that his fall would enable Christianity to spread and flourish. However, Infidelity, the American Revolutionary War, and British discoveries and sea power all received eschatological significance. After George Faber began speculating on political events, Anglican eschatological adducements for missions also assumed more importance.

---

196 W. T. Gidney, *The History of the London Society for Promoting Christianity amongst the Jews from 1809 to 1908* (London: 1908) remains the standard work on the subject.

In an age of expectancy old interpretations of prophecy were reprinted and new ones published. Anglicans relied on Bishops Newton and Horsley and dissenters on Robert Fleming, Jr., Edwards, and Willison. Among evangelical missionary leaders Henry Hunter, David Bogue, and Andrew Fuller wrote extensively on apocalyptic themes.

The themes of British chiliasm as expressed in the missionary sources have little new to offer. Well known texts depicting the world-wide dominion of Christ and portraying the coming of the nations to the Lord were frequent sources for sermons. There was an emphasis on the proliferation of the knowledge of Christ during the millennium, and the major new societies understood as their major responsibility the proclamation of that knowledge. Millennial hopes as grounded in prophecy were "encouragements" to missionary figures and were regarded as motives and calls to missions. A resurgence of interest in the conversion of the Jews, stimulated by William Cooper, Joseph Frey, Henry Hunter, and Claudius Buchanan, was perhaps the major new emphasis of the period; near the end of the period covered in this chapter it received the luster of Charles Simeon's endorsement. Among evangelical leaders the term "millennium" occurred with more frequency than it had before.

Excited by prospects of the fall of Babylon during the French Revolution, therefore, British Christians established the agencies for spreading the kingdom for which they had been praying. It was to be a kingdom among both Jews and Gentiles, and missionary societies were organized accordingly. The societies are the monuments to British faith and hope that the Lord of history was establishing his kingdom, and through them were expressed some of the noblest instances of benevolence and self-sacrifice ever recorded in the annals of the Christian church. Their existence indicates not only the British understanding of the world-wide nature of the kingdom, but also the priority given to the propagation of Biblically grounded truth as the leaven of the kingdom.

Chapter VI

All things new
(1776-1810, America)

A. General Background

The American churches paid a high price for the pursuit of victory during the Revolutionary War. Spirituality suffered when ministers marched away from their congregations and became officers and chaplains in the colonial army. Church property was often razed by retreating armies, and families and congregations were fragmented. Deism and the cult of reason, which many evangelicals said had been carried into American homes by the British troops quartered there before the war and by French allies, swept through the mobilized colonies. Yale and other colleges became hotbeds in Infidelity both during and after the war. With the coming of peace, American leaders became involved in reorganizing ecclesiastical structures along indigenously American lines. While scarcely a problem for Congregationalists, it became such for groups formerly under European direction and precluded any immediate address to the rationalistic spirit of the age by evangelicals. Among those still identified with the Christian church, universalism and a trend toward unitarianism were divisive complicating factors. Religious indifference prevailed.

Stirrings of reaction did not appear until the late eighties and nineties. Ministers horrified by the flagrant ridicule of the Christian faith in the name of reason and enlightenment issued warnings and appeals for reform and revival. Timothy Dwight, who became President of Yale in 1795, turned the tide of Infidelity there by his convincing apologetic for Christianity.[1] A series of revivals reintroduced evangelical piety to that campus after 1800. Jedidiah Morse, the geographer and missionary leader, aroused considerable opposition to the Illuminati and Jacobian societies, which he claimed were undermining not only Christian faith and morality but also the new republic.[2] In the late 1780's awakenings appeared on several Methodist circuits in the South, and colleges and other denominations were

---

1 Dwight lectured on "The Nature and Danger of Infidel Philosophy," "Is the Bible the Word of God?" and preached a four-year series of theological sermons in the college chapel. Sweet, 226.

2 On the Illuminati see Vernon Stauffer, *New England and the Bavarian Illuminati* (New York: 1918).

soon affected by the same spirit. In Lee, Massachusetts, an eighteen-month awakening beginning in 1792 added more than one hundred new members to the Congregational church.[3] A concerted drive against religious indifference was made by Connecticut clergy,[4] and after 1797 revivals became more frequent and widespread throughout various New England states. Although they carefully avoided the excesses of the Great Awakening, ecclesiastical leaders along the eastern seaboard[5] witnessed several peaks of awakening during the first decade of the new century. Many of the student leaders in foreign missions were converted during these revivals, and it is in the context of revival and concerts for prayer that the American missionary movement sprang to life.

This relationship between missions and revivals is largely explainable by the Edwardean roots of the Second Great Awakening. Many of the revival leaders of New England were professed disciples of Edwards. The group had grown from four or five theologians in the 1750's to between forty and fifty ministers before the war. By 1796 it numbered more than one hundred.[6] The leaders were Joseph Bellamy, Samuel Hopkins, Stephen West, Nathaniel Emmons, John Smalley, Timothy Dwight, and Jonathan Edwards, Jr. Although each man made his own improvisions on Edwards' thought and imparted them to the divinity students studying under him, the theology of the movement was based on Edwards and was known collectively as the "New Divinity."[7] By 1800 its adherents outnumbered Old School ministers in Connecticut and western Massachusetts, and in its Hopkinsian form it was making inroads into eastern Massachusetts. As the movement spread, so did revivals. From revivals flowed the power and the will to begin foreign missions. As had Jonathan Edwards, the Edwardeans generally saw missions as the logical extension of revival. It is not surprising, therefore, that they and their students became the leaders of the new

3   H. Shelton Smith, Robert T. Handy, Lefferts A. Loetscher, *American Christianity*, 2 vols. (New York: 1960 and 1963), I, "Revival at Lee," 525-529.

4   Charles Roy Keller, *The Second Great Awakening in Connecticut* (New Haven: 1942), 36f. Keller masterfully traces the transition from complacency to the era of benevolence, evangelical revival, and social action.

5   The frontier revivals of the same period were characterized by greater excesses. See Catherine C. Cleveland, *The Great Revival in the West, 1797-1805* (Chicago: 1916). They were not directly connected with the foreign missionary awakening in America and remained in themselves self-contained, local missionary movements.

6   Keller, 33.

7   See Benjamin B. Warfield's article, "Edwards and the New England Theology," *Encyclopaedia of Religion and Ethics*, 13 vols., James Hastings (ed.) (Edinburgh: 1908-1926), V, 221-227. The term "Hopkinsian" or "Hopkintonian" has been incorrectly used as a synonym for "New Divinity" or "Edwardean," when in fact it refers only to Hopkins' thought and not to that of the entire group. See Keller, 33. On the transmission and development of the New Divinity see Mary Latimer Gambrell, *Ministerial Training in Eighteenth-Century New England* (New York: 1937).

movement.[8] Missions were further aided by the leveling influence of revivals on Congregational-Presbyterian differences. In 1800 Jonathan Edwards, Jr., acting in his capacity as delegate from the Presbyterian General Assembly, proposed the Plan of Union to the Congregational Connecticut General Association. Ratified by both bodies the following year, it provided the basis for co-operation in Christianizing the frontier.[9] Co-operation was reflected in the A.B.C.F.M. a decade later.

Missions imbibed the optimism and vigor with which the young country was reaching out into new commercial and diplomatic ventures. They were born in an era of new opportunity, when English explorers were bringing home startling reports on Asia and the South Seas and when Lewis and Clarke had opened the West for caravans of pioneers.[10] Not to understand missions as a child of this age would be a mistake. But perhaps a more serious error is not to appreciate the antithetical alternative which evangelical Christianity posed to the humanistic expectations of the Enlightenment.[11] On the one hand the New Divinity waged a ceaseless polemical war against the spirit of the Enlightenment, particularly as it was manifested in Infidelity. On the other hand Hopkins' "consistent Calvinism" was at most the adaptation of methodology to a system of truth resting on radically different presuppositions from those of rationalism. Essentially, therefore, the New Divinity reached back into her heritage of Biblically based expectations for her certainty that through missions God's kingdom would spread to all nations.

B. *Millennial Expectations*

The leaders of the New Divinity and of evangelical orthodoxy in general were not the only protagonists of optimism regarding the future. Sons of the Enlightenment espoused a utopianism and believed in the gradual improvement of man. William E. Channing, parishioner of Samuel Hopkins, inclined toward a humanized version of his pastor's more traditional New England millennialism and harbingered a still more complete secularization

8 Speaking more strictly of Hopkinsians, Kawerau says, 103, "Sie waren die Träger des Missionsgedankens und betonten die Notwendigkeit des Revivals."

9 On the Plan of Union see Sweet, 210-212.

10 The Lewis and Clarke Expedition occurred in 1804, following the Louisiana Purchase in 1803.

11 Wolfgang Eberhard Löwe, *The First American Foreign Missionaries: "The Students," 1810-1820* (Unpublished doctoral dissertation submitted to Brown University, 1962) excessively stresses the spirit of the age in his appraisal of the American missionary movement's origins. See especially Chapters I and V, "The Zeitgeist of the Eighteenth Century" and "The Influence of Eighteenth Century Thought on the General Character of the Mission Theology of the Students."

of evangelical expectations.[12] Joseph Priestly, heretical Presbyterian clergyman who settled in Pennsylvania in 1794, shocked Englishmen with his
defense of the French Revolution, which he interpreted in terms of prophecy.
In articulating his universalism, Charles Chauncy used the double resurrection associated with the millennium in Revelation 20 to postulate a cycle
of deaths, punishments, and resurrections continuing until all men would be
raised to eternal life.[13] Nor did millennial expectations apply only to the
rise and understanding of the missionary movement. Americans hoped that
the millennium would be born out of the Revolutionary War.[14] Their
country was regarded as the potential seat of Christ's rule in that era, and
evangelicals were compared with Cromwell's Roundheads for their consciousness of being divine instruments in realizing that day. Furthermore, through
the fear and perplexity occasioned in some Americans by the French
Revolution, there was a resurgence of premillennialism.[15]

Among these divergent and widespread millennial views the simple
chiliasm of evangelicals especially concerns us. It was integrally bound up
with the rise of missionary organizations in America. Traditional expositors
such as Brightman and, on some points, Mede were consulted. The senior
Fleming's view of history was recommended in the American missionary
periodicals, as were the writings of such recent authors as George S. Faber
and Bishops Horsley and Newton. Both Old School Calvinists, who were
unaffected by either the Edwardean or the liberal modifications in New
England theology, and the leaders of the New Divinity were motivated to
missions by simple chiliasm. Edwards' influence was also reflected in
Presbyterian leaders in the middle states. John Livingston, Dutch Reformed
leader in New York, was an active supporter of missions and was stimulated
by millennial motifs. Baptists, many of whom had left Congregationalism
at the time of the Great Awakening, followed either John Gill or Andrew
Fuller in their eschatology. During the pervasive 1806-1807 awakening
David Tappan, Hollis Professor of Divinity at Harvard, addressed a
concert for prayer on the second petition of the Lord's Prayer in a sermon
defining his millennial views.[16]

It was this chiliasm, prevalent among evangelicals of various denominations, regions, and theological emphases, which in the context of revival
and in imitation of the British stimulated missionary interest in America.

12   Niebuhr, 152-153.
13   [Charles Chauncy], *The Mystery hid from Ages and Generations* (London:
1784).
14   Heimert, 396.
15   *Ibid.,* 535; *P.F.F.,* II, 723-782.
16   David Tappan, *Sermons on Important Subjects* (Boston: 1807), 229-245.

C. *Mission Efforts*

Compared with the British missionary awakening the formation of new American societies occurred more gradually and naturally and was often initiated by and associated with the instituted church. Missions to non-Christians overseas were preceded by the decades-old practice of sending ordained men on tours of frontier areas. There was a continuing sense of responsibility by Congregational associations and Presbyterian synods for the white settler of new areas. As the frontier pushed steadily westward and short tours became impossible, men were appointed for longer terms. Some were even appointed on a full-time basis. Baptists met the needs of the frontier through their lay or farmer preachers and Methodists through their circuit riders. All these groups demonstrated concern for Indians and Negroes. Foreign missions was the addition of another dimension to the outreach of American churches revitalized by awakenings.

During and after the war older Baptist associations sent men into frontier areas. Already in 1774 the Connecticut General Association of Congregationalists designated two men to minister to new settlements in the North and West.[17] In 1792 she appointed a committee on missions and in 1798 incorporated herself as the Missionary Society of Connecticut. Soon thereafter Congregationalists in Massachusetts and Rhode Island organized societies with Nathaniel Emmons and Samuel Hopkins as their presidents. Massachusetts Baptists established a society in 1802, the same year that the General Assembly of the Presbyterian Church appointed a standing committee on missions.

Several larger societies had more conglomorate compositions and were less closely bound to ecclesiastical structures. In 1787 the Society for Propagating the Gospel among the Indians and Others in North America was granted a charter by the Massachusetts legislature.[18] This first American missionary society included Boston-area religious leaders of various theological tinctures, many of whom had served the S.S.P.C.K. and advocated the aborted 1762 society. Her aim was to reach unchurched whites as well as Indians. The New York Missionary Society dated from 1796, was stimulated by the L.M.S. example, and included Dutch Reformed, Associate Reformed, Presbyterians, and for a time Baptists in her membership.[19] The society sponsored work among the Chickasaw Indians of Georgia. Not until several Williams College students pledged themselves to foreign mission service were the foundations laid for America's first foreign missionary society. After graduating from Andover Theological Seminary, a school founded jointly by Old Calvinists and Edwardeans in reaction to

17 Keller, 71.
18 Hereafter abbreviated S.P.G.N.A.
19 Beaver, *Pioneers in Mission,* 235-238.

growing liberalism at Harvard, the students approached the General Association of Massachusetts. They proposed American participation in the foreign missionary movement. The association adopted a plan for the formation of the Board of Commissioners for Foreign Missions. The 1810 plan called for five commissioners from Massachusetts and four from Connecticut, but soon Presbyterians and Dutch Reformed as well as Congregationalists were active in the new society. Two years later it sent out America's first foreign missionaries, and its birth marks the point at which we terminate our survey.[20]

Writing to Andrew Fuller in October, 1799, Samuel Hopkins listed five missionary societies in America, four of which were Edwardean in theological character.[21] Fifteen years later that number had risen to almost a score. These in turn were supported by clusters of local, auxiliary societies. For a time virtually every major society produced its own missionary magazine.[22] A mass of annual sermons was delivered, demonstrating the pervasiveness of the missionary spirit.

The periodicals and sermons of the major societies and the eschatological views of missionary leaders from the various American denominations provide us with sufficient material to characterize the millennial expectations in American missions during this period.

D. Missions and Millennial Expectations

In assessing American missions in their eschatological dimension, we shall first consider the contribution of the Edwardeans, particularly Samuel Hopkins, concerning whom there exists some disagreement. In the second section cognizance will be taken of the impact of British eschatological discussions in stimulating American missions. That the views of the Edwardeans and of the British expositors and missionary figures were widely influential in missionary societies, magazines, and sermons will then be demonstrated. Three major millennial concepts as elaborated by three missionary propagandists will be sketched in separate sections. That the A.B.C.F.M., the capstone in the rise of American foreign missions, was in large measure founded and sustained in the hope of realizing the

---

20 *Ibid.,* 249-257, on the American Board, hereafter abbreviated A.B.C.F.M.; see Kawerau's study, III, "Die Periode des Aufbruchs (1790-1819)," for a full discussion of the A.B.C.F.M.; Oliver Wendell Elsbree, *The Rise of the Missionary Spirit in America, 1790-1815* (Williamsport, Pa.: 1928) still remains the best comprehensive study of American missions during this period.

21 Löwe, 73.

22 Elsbree lists more than twenty of these magazines, most of whose life-spans fell between 1800 and 1815.

millennial expectations of the students and of the board's leaders will be treated finally.

1. Samuel Hopkins — a tradition embellished

While they differed from one another and from their teacher on a number of issues, the Edwardeans in general "were content to follow their master in eschatology."[23] They consulted the same sources as Edwards himself had and derived the main lines of their position from him. Like Emmons the others in turn impressed these ideas on their students.[24] Dwight emphasized the glory of the church in the latter days both in his sermons[25] and in his hymns. This emphasis is evident in "I Love Thy Kingdom, Lord," perhaps his most loved composition:

> Sure as Thy truth shall last,
>   To Zion shall be given
> The brightest glories earth can yield,
>   And brighter bliss of heaven.[26]

In 1798 he preached a sermon asserting that the current crises and miraculous events indicated the nearness of the Moslems' capitulation, the Jews' conversion, and the coming of Christ in the latter-day glory.[27] Bellamy's 1758 sermon on the millennium was republished in 1794 by David Austin, who expected an imminent realization of the conditions it described.[28] Samuel Hopkins wrote several important pieces on the subject. All these men defended an Edwardean view of the last days, and therefore it comes as no surprise that they were among the leaders in the revivals and the missionary movement.

It might be considered enigmatic, therefore, that Hopkins has been traditionally singled out by historians for extraordinary recognition as a missionary leader. The problem can be traced in large measure to the rather loose and indiscriminate usage of the term "Hopkinsian" by Hopkins' biographer, Edwards A. Park. Park applied the term to many missionary figures who, although associated with Hopkins and his loyal admirers, could never accept the various modifications of Edwards' thought which

---

23   Goen, 38.
24   Gambrell, 132.
25   See especially Timothy Dwight, *Sermons*, 2 vols. (Edinburgh: 1828), I, Sermon XIV., "On Revivals of Religion," 231-249.
26   Our citation of this hymn, which still appears in many American and English hymnals, is from *Psalter Hymnal*, 558.
27   Löwe, 96.
28   Heimert, 536-537; and Löwe, 68, n. 38.

Hopkins made.[29] Elsbree adopted this loose usage and consequently accented Hopkins' role in American missions.[30] Kenneth Scott Latourette relied on Park and Elsbree when reporting Hopkins' contributions.[31] And more recently Kawerau and Löwe, although more discriminate in their terminology, have treated Hopkins as the link between Edwards and the American phase of the missionary awakening.[32] Charles Keller has called for a more circumscribed and careful usage of "Hopkinsian," for applying it to all Edwardeans "implies an agreement in doctrines and a dependence on Hopkins which did not exist."[33] Proceeding with similar discernment, Dick Van Halsema has appreciated the complexity of the rise of American foreign missions and has been unwilling to ascribe the central or key position in that movement to Hopkins alone.[34]

We take full cognizance of the restricted character of Hopkins' influence in missions and fully acknowledge that the missionary movement was the combined effort of many Edwardeans and indeed of many evangelicals influenced to a still less degree by Edwards' thought than his own disciples. Nevertheless, in the remainder of this section we too choose to focus specifically on Hopkins for several reasons. First, as a younger contemporary and intimate friend of Edwards and as Edwards' designated trustee of his papers and manuscripts, Hopkins was assured of a hearing by those who may not have agreed with him. His devotion, clear thinking, and mission zeal were held up as examples to New Englanders.[35] Secondly, he was one of America's most consistent exponents of humanitarian and missionary causes throughout the last half of the eighteenth century. Finally and most importantly, although Edwardeans were in essential agreement on eschatology, Hopkins was more engrossed in the subject than the others, and his writings on it contributed an important new emphasis to the doctrine.

Hopkins' earlier involvement in mission causes has been noted in another connection.[36] That involvement continued until the end of his life. Throughout his Newport pastorate Hopkins preached and wrote against the evils of the slave trade, urging his parishioners and fellow Americans to liberate,

29 See, for example, Park's ascription of Hopkinsianism to West, Emmons, and the majority of the members of the Massachusetts Missionary Society. Park, I, 60 and 64.

30 For examples of Elsbree's application of "Hopkinsian" see Elsbree, 92-93, 95, 139.

31 Kenneth Scott Latourette, *A History of the Expansion of Christianity*, 7 vols. (New York and Evanston: 1937-1945), IV, 77-79.

32 Kawerau, II, "Samuel Hopkins (1721-1803)"; also see Löwe, Chapter III, "Missionary Elements in the Theology of Samuel Hopkins."

33 Keller, 33.

34 Van Halsema, 350-356.

35 *The Massachusetts Missionary Magazine*, I, 1803, 363-364.

36 *vide supra*, 140.

convert, and colonize their black brothers. After convincing broad-minded, irenic, neighboring minister Ezra Stiles of the feasibility of the scheme, Hopkins published a joint appeal with Stiles for public support for educating two Negroes, Bristol Yama and John Quamine, and for sending them to Africa as missionaries. Van Halsema judges that the emphasis of this initial appeal "did not lie on political or social measures" but that its "thrust is completely missionary or religious in character, and has to do with the negroes' need for the Christian Gospel...." [37] In 1776 Hopkins and Stiles repeated this appeal. The same year Hopkins published "A Dialogue Concerning the Slavery of the Africans," dedicated to the Continental Congress. He felt that while colonists were fighting for their own liberty, they should "feel the consistency of giving freedom to their own bondsmen." [38] If Europeans and Americans had spent one half as much money on Christianizing Africans as on enslaving them, "that extensive country... would have been full of gospel light...." [39] Numbered among Hopkins' anti-slavery writings are a number of newspaper articles written throughout the following decades. His 1793 "A Discourse upon the Slave Trade and the Slavery of the Africans" contained a positive mission thrust, which was based on the Great Commission. Elsbree identified Hopkins' interest in freeing the slaves and sending missionaries to Africa with "the earliest foreign mission field to be contemplated by Americans." [40] In 1791 Hopkins was again unsuccessful in an attempt to send Yama to Africa, this time with Salmur Nubia, another freed slave.

Even during the unsettled conditions of the Revolutionary War, when Hopkins was forced to leave Newport, he did not forget missions. He settled temporarily in North Stamford, "which was then a missionary field." [41] As late in his life as 1801 Hopkins "was to a large extent responsible for the formation of the Missionary Society of Rhode Island." [42] He became the society's first president.

It is only against the background of fifty years of interest in missions that Hopkins' thought on the millennium can be properly appreciated. Like Edwards Hopkins saw the integral relation of revival, missions, and the millennium. That the millennial ideal, as well as his emphasis on rejecting all self-interest for Christ's sake as expressed in his concept of disinterested benevolence, [43] compelled him to call for revival and advocate his missionary

37 Van Halsema, 252.
38 Park I, 117.
39 Hopkins, "A Dialogue Concerning the Slavery of the Africans," in Park, II, 457.
40 Elsbree, 109.
41 Park, I, 97.
42 Elsbree, 66.
43 Elsbree finds that Hopkins' idea of disinterested benevolence is at the heart of American missions. (146-152) Van Halsema correctly ascribes the concept to

and benevolent schemes is particularly apparent from the writings of the last decade of his life. His 1793 address to the Providence Society for Abolishing the Slave Trade concluded with a reference to the millennium. He "declared that the slow progress of his day in Christianizing the African would give way eventually to the glories of a millennial era, when the Church would fully appreciate the privilege of bringing the Gospel." [44] For Hopkins missions would bring the millennium and the millennium would be characterized by heightened mission work.

In 1793 Hopkins' two-volume work on systematic theology also appeared. It contained a lengthy appendix entitled "A Treatise on the Millennium." The piece validates the observation made by his young parishioner and critic William Ellery Channing that "the millennium was his chosen ground," a subject with which Hopkins was thoroughly familiar.[45] Although the subject may have been "more than a belief" and may have assumed "the freshness of visible things" for the aging theologian,[46] by his own admission Hopkins treated it for its doctrinal merit. Doctrine for Hopkins was designed to strengthen Christians in their faith, and in his appendix he treated the millennium doctrinally, since

> it appears not to be believed by many; and not to be well understood by more; or attended to by most, as an important event; full of instruction; suited to support, comfort and encourage christians, in the present dark appearance of things, respecting the interest of Christ, and his church; and to animate them to faith, patience and perserverance in obedience to Christ; putting on the hope of salvation for an helmet.[47]

Even though the purpose of the piece was not to motivate men to mission activity, therefore, Hopkins not only hoped to excite men "to pray for the advancement and coming of the kingdom," but he also made repeated allusions to the truth that it would come through human means or agents.[48] Missions were a logically necessary consequence of Hopkins' doctrine of the millennium as given in "A Treatise," therefore. It was particularly his expanded description of the millennium, a new note in the development of the doctrine, which inspired the church with visions of the age to be inaugurated through her mission.

Hopkins was concerned with four basic questions regarding the millen-

Edwardeans in general and underlines other elements in Hopkins' theology of missions. (350-356).

44   Van Halsema, 272.

45   As quoted by Niebuhr, 143-144, from *The Works of Samuel Hopkins* (Boston: 1888), I, 427.

46   *Ibid.*

47   Hopkins, II, 6 [appendix].

48   *Ibid.*, and 7, 115, 116, 122, 152, 153, 154.

nium: 1. Is it grounded in Scripture? 2. What will be its character? 3. When will it begin? 4. What must happen before it begins? These four questions provided the outline for his treatise.

In Section I Hopkins "proved from Scripture, that the church of Christ is to come to a state of prosperity in this world" unattained before and destined to continue for a minimum of a thousand years.[49] He found the doctrine implied or stated in every major section of the Bible and culminating in the enthronement of Christ in Revelation 19.

In Section II he opted for a figurative interpretation of Christ's reign in Revelation 20. The section is divided into two parts. The first explicates what is clearly revealed in prophecy regarding Christ's millennial reign. Here Hopkins discussed such characteristics as glory, holiness, benevolence, peace, knowledge, concord, unity, happiness, and joy. The second, to which we shall return momentarily, describes the conditions implied by prophecy.

Hopkins asserted in Section III that it could be ascertained "within a thousand, or hundreds of years" when the millennium would begin.[50] Working with the various numbers given in Daniel and Revelation, he calculated that Antichrist's fall, already in progress, would be completed sometime between 1866 and approximately 2000. The difference between Daniel's figures 1290 and 1325 denotes the period after Antichrist's fall when the perfect church will spread true Christian principles throughout the earth and when their acceptance will be guaranteed in the millennial sabbath.[51] Hopkins assured his readers that "these great events will come on within two hundred years."[52] Hopkins produced the most extended Edwardean study of the symbolic numbers in apocalyptic literature, therefore, and the charge that he fostered "speculation about the time of the millennium"[53] is not without foundation. He never committed himself to specific years, however, and it must be remembered that he was doing no more than a number of his English contemporaries and that even Edwards had ventured to suggest that the Great Awakening was perhaps the inception of the millennium.

---

49   *Ibid.,* 9.

50   *Ibid.,* 84.

51   For many expositors, including Hopkins, creation in seven days was a figure of the seven-millennia existence of the world. The Genesis account was then interpreted in the light of II Peter 3:8, "...with the Lord one day is as a thousand years, and a thousand years as one day." (*Ibid.,* 85-86) Ussher's chronology fixed creation at 4004 B.C., a date almost universally accepted by Anglo-American Protestants throughout the period of our survey. On the basis of the thousand years=one day principle Hopkins' calculation that the millennium would begin approximately 2000 A.D. harmonized with Ussher's findings.

52   Hopkins, II, 95 [appendix].

53   Beaver, "Eschatology...," 67. Beaver's conclusions here that Hopkins' millennialism stood outside the mainstream of Edwardean eschatology and that it had a

The sixth vial will be accompanied by unclean spirits proceeding from the mouths of the beast, dragon, and false prophet, Hopkins reminded his readers in Section IV. Those spirits were identified as the godless forces of his own day. During the seventh vial they would be defeated by the church in the battle of Armageddon.

The most significant new element in Hopkins' treatise was his discussion of the character of the millennium as implied in prophecy. He demonstrated remarkable insight into the potentials of the science and technology just beginning to develop in his day and perceived the implications of contemporary discoveries and commerce for the unity of mankind.

He said that people would be prosperous, all their needs being adequately met and their comfort and convenience fostered. This rests on "the kindness and peculiar blessing of God in his providence" [54] and on "the great degree of benevolence, virtue and wisdom, which all will then have and exercise, with respect to the affairs of this world." [55] War and lawsuits will be eliminated. Temperance will lead to absence of "expensive, distressing, desolating pestilence and sickness; but general health will be enjoyed; by which much expense of time and money will be prevented." [56] Agriculture will be improved to the point that barren lands will blossom, and increase will be multiplied a hundredfold in some places. All excesses, intemperance, and waste will be abolished. Prudence and economy will prevail. Mechanical arts, crafts, and trades will be vastly improved, all of life benefiting from them. Inventions will multiply. Rocks and stones will be cut, moved, and used in most unbelievable ways. Work will be limited to several hours a day. Leisure will be used to the greatest profit, especially in reading, improvement of self, and religious improvement. Benevolence will be so largely engaged in as to eliminate all want.

"In that day mankind will greatly multiply and and [sic] increase in number, till the earth shall be filled with them." [57] Instead of spending their time in subduing and killing each other in "impiety, intemperance, folly and wickedness," [58] men will fulfill God's command to Adam and Noah to multiply, fill the earth and subdue it. They will enable the earth to maintain a thousand people to the one it now supports. Seas will be drained and millions supported from the produce of these once salty wastes. All needs will be met. All people will live happily as one family. Even death will not be regarded as an evil which brings fear and distress to survivors. Pain and sickness will be greatly alleviated.

---

negative effect on the church's mission must be reassessed in the light of Hopkins' later writings, which we shall treat below. See also *Pioneers in Mission*, 25.

54 Hopkins, II, 70 [appendix].
55 *Ibid.*
56 *Ibid.*, 70-71.
57 *Ibid.*, 73.
58 *Ibid.*

"In the Millennium, all will probably speak *one language*." [59] All the time wasted in teaching and learning languages will be saved. The most recognized scholars will determine the best language. It will become universal, and all knowledge worth preserving will be translated into it. This knowledge will in turn improve the language. Understanding and hence good will will be fostered. Techniques for teaching this language to children will be devised. Knowledge and books, especially the Bible, will spread rapidly and cheaply. Mankind will be more readily unified. God's blessings will flow to him in greater measure. God will be praised in one language, as with one voice.

> The church of Christ will then be formed and regulated, according to his laws and institutions, in the most beautiful and pleasing order... There will then be but one universal, catholic church, comprehending all the inhabitants of the world, formed into numerous particular societies and congregations, as shall be most convenient, to attend on public worship, and the institutions of Christ. [60]

There will be no schisms, but agreement in doctrine and worship will prevail. All children will be baptized, easily educated, and confess their love for Christ at an early age. Discipline will be charitable and pure.

Hopkins' description was not mere utopianism. It was grounded in the emphases of evangelical Protestantism. These blessings would come only after the majority of men had heard the gospel, repented and were converted, and lived their Christianity in lives of disinterested benevolence. He went on to describe the radical spiritual transformation upon which material blessings were contingent. But this note had been sounded before. Hopkins contributed to Anglo-American eschatology by showing the implications of the spread of Christian knowledge. His contribution could only add incentive to the missionary enterprise. But outside stimuli were needed to clarify for Hopkins the missionary implications of his own study, which had minimized the conversion of the nations and the global spread of Christianity.

Hopkins' correspondence with Andrew Fuller after the founding of the B.M.S. was his tangible link with the British missionary awakening. The British movement deeply influenced Hopkins personally. He acknowledged to his Baptist correspondent, "I believe all the missionary societies lately formed in America owe their rise to those formed in England, and their extraordinary exertions." [61] He not only "seemed to feel" that Carey had been molded by Edwards' thought, [62] but he recognized in him a brother.

---

59 *Ibid.*, 75.
60 *Ibid.*, 78.
61 Hopkins' 1799 letter to Fuller, as quoted by Van Halsema, 355.
62 Löwe, 2.

Both men were theological sons of Edwards. Like so many other Americans, Hopkins received new insight into his own eschatology from Carey's appeal to use means in spreading the kingdom of Christ to the ends of the earth. This note, only casually struck in Hopkins' 1793 appendix, became dominant in a sermon which he wrote in 1801.[63]

Christ will reign until his enemies are subjugated and until all earthly kingdoms "become his own kingdom," asserted Hopkins.[64] Assured of this by the Bible, he was supported and consoled in spite of the large masses of non-Christians, papists, and Eastern Orthodox believers. Since it is the "preceptive will of God" that all should be saved, Christ sent his disciples to all nations. Despite human opposition to the gospel "it is the duty of Christians to exert themselves, and take every proper method to propagate it far and wide, to the utmost of their power, looking to and trusting in Christ, to cause his word to run and be glorified."[65] Whatever the price in terms of difficulty, disappointment, and loss of life, and "though Israel be not now gathered," by enlisting in missions Christians will "be acceptable" to God.[66] Their effort

> will, in some way, though now unknown to us, serve to promote and hasten on the happy day when the Heathen shall be given to Christ for his inheritance, and the uttermost parts of the earth for his possession.[67]

Although Hopkins believed that he was living during the pouring of the sixth vial, two hundred years from the day he had described eight years earlier, he had come to see that contemporary effort was vital to the realization of the millennium. His publications had neither the missionary urgency of David Bogue's nor the millennial immediacy of Henry Hunter's writings. But they provided a pleasing panorama of the new age for New England's missionary figures and reinforced Carey's emphasis on the necessity of missions in realizing the millennium.

2. Stimulation from Britain

From the time Hopkins acknowledged America's debt to Britain, the stimulation which American missions received from the example of the new British societies has been emphasized by many historians of missions.[68]

---

63 Entitled "The Author's Farewell to the World," the sermon was published in Hopkins' *Twenty-one Sermons* (Salem: 1803).
64 *Ibid.*, 357-358.
65 *Ibid.*, 360.
66 *Ibid.*, 361.
67 *Ibid.*
68 For a recent example see Kawerau, 150f.

Americans were fascinated by the example of Carey and by the writings of Buchanan. From the English propaganda they borrowed copy for their own missionary publications. They sent significant sums of money to the headquarters of the new British societies. And when Americans established their own foreign missionary societies, they patterned them after the British models, learned from British experience, and consulted with British leaders to avoid duplication of effort.

A significant dimension of this stimulation was the British eschatological heritage. Two centuries of Anglo-American thinking on the millennium contributed to a renewal of American aspiration for the latter-day glory of the church among all nations. The earliest as well as the most recent British commentators and theologians were read and recommended for study in the American missionary awakening. These British sources must be seen as reinforcing the Edwardean and more broadly evangelical eschatology already accepted by Americans and as calling Americans to assume the missionary responsibilities implied in their eschatology.

Preaching before the S.P.G.N.A., Jedidiah Morse expressed his debt to Joseph Mede's works, to Robert Millar's *The History of the Propagation of Christianity*, and to Dwight's 1798 sermon referred to above. He concurred with Francis Bacon, who in *Advancement of Learning* contended that prophecy is not fulfilled punctually but gradually and in increasing degrees.[69] The first issue of *The Panoplist* acquainted its readers with Thomas Brightman through a sketch of his life and recommended his writings.[70] *The Fulfilling of the Scripture* by Robert Fleming, Sr., was reprinted and called to the attention of American readers.[71] The writings and missionary example of John Erskine were eulogized in an extended obituary written by Morse.[72] The thinking of such British contemporaries as Bishop Horsley and George S. Faber were reported in reviews of their books, and the controversy surrounding Faber's views in Anglican circles was followed with interest in the American journals.[73] The ideas of British expositors were soon given extensive attention in American sermons and lectures.[74]

American and British sources on the latter days intertwined to give an eschatological interpretation to the French Revolution in Europe, to the

69   Jedidiah Morse, *Signs of the Times* (Charlestown: 1810).
70   *The Panoplist*, I, 1806, 478-479.
71   *Ibid.*, 408-410; and *The Massachusetts Missionary Magazine*, IV, 1806, 76.
72   *The Massachusetts Missionary Magazine*, I, 1803, 38.
73   *The Panoplist*, II, 1807, 190; *The Panoplist and Missionary Magazine United*, IV, 1808 [In 1808 *The Panoplist* and *The Massachusetts Missionary Magazine* were united. Numbering continued from the old paper *The Panoplist*.], 35-40, and X, 1814-1815, 205. The first American edition of Faber's *A Dissertation on the Prophecies* appeared in 1808.
74   See for example the two lectures of Joseph Lathrop, *The Prophecy of Daniel* (Springfield, Mass.: 1811), 7, 11, 15.

Infidelity on both sides of the Atlantic, to the revivals, and to the missionary movement. These were seen as signs of further progress in the rapid approach of the millennium. And an awareness of the impending climax of history gave new urgency to missionary and benevolent enterprises.

3. A pervasive ideal

To this point in the present chapter we have examined the British and American sources of the millennial ideal in the American missionary awakening during the 1790's and early 1800's. We dealt in some detail with the contributions of the Edwardean Samuel Hopkins. Having exposed the taproots of that ideal, we shall note its pervasion of American Christianity and mention its major emphases in this section. The three following sections will focus on three new and important eschatological emphases in American missionary circles.

It scarcely needs to be indicated that an exhaustive investigation of the missionary sources of this period — whether magazines or sermons — is not feasible within the scope of our study. Nor is such an investigation requisite in order to determine either the breadth of millennial expectations in American missionary organizations or the general character of those hopes. In general it can be said that millennial hopes were stimulated wherever evangelical Protestantism, particularly those denominations most influenced by the Edwardean tradition, experienced new revivals. Millennial hopes in turn created a new sense of urgency and responsibility for missions culminating in the formation of new societies. Having investigated the annual sermons delivered to the various new missionary societies, Beaver concludes, "Fifty-two sermons out of seventy selected at random give more than passing attention to eschatology, usually in the form of millennialism." [75] In a chapter devoted to the subject Elsbree concludes that widespread interest in Biblical prophecy "constituted a not inconsiderable part of the dynamic of missions." [76] In a series of short paragraphs we shall show that the missionary concern of the leaders of various missionary and denominational organizations was inextricable from millennial motifs. Their views are reflected in representative sermons and periodical articles.

In 1805 Joseph Eckley reminded the Boston-based S.P.G.N.A. of "the most animating motives" for missions which divine promises regarding the church tendered.[77] He cited successes already made as added incentives to

75 Beaver, "Eschatology . . . ," 68.
76 Elsbree, 122. See Chapter VI, "Prophecy, Prayer, and Propaganda," 122-145.
77 *The Panoplist,* II, 1807, 132; and Elsbree, 132. For a list of preachers before the S.P.G.N.A. see *The Society for Propagating the Gospel among the Indians and Others of North America* ([no place]: 1887), 11.

work for the fast-approaching day when the knowledge of the true God would fill the earth. Three years later Abiel Holmes, choosing Psalm 72 : 17 as his text, movingly proclaimed that all nations would soon be embraced in Christ's kingdom.

> Yes: The time will come, and 'will not tarry,' when the Pagan idolater shall 'cast his idols to the moles and to the bats'; when the Indian Powows shall be silenced by the songs of Zion; when the Vedas of the Hindu, the Shasters of the Gentoo, and the Koran of the Mahometan, shall be exchanged for the Holy Bible; when the religion of Brahma, the Institutes of Menu, the rites of the Lama, the Zend of Zoroaster, and even the laws of Confucius, shall be superseded by 'the glorious Gospel of the blessed God.' [78]

In 1810 Jedidiah Morse exposed for the society the missionary imperative contained in the signs of the times.

Joseph Barker's 1806 sermon to the Massachusetts Missionary Society was based on Psalm 67 : 7 and dwelt on the same theme as Holmes' sermon. Man therefore has "great encouragements" to advance Christ's millennial kingdom, he concluded.[79]

In his 1797 sermon to the New York Missionary Society John Mason found Infidelity an indication of the end of the old age and a harbinger of "Hope for the Heathen." [80] John Livingston, Dutch Reformed minister in New York, developed the concept of the everlasting gospel, which would make unprecedented progress among all nations during the millennium. His sermon to the New York Missionary Society in 1804 will be treated in a separate section below.

The annual report submitted by the Trustees of the Hampshire Missionary Society in 1805 reflected current theory on the spread of Christianity in the gospel age. They noted that the conversion of frontier whites would "allure" their Indian neighbors to embrace the Christian religion.[81] A Presbyterian minister addressing the society two years later surveyed the periods of Christian progress and looked forward to the even more remarkable period yet to come.[82] Jonathan Pomeroy noted the signs of the times, concluded that the latter days had arrived, and expected that Christian knowledge would soon be universal, that worship would be reformed, and that men would unitedly worship God in one language.[83]

---

78   Abiel Holmes, *A Discourse Delivered before the Society for Propagating the Gospel among the Indians and Others in North America* (Boston: 1808), 36.
79   *The Massachusetts Missionary Magazine*, III, 1805, 17.
80   Elsbree, 123.
81   *The Panoplist*, I, 1806, 275.
82   *Ibid.*, III, 1808, 414.
83   *Report of the Trustees of the Hampshire Missionary Society* with an appended sermon by Jonathan L. Pomeroy (Northampton: 1806).

As late as 1820 Sereno Edwards Dwight addressed a local Boston group, the Foreign Mission Society of Boston and the Vicinity, on "Thy kingdom come." He interpreted this petition of the Lord's Prayer as referring to the reign of peace, joy, and righteousness still to appear through human means.[84]

The 1795 circular letter of the Philadelphia Baptist Association expressed the hope that the glorious spread of the gospel over the entire earth was not far off.[85]

That the Christianization of the world would occur gradually, that the conversion of the Jews was near, and that the gathering of the Gentiles was an indisputable theme of prophecy were three truths elaborated by William Collins before the Baptist Missionary Society in 1806 in Boston.[86]

The Presbyterian General Assembly listened to Eliphalet Nott apply Ezekiel 37 to the Indians and make a startling suggestion regarding the duration of the millennium.[87] Edward Griffin had addressed her on Christ's kingdom in another missionary sermon the year before. He adopted the English interpretation of prophecy which regarded 1792 as the birth of a new era in world history.[88]

Occasionally millennial themes were applied to missions under pseudonyms. "Theophilus" wrote on the sixth vial, "Observator" read the arrival of the missionary era in the signs of the times, and "Silas" scrutinized the doctrine and sacramentalism of the Roman Catholic Church and recommended prayer for her downfall and for the spread of Reformed religion.

For a decade before the founding of the A.B.C.F.M., therefore, the millennial ideal pervaded evangelical Protestantism. Among Congregationalists, Baptists, Presbyterians, and the Reformed in New England and the middle Atlantic states it became an important concept and motive for evangelistic outreach. Only when the spirit and scope of this ideal are grasped can the deep commitment of the young Andover students who pledged themselves to foreign missions be understood and appreciated. These young men were totally dedicated to the realization of God's glorious kingdom in all nations. The spontaneous support which they won from church leaders, parents, and friends indicates that their ideal had become an unquestioned element of missionary theology for American evangelicals.

4. "Theophilus" and the sixth vial

The conviction that the times were pregnant with events soon to produce

---

84 Sereno Edwards Dwight, *Thy Kingdom Come* (Boston: 1820).

85 Charles L. Chaney, "An Oral Statement" (Mimeographed proposal for a doctoral thesis to be presented to the University of Chicago: 1967).

86 Elsbree, 125.

87 *vide infra*, 220-222.

88 Elsbree, 129-130.

missionary successes had accompanied each new wave of missionary effort in the Anglo-American religious tradition since the mid-1640's. The years after 1800 in America were no exception to this rule. Theologically this conviction was expressed in the concept of the sixth vial. It will be remembered that in the momentous awakenings of his day Edwards believed that two vials remained to be poured out against Rome, the sixth and the seventh.[89] Adjusting figures to compensate for intervening years, Hopkins followed his master in this regard. He calculated that by his day the sixth vial had been roughly two-thirds emptied.[90] But it was "Theophilus" who explained to his contemporaries the missionary implications of this concept in a clearer way than either Edwards or Hopkins had, though he may well have depended on both men for his basic understanding of the apocalyptic figure.

The identity of this contributor to *The Panoplist* remains a mystery. He may have been a Scot, for several years earlier a "Theophilus" had contributed to a Scottish journal a series of articles similar in content to those under consideration here.[91] On the other hand the manner in which he identifies himself with America in his warnings to her argues for his citizenship in that nation. In any case his exposition of the times unmistakably linked missions to his age for American readers.

The Infidelity and consequent immorality which will result from the pouring of the sixth vial are the marks of our day, began the writer. It is obvious, therefore, that Revelation 16 : 12-16 applies to our day. He interpreted Babylon, against whom all the vials were directed, as Rome; the Euphrates, the object of the sixth, as "any sources of riches and strength, which have rendered her formidable"; and the kings of the east, those who cross the dried Euphrates to destroy Babylon, as "her enemies in general."[92] That the Euphrates has been drying up for some time is apparent from such events as "the abolition of convents and of the inquisition" in Catholic countries, the disbanding of the Jesuits, the spread of commerce and knowledge, and especially the overthrow of Louis XVI.[93] According to the apostle John three impure spirits would attempt to unite the kings of the earth against God during the running of the sixth vial. They were to proceed from the mouths of the dragon, the beast, and the false prophet, whom "Theophilus" interpreted as the pagan Roman empire, the papal Roman establishment, and the Catholic hierarchy. The first two have long formed a coalition of temporal and spiritual power best typified by present-day Germany, he added. Germany must be revolutionized before

89   See "Die sechste Schale" in Kawerau's chapter on Edwards, 54f.
90   Hopkins, "The Author's Farewell...," 368.
91   They were entitled "On the Coming of Christ's Kingdom" and appeared in *The Missionary Magazine*, III, 1798, 295-298; and IV, 1799, 243-246.
92   *The Panoplist*, II, 1807, 10.
93   *Ibid.*, 11.

pure Christianity can spread there. Perhaps the new France will effect the necessary changes through present Franco-German hostilities, he added. Whether the battle of Armageddon as stirred up by the three spirits indicates either a literal or a figurative war, present European political and spiritual struggles correspond to the decisive battle. Especially the two most recent wars "have had a more remarkable effect... in subverting the papal power" than any before, indicated the writer.[94]

On the basis of his investigations as recorded in his first two articles, "Theophilus" was led "to expect great changes in the world." [95] The fall of the papacy would be quickly followed by the fall of the Turkish empire, as Scripture seems to indicate. John's warning of Christ's unexpected return should foster caution in America's political and religious conduct, therefore. To be prepared for his return she should avoid Europe's sins. Then she would also escape the current divine judgments on that continent. Yet even these judgments were "removing the obstructions, which have long lain in the way of a general reformation." [96] God was busy shaking the nations. The current missionary awakening in Europe would be the instrument for spreading that reformation which is soon to follow the shakings of the nations.

> As the object of the missionary societies is pious and benevolent, as their number is great, and as their rise in different parts was without concert, as they have met with liberal encouragement, and happy success; we cannot doubt but the hand of God is with them.[97]

"Theophilus" felt that God was definitely preparing for the great, worldwide reformation through current events, including the rise of the missionary movement. He showed American readers that they stood at that crossroads in history where missions was the logical and most promising course to follow.

5. John Livingston and the everlasting gospel

The contention of "Theophilus" that the age of missions had arrived was reinforced by John Livingston's sermon on Revelation 14 : 6-7. Delivered to the New York Missionary Society and later published with a number of appendixes elaborating crucial points in the sermon, the address offered a theological explanation of what God was doing in the young missionary movement and presented to the society "a NEW MOTIVE for strenuous

94 *Ibid.,* 71.
95 *Ibid.,* 115.
96 *Ibid.,* 117.
97 *Ibid.,* 118.

and persevering exertions in [their] missionary engagements."[98] The explanation and motive both rested on the concept of "the everlasting gospel."

The concept had been given a missionary connotation in earlier Anglo-American missionary sources[99] and was therefore not as new as the preacher supposed. Livingston's sermon was, however, the first systematic and extended explanation of the term which we have seen in connection with missions. It ascribed a missionary essence to the period between his day and the millennium and contended that the latter would be the product of faithful mission efforts during the next two hundred years.

The text from which the concept is derived describes the second of three visions seen by John and recorded in Revelation 14. The second depicts an angel flying through the heavens with an everlasting gospel, which he is to preach in a loud voice to men everywhere. Livingston explained the symbols in the text: heaven meant "the Church under New Testament dispensation"; angel, "the character and duty" of the messengers or preachers of the gospel "in the aggregate"; flying, speed; continuous flying, "uninterrupted and increasing progress"; and the angel's loud voice, "earnestness, zeal, and authority."[100] The meaning of the vision for the New York preacher becomes obvious.

> John foresaw a period when a zealous ministry would arise in the midst of the Churches, with a new and extraordinary spirit; a ministry singular in its views and exertions, and remarkable for its plans and success; a ministry which would arrest the public attention, and be a prelude to momentous changes in the Church and in the world.[101]

This corps of ministers will carry the gospel to the most remote corners of the world on a scale and with a zeal unprecedented in the history of the Christian church, he continued.

When will this period commence? Livingston felt that commentators had generally given confused answers to this question. Some applied the vision to the Reformation and others to the millennium. Arguing that the three visions in Revelation 14 must be understood in historical sequence and that the first applies to the Reformation and the third to the millennium, which he expected would begin about the year 2000, the preacher applies this vision to the intervening five hundred years. Yet nothing occurring prior to 1800 compares with it, he indicated. Therefore within the next two hundred years "the angel must begin to fly in the midst of the Churches, and preach

98 John H. Livingston, *A Sermon Delivered Before the New York Missionary Society* (New York: 1804), 7.
99 *vide supra*, 54 and 103.
100 Livingston, 9.
101 *Ibid.*

the everlasting Gospel to all nations, and tongues, and kindred, and people in the earth." [102] Several considerations convinced Livingston that the beginning of the angel's flight must be placed near his own day. Since the four events which must precede the millennium — the divine judgment of the nations which assisted Antichrist in oppressing God's servants, the conversion of the Jews, the fulness of the Gentiles, and the fall of Babylon — will be achieved gradually and through the use of human means, sufficient time must be allotted for their accomplishment, he explained to his readers. Relying on the same entry in the 1793 volume of the *Evangelical Magazine* which had impressed L.M.S. leaders,[103] he said that "the righteous Jehovah has taken vengence" on France in the revolution for the countless number of saints martyred in that country.[104] Furthermore, extensive proclamation of the gospel, with which the missionary awakening accords, will precede the latter three events. Livingston asked, therefore, "may we not exclaim, Behold the angel! his flight is begun!" [105] He was convinced that it had. Several pages later he answered his question. "This time, we believe is arrived. The present exertions in the Churches, we are persuaded, are the first stirrings, the gradual beginnings for accomplishing" the universal proclamation of the gospel.[106]

Livingston was not mistaken in finding in his explanation a strong motive for "strenuous exertions to propagate the Gospel." [107] As such his explanation functioned as numerous other sermons on many other eschatological passages. And when he indicated that all other missionary motives derived "additional force and energy from this word of prophecy," [108] he formulated a truth which could have been asserted about any one of those texts. It meant, as he stated, that the missionary societies held a position of pre-eminence among Christian organizations. To facilitate the accomplishment of their objective as defined in his text he recommended the establishment of a school for training missionaries similar to those existing in Rome, Gosport, and Rotterdam.

6. *Eliphalet Nott and a new ratio*

If "Theophilus" showed that the time had arrived for missionary activity, and if Livingston demonstrated that a two-hundred-year era of missions would be a prelude to the millennium, Eliphalet Nott, minister in Albany,

102 *Ibid.,* 17.
103 *vide supra,* 183.
104 Livingston, 67.
105 *Ibid.,* 22.
106 *Ibid.,* 31-32.
107 *Ibid.,* 32.
108 *Ibid.,* 34.

New York, and successor of Jonathan Edwards, Jr., as President of Union College, spoke on the character and length of that era as an incentive for mission work.

Although his text was the clause "always abounding in the work of the Lord" (I Corinthians 15 : 58), Nott's point of departure was the dry bones passage of Ezekiel 37. He indicated that the latter text refers not only to Israel's restoration from Babylon in the fifth century before Christ, but to the "moral resurrection" which occurs when men in any age are spiritually reborn under the proclamation of the gospel.[109] Looking at "yonder wilderness," Nott admitted that to him it was "a valley of dry bones."[110] He expressed confidence in the Scriptural promises that even the Indian dry bones would live in the millennium. His description of the new Indian shares the spirit of Hopkins' description of the new age.

> Then shall the bow of war be unbent, and the arrow of death loosed from its string. Then shall the huntsman, attracted by the sound of salvation, relinquish the pleasures of the chase, and the hoary warrior, touched by sovereign grace, shall lose his wonted cruelty; and turning from conquest with the benignity of heaven on his countenance, consecrate to charity the spoils he had taken, and, bowing, lay his tomahawk and scalping-knife as a trophy at the foot of Jesus.[111]

Nott moved from a discussion of the character to a treatment of the length of the new age. Here he was more unconventional. Although he conceded that Christians were probably generally "united in the opinion" of a thousand-year reign of Christ, Nott suggested that the Messiah would reign for a millennium of prophetic years, that is, for 360,000 years.[112] He found it incredible and inconsistent with Genesis 3 : 15 that Satan should reign on earth for six thousand years and Christ for only one thousand. Nott cited many other prophecies indicating the predominance of Christ's reign, "in comparison with which, all preceding reigns will appear transitory and unimportant."[113] It hardly appears that in another thousand years the earth will have " 'grown old as doth a garment' " and be discarded as unfit for use, he added.[114] On the contrary, promises indicate that the righteous will inherit the earth and dwell on it forever.

Nott's new ratio of the relative lengths of Satan's and Christ's reigns of necessity brought a re-evaluation of the ratio of the saved to the lost. This question had engaged New England theologians from the beginning

---

109 Eliphalet Nott, *A Sermon Preached Before the General Assembly of the Presbyterian Church in the United States of America* (Philadelphia: 1806), 6.
110 *Ibid.,* 8.
111 *Ibid.,* 8-9.
112 *Ibid.,* 11.
113 *Ibid.,* 16.
114 *Ibid.,* 18.

of the eighteenth century. The liberals among them initially maintained that a loving God could not and did not condemn to hell innocent souls dying in infancy. Subsequent discussions on this issue became one of the roots of American universalism. Even Bellamy and Hopkins were intrigued by the question and concluded, on the basis of the population explosion expected during the millennium and on the basis of the predominance of believers over unbelievers during that era, "that many more will be saved, than lost, perhaps some thousands to one." [115] Nott's position on the issue was incorporated into his sermon under consideration here. Although the percentage of those converted and saved during the initial six thousand years of human history is small, in the millennium apostacy and its consequences will be comparatively insignificant, he maintained. There will be "superabounding happiness of myriads of myriads without number, and without end...." [116] He believed that that day was at hand and urged his hearers to "hasten its approach" through charity, prayer, and missions.[117]

Years earlier Thomas Prince had suggested a 360,000-year millennium.[118] His view had apparently met with little favor, and Nott also acknowledged, as we have already noted, that his position was exceptional. It must be seen as part of a resurgence of interest in the millennium itself, which in evangelical circles was usually developed as an incentive for missions. As such Nott's sermon was reviewed in *The Panoplist*, where the reviewer conceded that "every friend to the best interests of men would rejoice at finding this opinion supported by Scripture." [119] Whether it is or not, he left to the readers' discretion. Nevertheless he recommended the sermon highly, and we may be sure that its novel suggestion caused debate and excitement regarding the potential of missions.

7. A structure for hope — the A.B.C.F.M.

It was among New England students in the Edwardean milieu that the initial impulses toward the founding of the A.B.C.F.M. appeared. These young men were products of a theological tradition which saw the significant issues and events of the day from a millennial perspective. Infidelity at home and political events in Europe were interpreted as signs of the approaching end of the age. In a spirit of alarm for the church and the country, preachers called for repentance, reform, and revival as guarantees of divine blessing and requisites for the new age. Many of the students

---

115 Hopkins, *The System of Doctrines*, II, 166, where he refers to Bellamy's sermon on the millennium. Also see I, 364-365.
116 Nott, 19.
117 *Ibid.*, 34.
118 *vide supra*, 140.
119 *The Panoplist*, II, 1807, 227.

dated their conversions from one or another of the revivals.[120] Samuel Mills, Jr., was converted by his father's preaching in 1798 and came to share his father's admiration for Hopkins' theology and African mission scheme.[121] Like many other Yale students Jeremiah Evarts was converted during the 1801-1802 revival at Yale College and became an ardent Edwardean.[122] Yale's president, Timothy Dwight, also promoted revival and preached on millennial themes to students on campuses outside New Haven. He addressed the Andover Theological Seminary community at the opening of that school, when he explained how the conversion of the Jews and their restoration to Palestine was contingent on the conversion of the Gentiles.[123] In summary it can be said that the revivals occurring in the eastern part of the country during this period centered on the Congregational and Presbyterian campuses where Edwardean ideas dominated.[124]

Coming from these campuses, students whose devotion to missions had been quickened in part by the pervasive vision of the new age enrolled at Andover. At the seminary Mills and several other alumni from Williams College continued their secret society for prayer and the discussion of missions. Out of this coterie the first steps toward the formation of an American foreign missionary society were taken.[125] It was particularly Mills, a leader in the group, who argued for indigenous American support for American missionaries. The students aroused the interest and support of Professor Moses Stuart, who himself had been trained under Dwight. Prior to the annual meeting of the General Association of Massachusetts in 1810 Stuart invited Evarts, Samuel Worcester, and Samuel Spring to his home to consider a document which the students desired to submit to the association. All three men were mission enthusiasts. Since his days at Yale lawyer Evarts had become editor of *The Panoplist and Missionary Magazine*. Spring and Worcester were prominent Congregational clergymen. Spring had studied under Witherspoon, Hopkins, Bellamy, and West,[126] and Worcester has been described as "an inflexible Hopkinsian Calvinist."[127] These leaders endorsed the students' expression of their commitment to missions and their request for advice on how to implement their convictions. They encouraged the young men to present it to the association. Signed by

120 Löwe, 114-115.
121 Elsbree, 36 and 110.
122 *Ibid.,* 36.
123 *Ibid.,* 132, n. 24.
124 "...das Second Awakening ist eine akademische Bewegung gewesen; Schüler, Studenten, Pfarrer und Theologieprofessoren waren revivalistisch gesinnt, und durch sie verbreitete sich das Revival von den theologischen Bildungszentren aus über das ganze Land." Kawerau, 90.
125 Elsbree, 110-114; Beaver, *Pioneers in Mission,* 250-253; Kawerau, 119-125.
126 *D.A.B.,* XVII, 481.
127 *Ibid.,* XX, 529.

Mills, Samuel Newell, Adoniram Judson, and Samuel Nott, nephew of Eliphalet, it was presented to the association, discussed, and assigned to a committee of three which included both Spring and Worcester. The committee subsequently proposed the plan for the A.B.C.F.M., which the association adopted. Spring, Worcester, and Dwight were all appointed to the original, nine-member board of directors. Worcester became the board's first corresponding secretary, a position in which he was succeeded by Evarts. Early in 1812 the new society's first missionaries sailed for India. Among them were Judson, Newell, and the younger Nott.

That the society was founded as a structure for realizing the millennial hopes of Edwardean leaders and students is evident from their personal writings and from the board's official communications. These sources afford us a general impression of the character and scope of millennial hope in A.B.C.F.M. circles.

Preaching on Daniel 2 : 44, Worcester counseled the local missionary society of Salem to assist in the destined extension of Christ's kingdom over the entire world.[128] The same year as the society was founded Jedidiah Morse, one of her commissioners and founder of *The Panoplist*, propagated the Hopkinsian position on the waning of the eastern and western Antichrists by 1866. His address to the S.P.G.N.A. continued by postulating the subsequent return of the Jews to Palestine, conversion of the Gentiles, and arrival of the millennium.[129] In a sermon to the local Boston missionary society he explained the young missionary movement as the inception of the "long desired and glorious era" assured by prophecy.[130] As early as 1802 Spring examined the relationship of the conversion of the Jews and of the Gentiles in a sermon to the Massachusetts Missionary Society. Like Dwight but in opposition to Livingston, he concluded that the Gentile conversions would be prior.[131] Newell and Gordon Hall, two of America's first five overseas missionaries, were the authors of a book pointing to the imminence of the millennium and indicating a need for thirty thousand missionaries to realize that age in the heathen nations.[132] In *The Panoplist* Morse not only gave extensive coverage to Joseph Frey's work among London's Jews,[133] but encouraged rumors of the old hypothesis of the Indians' Jewish origin. This occurred in a series of letters addressed to Morse by missionary Gideon Blackburn, whose vivid account of the Cherokees'

---

128   Samuel Worcester, *The Kingdom of the Messiah* (Salem: 1813).
129   Elsbree, 129.
130   Jedidiah Morse, *The Gospel Harvest* (Boston: 1815), 12. Morse drew evidence from Dan. 2 : 34-44; Dan. 12; Ps. 22 : 27-28; Ps. 72 : 8-11, 17; Isa. 2 : 2; Lev. 26 : 44-45; and Rom. 11 : 25-27.
131   Elsbree, 132.
132   Löwe, 6.
133   Elsbree, 133. *The Connecticut Evangelical Magazine* also publicized Frey's work.

"Eagle-tail dance" suggested that Indian ceremonies were "evidently Jewish." [134]

The central place of millennial expectations in the activities and thought of the A.B.C.F.M. appears in her earliest records. On February 6, 1812, Leonard Woods, Professor of Theology at Andover, delivered the sermon at the ordination of the board's first five missionaries. That all nations and people would praise and fear God and that he would bless them and make his salvation known among them was the thrust of Woods' text, Psalm 67. The true Christian has "enlarged views," "benevolent desires," and "pleasing anticipations" like the Psalmist; his longing for "the diffusion of Christian knowledge and happiness" is "insatiable and unbounded." [135] As long as any nation has not acknowledged Christ, the Christian must pursue "his unalterable object" of the universal knowledge of Christ.[136] That the "object" of missions was for Woods nothing less than the realization of the millennium is apparent from the last of the six motives which he discusses. Divine prophecy guarantees an era of millennial glory for the church, he reminded his hearers.[137] "All the passing events of the civil and religious world, in connection with prophecy, indicate the approach of better days," he said, assessing the events of his day.[138] God's deepest concern in history is for the growth of "the kingdom of grace," which is centered in the church. Human kingdoms and empires will be shaken and fall, but this kingdom will grow and increase. In his closing comments directed to the young missionaries, the Andover professor asked them to consider "how it will be in Asia a century or two hence." [139] Done in the strength of Christ, their work would become the parabolic leaven and grain of mustard seed of the kingdom. With these reflections on the great significance of their work for the coming of God's kingdom, these recent graduates began a new venture in the history of American Christianity. But like Worcester, who gave them the right hand of fellowship at the service, they were certain with the certainty of faith in God's unbreakable

134 *The Panoplist*, III, 1808, 568. Only after 1810, however, was this theme revived on a significant scale. See Elias Boudinot, *A Star in the West* (1816); Elias Smith, *View of the Hebrews: or the Ten Tribes of Israel in America* (1825); Israel Worsley, *A View of the American Indians Showing them to be the descendants of the Ten Tribes of Israel* (1828); B. A. Simon, *The Hope of Israel* (1828) and *The Ten Tribes of Israel Historically Identified with the Aborigines of the Western Hemisphere* (1836).

135 Beaver, *Pioneers in Mission*, 257-258.

136 *Ibid.,* 258.

137 *Ibid.,* 262-266. The first five motives were concern for the souls of unbelievers, Christ's atonement, his command to preach to all men, the example of previous missionaries, and the suitability of Christianity to be the universal religion.

138 *Ibid.,* 266.

139 *Ibid.,* 267.

promises that they were " 'but the precursors of many' " who would imitate them " 'in this arduous, glorious exercise.' " [140]

A report drafted by the board in the first year of her life explained the current shakings of the nations and the "unprecedented exertions" for propagating Christian knowledge and converting the nations as indications that the prophesied millennium was approaching.[141] In subsequent years Morse, Worcester, and Evarts annually presented "An Address to the Christian Public . . ." on behalf of the A.B.C.F.M. In 1811 they interpreted political events, the weakening of the eastern and western Antichrists, and the missionary movement itself as signs that the world was ripe for efforts to realize the kingdom.

> Now is the time for the followers of Christ to come forward boldly, and engage earnestly in the great work of enlightening and reforming mankind. Never was the glory of the Christian religion more clearly discernible, never was the futility of all other schemes more manifest; never were the encouragements to benevolent exertion greater, than at the present day.[142]

By virtue of her religious tradition and her "social and civil enjoyments" New England is in a uniquely favorable position to accept missionary responsibility, the trio concluded. In their address the following year they reiterated the same major themes but also acknowledged that the task was too large for any one country to undertake alone. "All the power and influence of the whole Christian world must be put in requisition during the course of those beneficent labors, which will precede the millennium." [143]

The conviction that Christ's reign would be universal in the millennium continued to impel the A.B.C.F.M. for many years.[144] As late as 1841 Rufus Anderson, undoubtedly the board's most illustrious personality and America's greatest missionary leader during the nineteenth century, consulted the signs of the times and projected a great, mission-enhancing effusion of the Spirit in the latter days.[145] The vision was shared by younger missionary societies and boards.[146]

It is indisputable, therefore, that Edwardean millennialism gave the American missionary movement a global vision and directed her leaders

140 *Ibid.,* 253.

141 *The Panoplist and Missionary Magazine,* VI, 1810-1811, 183.

142 *Ibid.,* VII, 1811-1812, 244.

143 *Ibid.,* VIII, 1812-1813, 251.

144 See the annual sermon by Alexander Proudfit *The Universal Extension of Messiah's Kingdom* (Boston: 1822).

145 Rufus Anderson, *The Promised Advent of the Spirit* (Boston: 1841).

146 Keller also interprets Bible, tract, education, and various moral and social reform societies in terms of the Second Great Awakening, which stimulated millennial ideas. See Chapter V, "Orthodoxy Forges New Weapons," and Chapter VI, "Design for Reform."

to the prophecies of the kingdom for the faith and strength for implementing their newly realized task.

8. *Summary*

The foreign missionary movement in America began with the formation of the A.B.C.F.M. in 1810. It was the result of a number of forces. In post-Revolutionary War America evangelicals reacted to religious indifference by issuing calls to reform and revival. The ensuing revivals stimulated missionary overtures to white settlers pushing into the wilderness and to Negroes and Indians. For this work new societies were formed, and they must be regarded as precursors to the organizations which engaged in overseas missions. Revivals also stimulated interest in eschatology, which was developed along Edwardean lines and with close attention to British millennial discussions.

In 1793 Samuel Hopkins, who had pressed missionary causes for decades, gave systematic development to the Edwardean doctrine of the millennium. He embellished the tradition with a detailed description of the new age. His position was regarded as authoritative, and when Edwardean eschatology was popularized in ensuing revivals he and other New Divinity leaders demonstrated the missionary implications of their millennial hopes.

Particularly the British missionary awakening with its strong emphasis on millennial motifs stimulated American desires to participate in the new movement. The local societies for frontier missions and their monthly magazines became the channels through which millennial motives to bring all nations to the knowledge of Christ pervaded the American scene. In the discussions of eschatology in these sources many time-proven themes in Anglo-American millennialism were reviewed. The need for missions was also deduced from such novel concepts as the pouring of the sixth vial, the flight of the angel bearing the everlasting gospel, and a millennium extending for 360,000 years and embracing uncountable myriads of saints.

At Andover Theological Seminary students and religious leaders strongly influenced by Edwardean eschatology contributed to the formation of the A.B.C.F.M. The society became a structure for realizing the millennial hopes of evangelical Americans, even though it was openly acknowledged that the new era lay some two hundred years off.

Epilogue

The Biblical message is such that it compels the serious Christian to formulate an opinion regarding the future. Going one step further, we can say that Scripture requires the true believer to acknowledge — both in his heart and by his actions — the ultimate triumph of his Lord and King over all opposing forces. Various understandings of the Biblical data on this point underlie the often widely divergent doctrines of the last things which have at one time or another won currency in the Christian church. Throughout the period which we have covered, millennial hopes oscillated between a highly complex chiliasm or premillennialism with adventist tendencies and a low-keyed postmillennialism with its belief in the gradual improvement of human conditions through Christian benevolent and educational programs. The former tendency was present in the thought of a number of theologians. The latter tendency can be found in the S.P.C.K., the S.P.G., and the S.S.P.C.K. circles. Canon Max Warren has correctly indicated that of the traditional Christian perspectives on the end of time neither the adventist nor the ethical or humanitarian position is completely satisfactory.[1] The adventist viewpoint tends toward world flight and world renunciation. It consigns the present world order to the jurisdiction of the Evil One and conceives of salvation and hence of the mission's predominant concern as the saving of souls from the present evil order. This resignation is compatible neither with Scripture's view of the whole man, both in his total need and in his total deliverance, nor with the profession of Christ's Lordship over all of history. On the other hand, the ethical eschatology tends toward a constriction of the kingdom to the purely secular. It operates with a naive optimism regarding the course of history and is blind to the radical nature of sin with its effects on the human mind and will. It conceives of the church's mission largely in terms of the application of human skills to social and cultural problems. The humanitarian definition of the church's mission does injustice to the clear, central, Biblical emphasis on the purification of thought and motive through a total conversion.

It is noteworthy that in the Anglo-American missionary tradition of the seventeenth and eighteenth centuries millennial expectations generally fell

---

1   Max Warren, *The Truth of Vision* (London: 1948), 38f.

somewhere between the adventist and the ethical poles. As such they partook of the strengths and avoided many of the weaknesses of these extremes. They asserted the worth of the world as created and as in the process of being redeemed by God. Both Jews and Gentiles were being called and would eventually become one people of God. Christ's triumph would be made visible among all nations. It would occur in history, before the end of time. Yet this would not be achieved without bitter struggle and unflagging effort, for the Antichristian forces in all their craft and power would first have to be abolished. Christ's victory would come through the spread of knowledge. This knowledge was generally defined not in the categories of the Enlightenment but as a personal knowledge of the living God, from whence sprang full knowledge of self and the world. Through this full-orbed knowledge God would effect a new and glorious age. In general, therefore, these expectations were a healthy balance between other-worldly and secularized hopes, between capitulation to and underestimation of the forces of evil, between the eternal and the temporal dimensions of salvation. It was these balanced views which compelled men to confidently but realistically conduct missionary activity.

After 1810 millennial expectations continued to afford Christian missions vision and inspiration. Gradually eschatological discussions became more polarized, however. British church leaders such as Henry Drummond and Edward Irving popularized an extreme form of premillennialism, which in some cases was wedded to dispensationalism. In America William Miller calculated that Christ would visibly return in 1843, and from Miller's following the adventist movement developed. By 1850, therefore, premillennialism had become widespread. Meanwhile the Christian Socialist movement in England and later the Social Gospel movement in America were built on expectations which were more historical and which were compatible with nineteenth-century optimism regarding man's future.

Although the eschatology which had strengthened the rise of Anglo-American missions became increasingly polarized during the nineteenth century, seen in retrospect, the past one hundred seventy-five years in world missions can be interpreted as an age when at least some of the hopes of the early pioneers in missions have been implemented. Christian knowledge has been propagated as succeeding generations of missionaries preached the gospel, established schools, taught the masses to read, translated the Scriptures, and founded centers for producing and distributing Christian literature. As an institution found on all six continents, seriously searching for inner unity, and attempting to be of benevolent service to her fellow men, the Christian church may be said to have received a measure of that glory which the founders of the missionary societies regarded as her destiny. The ministry of medicine has brought health and extended lives. In the third world progress has been made in the political, economic, educational, industrial, and technological fields. The potential for taking still further strides in these areas is greater than ever before. Nations are inclined to resort to the council table rather than to the battle field to settle their differences. The leaders of younger churches are making significant contributions to discussions in Christian theology. Jews have returned to Palestine. Nations have heard the good news of salvation in Christ. Although many of these facts should also be seen from a less optimistic perspective, it can perhaps be suggested that, were they alive today, the men considered in our study might be startled by the seeming accuracy of a number of their prognostications.

To acknowledge that the vision of these early leaders has to some degree been fulfilled is not to recommend their eschatology, however. That can only be done on the basis of answers to the complex hermeneutical, exegetical, and doctrinal questions involved — questions which lie beyond the scope of this study. Nor is this acknowledgment designed to camouflage the serious blunders and lapses in the history of missions. They are all too prominent to be ignored or to be excused. To indicate that which has been achieved through missions, moreover, is certainly not to imply that the church has completed her mandate or fulfilled her obligations in history. If anything her responsibilities today are more awesome and the problems she faces more imposing than they were two hundred years ago. The spirits and powers and principalities that oppose her are wilier and more concerted. Each fruition of Christian hope mentioned in the preceding paragraph must be counterbalanced with evidence proving that her achievements have only been partial and that they do not partake of the fulness of the kingdom. And furthermore, meeting the modern issues with the new potentials at her disposal requires that the church reappraise the structure of her mission.

But to recognize the expectations of the early leaders in Anglo-American missions and to assess the degree to which those hopes have been realized is to receive inspiration for the new tasks and the new issues of today. That those hopes have in some measure been realized is a tribute to the faith of the generations of missionaries whose sacrifice proves that Christian hope is not ephemeral. Furthermore, their realization is cause for thanksgiving and rejoicing before the Lord who establishes and quickens faith, who gives strength, and who works through the hope of his followers. Today no less than at earlier periods in her mission the church must live in hope. She can do no better than the early Anglo-American missionary leaders. She must return to the Christ of the Scriptures for her vision of mankind and of the rest of creation made new in him. She must draw her hope and her inspiration from those divine prophecies of the kingdom of God in Christ. She must pattern her program after divine ideals. Her mission will founder on anything less. But in Christ she can and she will triumph.

B.M.S.	Baptist Missionary Society
C.M.S.	Church Missionary Society
C.R.	*Corpus Reformatorum*
D.A.B.	*Dictionary of American Biography.* Dumus Malone (ed.). 22 vols. London and New York: 1928–1958.
D.N.B.	*Dictionary of National Biography.* Leslie Stephen and Sidney Lee (eds.). 63 vols. London: 1885–1900.
I.R.M.	*International Review of Missions*
L.M.S.	London Missionary Society
O.D.C.C.	*The Oxford Dictionary of the Christian Church.* F. L. Cross (ed.). London: 1958.
P.F.F.	*The Prophetic Faith of Our Fathers.* Leroy Edwin Froom. 4 vols. Washington: 1946–1954.
R.G.G.	*Die Religion in Geschichte und Gegenwart.* H. F. von Campenhausen *et al.* (eds.). 7 vols. 3rd revised edition. Tübingen: 1957–1965.
S.P.C.K.	Society for Promoting Christian Knowledge
S.P.G.	Society for the Propagation of the Gospel in Foreign Parts
S.P.G. (a.s.)	*A Sermon Preached before the Incorporated Society for the Propagation of the Gospel in Foreign Parts*
S.P.G.N.A.	Society for Propagating the Gospel among the Indians and Others in North America
S.S.P.C.K.	Society in Scotland for Propagating Christian Knowledge
V.R.G.	*Die Verkündigung des Reiches Gottes in der Kirche Jesu Christi.* Ernst Staehelin. 7 vols. Basel: 1951–1964.

Bibliography

The bibliography includes sources actually used in the writing of this dissertation, not necessarily all the works mentioned in the notes. As a general, though not an absolute, rule those works written during the time covered by the dissertation itself are designated "Primary Sources" and those written later, "Secondary Sources."

A. *Primary Sources*

Adres van het Zendings Genootschap te London, aan de Godsdienstige Ingezetenen der Vereenigde Nederlanden. [n.p.]: 1797.

Alsted, Johann Heinrich. *The Beloved City or, The Saints Reign on Earth a Thousand Yeares.* London: 1643.

Anderson, Rufus. *The Promised Advent of the Spirit.* Boston: 1841.

Archer, Henry. *The Personall Reign of Christ upon Earth.* London: 1642.

Baillie, Robert. *The Disswasive from the Errors of the Time, Vindicated from the Exceptions of Mr. Cotton and Mr. Tombes.* London: 1655.

Balfour, Robert. *Sermons on Interesting Subjects.* Glasgow: 1819.

Bellamy, Joseph. *Sermons Upon the following Subjects.* Boston: 1758.

Beverley, Thomas. *A Fresh Memorial of the Kingdom of Christ.* London: 1693.

——. *The Prophetical History of the Reformation.* London: 1689.

——. *A Sermon Upon Revel. 11.11.* London: 1692.

Bicheno, James. *The Probable Progress and Issue of the Commotions Which Have Agitated Europe Since the French Revolution.* London: 1797.

——. *The Restoration of the Jews, the Crisis of all Nations.* London: 1800.

——. *The Signs of the Times.* London: [1793].

Bogue, David and James Bennett. *History of Dissenters from the Revolution in 1688, to the Year 1808.* 4 vols. London: 1808-1812.

Bridge, William. *The Works.* 5 vols. London: 1845.

Brightman, Thomas. *The Workes of that Famous, Reverend, and Learned Divine, Mr. Tho. Brightman.* London: 1644.

Buchanan, Claudius. *Christian Researches in Asia.* Boston: 1811.

——. *The Works of the Rev. Claudius Buchanan, LL.D.* New York: 1812.

Calvinus, Ioannes. *Institutio Christianae Religionis.* W. Baum, E. Cunitz, and E. Reuss (eds.). 2 vols. (*Corpus Reformatorum,* XXIX and XXX). Brunswick: 1863 and 1864.

Carey, William. *An Enquiry into the Obligations of Christians to Use Means for the Conversion of the Heathens.* Leicester: 1792.

[Chauncy, Charles]. *The Mystery hid from Ages and Generations*. London: 1784.

——. *The Out-Pouring of the Holy Ghost*. Boston: 1742.

The Christian Observer. 9 vols. London: 1802-1810.

Coleman, Benjamin. *Twenty Sacramental Discourses*. London: 1728.

Cotton, John. *A Brief Exposition of the whole Book of Canticles, or, Song of Solomon*. London: 1642.

——. *The Churches Resurrection*. London: 1642.

——. *An Exposition upon the Thirteenth Chapter of the Revelation*. London: 1655.

——. *God's Promise to His Plantation*. London: 1630.

——. *The Powring Out of the Seven Vials*. London: 1642.

——. *The Way of Congregational Churches Cleared*. London: 1647/1648.

Cotton, John, Jr. Letter to Increase Mather dated September 10, 1688. (*Collections of the Massachusetts Historical Society*, Series IV, vol. VIII.) Boston: 1868.

Danforth, Samuel. "An Exhortation to All." *The Ministry of Taunton*. Samuel Hopkins Emery (ed.). 2 vols. Cleveland: 1853.

The Day-Breaking if not The Sun-Rising of the Gospell with the Indians in New England. London: 1647.

Donne, John. *The Works of John Donne, D.D.* Henry Alford (ed.). 6 vols. London: 1839.

Douglas, N[eil]. *Journal of a Mission*. Edinburgh: 1799.

——. *Messiah's Glorious Rest in the Latter Days*. Dundee: 1797.

Dury, John. *Israels Call to March out of Babylon unto Jerusalem*. London: 1646.

Dwight, Sereno Edwards. *Thy Kingdom Come*. Boston: 1820.

Dwight, Timothy. *The Nature and Danger of Infidel Philosophy*. Bristol: 1799.

——. *Sermons*. 2 vols. Edinburgh: 1828.

Edwards, Jonathan. *Miscellaneous Observations on Important Theological Subjects*. John Erskine (ed.). Edinburgh: 1793.

——. *The Works of Jonathan Edwards*. 8 vols. London: 1817.

Eliot, John. *A Brief Narrative of the Progress of the Gospel amongst the Indians in New-England, in the Year 1670*. London: 1671.

——. *The Christian Commonwealth*. London: 1659.

——. *A further Accompt of the Progresse of the Gospel amongst the Indians in New-England*. London: 1659.

——. *A further Account of the progress of the Gospel Amongst the Indians in New England*. London: 1660.

——. *A Late and Further Manifestation of the Progress of the Gospel amongst the Indians in New-England*. London: 1655.

Eliot, John and Thomas Mayhew. *Tears of Repentance. Or, A further Narrative of the Progress of the Gospel amongst the Indians in New England*. London: 1653.

Evans, Arise. *Light for the Jews*. London: 1664.

[Finch, Henry]. *The Worlds Restauration*. William Gouge (ed.). London: 1621.

Fleming, Robert, Sr. *The Fulfilling of the Scripture.* 5th ed. London: 1726.

Fleming, Robert, [Jr.]. *Apocalyptical Key.* London: 1809.

——. *A Discourse on the Rise and Fall of Papacy.* Edinburgh: 1809.

——. *A New Account of the Rise and Fall of the Papacy* in *Discourses on Several Subjects.* London: 1701.

Fuller, Andrew. *Miscellaneous Pieces on Various Religious Subjects.* Collected and arranged with notes by J. W. Morris. London: 1826.

Gill, John. *An Exposition of the Revelation of S. John the Divine.* London: 1776.

——. *The Glory of the Church in the Latter Day.* London: 1753.

Gillies, John. *An Essay on the Prophecies Relating to the Messiah.* Edinburgh: 1773.

——. *A Supplement to Two Volumes (Published in 1754) of Historical Collections.* John Erskine (ed.). Edinburgh: 1796.

Goodwin, Thomas. *An Exposition of the Revelation. The Works of Thomas Goodwin, D.D.* vol. 3. Edinburgh: 1861.

——. *The French Revolution Foreseen, in 1639.* London: [n.d.].

——. *A Sermon of the Fifth Monarchy.* London: 1654.

——. *The World to Come.* London: 1655.

Gookin, Daniel. *Historical Collections of the Indians in New England.* James Freeman (ed.). (*Collections of the Massachusetts Historical Society,* Series I, vol. I.) Boston: 1792.

[Gouge, William (ed.)]. *An Exposition of the Song of Solomon: called Canticles.* London: 1615.

——. *The Progresse of Divine Providence.* London: 1645.

Hayne, T. *Christ's Kingdome on Earth, Opened according to the Scriptures.* London: 1645.

Holmes, Abiel. *A Discourse Delivered before the Society for Propagating the Gospel among the Indians and Others in North America.* Boston: 1808.

Hopkins, Samuel [of Springfield]. *Historical Memoirs Relating to the Housatunnuk Indians.* Boston: 1753.

Hopkins, Samuel. *The System of Doctrines.* 2 vols. Boston: 1793.

——. *Twenty-one Sermons.* Salem: 1803.

——. *The Works of Samuel Hopkins, D.D. With a Memoir of his Life and Character.* Edwards A. Park (ed.). 3 vols. Boston: 1852.

Horne, Melville. *Letters on Missions.* Bristol: 1794.

Hunter, Henry. *The Rise, Fall, and Future Restoration of the Jews.* London: 1806.

——. *Sermons.* 2 vols. London: 1795.

Imrie, David. *A Strange and Wonderful Prophecy.* [n.p.]: 1756.

Jewel, John. *The Works of John Jewel.* 4 vols. Cambridge: 1845-1850.

Johnson, Edward. *The Wonderworking Providence of Sions Saviour.* London: 1654.

Knollys, Hanserd. *An Exposition Of the whole Book of the Revelation.* London: 1689.

——. *The World that Now is; and the World that is to Come.* London: 1681.

Koelman, Jacobus. *Sleutel ter opening van de donkerste Kapittelen in de Openbaaringe gedaan aan Johannis.* 2nd ed. Amsterdam: [1768].

l'Estrange, Hamon. *Americans no Iewes.* London: 1651/1652.

Livingston, John H. *A Sermon Delivered Before the New York Missionary Society.* New York: 1804.

London Missionary Society — annual sermons

    1. Bogue, David. "Address to Professors of the Gospel." *Sermons Preached in London, at the Formation of the Missionary Society.* London: 1795.

    2. Burder, George. "An Address to the serious and zealous Professors of the Gospel." *Sermons Preached in London, at the Formation of the Missionary Society.* London: 1795.

    3. Bogue, David. "Objections Against a Mission to the Heathen." *Sermons Preached in London, at the Formation of the Missionary Society.* London: 1795.

    4. Lambert, George. "The Greatest of Blessings, both in its Nature and Effects." *Four Sermons.* London: 1796.

    5. Findlay, John. "The Universal Diffusion of Divine Knowledge; with Its Happy Effects." *Four Sermons.* London: 1799.

    6. Mends, Herbert. "Dark Providences no just Reason of Discouragement in Missionary Exertions." *Four Sermons.* London: 1801.

    7. Bottomley, Samuel. "Advantages of Patience." *Four Sermons.* London: 1803.

The Massachusetts Missionary Magazine. 5 vols. Boston: 1803-1807.

Mather, Cotton. *Essays to do Good.* London: 1807.

——. *India Christiana.* Boston: 1721.

——. *Magnalia Christi Americana.* 2 vols. Hartford: 1855.

——. *The Negro Christianized.* Boston: 1806.

——. *Theopolis Americana.* Boston: 1710.

Mather, Increase. *The Mystery of Israel's Salvation.* London: 1669.

Mather, Increase *et al.* A letter to Governor Phips, October 2, 1693. (*Collections of the Massachusetts Historical Society,* Series III, vol. I.) Boston: 1825.

Mather, Increase, Cotton Mather, and Nehemiah Walter. *A Letter about the Present State of Christianity among the Christianized Indians of New England.* Boston: 1705.

Mather, Samuel. *The Life of the Very Reverend and Learned Cotton Mather, D.D. & F.R.S.* Boston: 1729.

Mede, Joseph. *Works.* 3rd ed. London: 1672.

Millar, Robert. *The History of the Propagation of Christianity.* 2 vols. 3rd ed. London: 1731.

The Missionary Magazine. Edinburgh: 1796f.

Morse, Jedidiah. *The Gospel Harvest.* Boston: 1815.

——. *Signs of the Times.* Charlestown: 1810.

New Englands first fruits. London: 1642/1643.

Nott, Eliphalet. *A Sermon Preached Before the General Assembly of the Presbyterian Church in the United States of America.* Philadelphia: 1806.

Owen, John. "The Shaking and Translating of Heaven and Earth." *The Works of John Owen, D.D.* vol. 3. Edinburgh: 1862.

The Panoplist. 3 vols. Boston: 1806-1808.

The Panoplist and Missionary Magazine United. Boston: 1808f.

Parr, Elnathan. *The Works of Elnathan Parr.* 3rd ed. London: 1633.

Periodical Accounts Relative to the Baptist Missionary Society. 6 vols. Clipstone: 1800-1817.

Prince, Thomas. *A Sermon upon the Death of the Honourable Samuel Sewall, Esq.* Boston: 1730.

———. *Six Sermons.* John Erskine (ed.). Edinburgh: 1785.

Proceedings of the Church Missionary Society. 5 vols. London: 1801-1805.

Proudfit, Alexander. *The Universal Extension of Messiah's Kingdom.* Boston: 1822.

Robe, James. *A Second Volume of Sermons in, Three Parts.* Edinburgh: 1750.

Rogers, John. *A Tabernacle for the Sun.* London: 1653.

Ryland, John. *Life and Death of the Reverend Andrew Fuller.* London: 1816.

Scott, Thomas. *The Holy Bible, Containing the Old and New Testaments; with Original Notes, and Practical Observations.* 4 vols. London: 1792.

Sewall, Samuel. *Phaenomena quaedam Apocalyptica.* 2nd ed. Boston: 1727.

———. *Proposals Touching the Accomplishment of Prophecies Humbly Offered.* Boston: 1713.

Shepard, Thomas (ed.). *The Clear Sun-Shine of the Gospel Breaking Forth upon the Indians of New England.* London: 1647/1648.

A Short Account of the Society in Scotland for Propagating Christian Knowledge in the Highlands and Islands. [Edinburgh]: 1809.

Sibbes, Richard. *The Complete Works of Richard Sibbes.* 6 vols. Edinburgh: 1862-1863.

Simeon, Charles. *Horae Homileticae.* vol. 11. 4th ed. London: 1841.

———. *The Jews Provoked to Jealousy.* London: 1811.

Smith, William. *A Discourse Concerning the Conversion of The Heathen Americans.* Philadelphia: 1760.

Snodgrass, John. *A Commentary, with Notes, on Part of the Book of the Revelation of John.* Paisley: 1799.

———. *Prospects of Providence Respecting the Conversion of the World to Christ.* Paisley: 1796.

Society for the Propagation of the Gospel — annual sermons. Unless otherwise indicated, these sermons are all entitled, *A Sermon Preached before the Incorporated Society for the Propagation of the Gospel in Foreign Parts.*

1. Stanhope, George. *The Early Conversion of Islanders, a wise Expedient for propagating Christianity.* London: 1714.
2. [Ash], George. London: 1715.
3. [Chandler], Edward. London: 1719.
4. Pearce, Zachary. London: 1730 [originally preached in 1719].
5. Waddington, Edward. London: 1721.
6. [Smallbridge], Richard. London: 1733.
7. [Benson], Martin. London: 1740.

8. [Thomas], John. London: 1747.
9. George, William. London: 1749.
10. [Trevor], Richard. London: 1750.
11. Osbaldiston, Richard. London: 1752.
12. Cresset, Edward. London: 1753.
13. Drummond, Robert. London: 1754.
14. Hayter, Thomas. London: 1755.
15. Terrick, Richard. London: 1764.
16. [Barrington], Shute. London: 1775.
17. [Bathurst], Henry. London: 1810.

Society in Scotland for Propagating Christian Knowledge — annual sermons.
1. Webster, Alexander. *Supernatural Revelation the Only Sure Hope of Sinners*. Edinburgh: 1741.
2. Robertson, William. *The Situation of the World at the Time of Christ's Appearance*. Edinburgh: 1755.
3. Gibson, John. *The Unlimited Extent and Final Blessedness of God's Spiritual Kingdom*. Edinburgh: 1768.
4. Brown, James. *The Extensive Influence of Religious Knowledge*. Edinburgh: 1769.

Society in Scotland for Propagating Christian Knowledge — annual sermons before the corresponding board in London.
1. Toller, Thomas. *The Coming and Enlargement of the Kingdom of God*. London: 1779.
2. Hunter, Henry. "The Universal Extent, and Everlasting Duration of the Redeemer's Kingdom." *Sermons*, I, 199-226. London: 1795 [the sermon was preached in 1780].
3. Jennings, Nathaniel. *Divine Tuition*. London: 1782.
4. Winter, Robert. *The Happy Tendency and Extensive Influence of the Christian Dispensation*. London: 1788.
5. Bogue, David. *A Sermon Preached at Salters-Hall, March 30th, 1792*. London: 1792.
6. Love, John. *Benevolence Inspired and Exalted by the Presence of Jesus Christ*. London: 1794.
7. Drummond, George Hay. *On Religious Indifference*. London: 1795.

Sterry, Peter. *The Comings Forth of Christ In the Power of his Death*. London: 1650.

———. *England's Deliverance From the Northern Presbytery*. London: 1651/1652.

Stoddard, Solomon. *An Answer to some Cases of Conscience Respecting the Country*. Boston: 1722.

———. *QUESTION Whether God is not Angry with the Country for doing so little towards the Conversion of the Indians*. Boston: 1723.

Strong, William. *The Vengeance of the Temple*. London: 1648.

Sutton, [Thomas]. *Lectures upon the Eleventh Chapter to the Romans*. John Downame (ed.). London: 1632.

Tappan, David. *Sermons on Important Subjects*. Boston: 1807.

Thorowgood, Thomas. *Iewes in America, or Probabilities that the Americans are of that Race*. London: 1650.

————. *Jews in America, or Probabilities, that those Indians are Judaical, made more probable by some Additionals to the Former Conjectures.* London: 1660.

Wesley, John. "The General Spread of the Gospel." *The Works of the Rev. John Wesley, A.M.* vol. 6. 3rd ed. London: 1829.

Whitefield, George. *George Whitefield's Journals.* London: 1960.

Whitfield, Henry (ed.). *The Light appearing more and more towards the perfect Day.* London: 1651.

————. *Strength out of Weakness; or a Glorious Manifestation Of the further Progresse of the Gospell amongst the Indians in New England.* London: 1652/1653.

Willard, Samuel. *The Fountain Opened.* 3rd ed. with an appendix by Samuel Sewall. [n.p.]: 1727.

Williams, Roger. *A Key into the Language of America.* London: 1643.

Willison, John. *The Balm of Gilead, for Healing a Diseased Land; with the Glory of the Ministration of the Spirit: And A Scripture Prophecy of the Increase of Christ's Kingdom, and the Destruction of Antichrist.* 8th ed. Falkirk: 1786.

————. *The Church's Danger and the Minister's Duty.* Edinburgh: 1733.

————. *Popery another Gospel.* Edinburgh: 1746.

Winchester, Elhanan. *A Course of Lectures, on the Prophecies that Remain to be Fulfilled.* 4 vols. London: 1789.

Winslow, Edward (ed.). *The Glorious Progress of the Gospel amongst the Indians in New England.* London: 1649.

Worcester, Samuel. *The Kingdom of the Messiah.* Salem: 1813.

B.   *Secondary Sources*

Beaver, R. Pierce. "The Concert for Prayer for Missions." *The Ecumenical Review,* X, 1957-1958, 420-427.

————. "Eschatology in American Missions." *Basileia: Walter Freytag zum 60.Geburtstag.* Jan Hermelink and Hans J. Margull (eds.). Stuttgart: 1959.

————. *Pioneers in Mission.* Grand Rapids: 1966.

Benz, Ernst. "Ecumenical Relations Between Boston Puritanism and German Pietism: Cotton Mather and August Hermann Francke." *Harvard Theological Review,* LIV, 1961, 159-193.

Bergema, H. "De Betekenis van Calvijn voor de Zending en de Missiologie." *Vox Theologica,* XXIX, 1958-1959, 44-54.

Biographisch Woordenboek van Protestantsche Godgeleerden in Nederland. J. P. de Bie *et al.* (eds.). 's-Gravenhage: [n.d.].

Blanke, Gustav H. "Die Anfänge des amerikanischen Sendungsbewusztseins: Massachusetts-Bay 1629 bis 1659." *Archiv für Reformationsgeschichte,* LVIII, 1967, 171-211.

Brown, Louise Fargo. *The Political Activities of the Baptists and Fifth Monarchy Men in England During the Interregnum.* Washington and London: 1912.

Brown, William. *History of the Propagation of Christianity among the Heathen since the Reformation.* vol. 3. 3rd ed. London: 1854.

Burleigh, J. H. S. *A Church History of Scotland.* London: 1960.

Campbell, Andrew J. *Two Centuries of the Church of Scotland, 1707-1929.* Paisley: 1930.

Catalogue of the Thomason Tracts, 1640-1661. 2 vols. London: 1908.

Chadwick, Owen. *The Reformation.* Grand Rapids: 1965.

Chaney, Charles L. "An Oral Statement." Mimeographed: 1967.

Clarke, W. K. Lowther. *A History of the S.P.C.K.* London: 1959.

Cleveland, Catherine C. *The Great Revival in the West, 1797-1805.* Chicago: 1916.

De Jong, Peter Y. *The Covenant Idea in New England Theology.* Grand Rapids: 1945.

Dickens, A. G. *The English Reformation.* London: 1964.

Dictionary of American Biography. Dumus Malone (ed.). 22 vols. London and New York: 1928-1958.

Dictionary of National Biography. Leslie Stephen and Sidney Lee (eds.). 63 vols. London: 1885-1900.

Eliade, Mircea. "Paradise and Utopia: Mythical Geography and Eschatology." *Utopias and Utopian Thought.* Frank E. Manuel (ed.). Boston: 1966.

Elsbree, Oliver Wendell. *The Rise of the Missionary Spirit in America, 1790-1815.* Williamsport, Pa.: 1928.

Encyclopaedia of Religion and Ethics. James Hastings (ed.). 13 vols. Edinburgh: 1908-1926.

Evans, Charles. *American Bibliography.* vol. 1. Chicago: 1903.

Ford, John W. (ed.). *New England Company: Letters from Eliot and Others, 1657-1714.* London: 1897.

Foster, John. "The Bicentenary of Jonathan Edwards' 'Humble Attempt.'" *International Review of Missions,* XXXVII, 1948, 375-381.

——. "A Scottish Contributor to the Missionary Awakening: Robert Millar of Paisley." *International Review of Missions,* XXXVII, 1948, 138-145.

Froom, Leroy Edwin. *The Prophetic Faith of Our Fathers.* 4 vols. Washington: 1946-1954.

Gambrell, Mary Latimer. *Ministerial Training in Eighteenth-Century New England.* New York: 1937.

Goen, C. C. "Jonathan Edwards: A New Departure in Eschatology." *Church History,* XXVIII, 1959, 25-40.

Hall, Basil. "Puritanism: the Problem of Definition." *Studies in Church History.* vol. 2. G. J. Cuming (ed.). London: 1965.

Haller, William. *Foxe's Book of Martyrs and the Elect Nation.* London: 1963.

——. *The Rise of Puritanism.* New York: 1938.

Heimert, Alan. *Religion and the American Mind.* Cambridge, Mass.: 1966.

Henderson, G. D. *The Burning Bush: Studies in Scottish Church History.* Edinburgh: 1957.

Hennell, Michael M. *John Venn and the Clapham Sect.* London: 1958.

Hewat, Elizabeth G. K. *Vision and Achievement, 1796-1956.* London: 1960.

Holmes, Thomas James. *Cotton Mather, A Bibliography of His Works.* 3 vols. Cambridge, Mass.: 1940.

Holsten, Walter. "Reformation und Mission." *Archiv für Reformationsgeschichte,* XLIV, 1953, 1-32.

Kawerau, Peter. *Amerika und die orientalischen Kirchen.* Berlin: 1958.

Kellaway, William. *The New England Company, 1649-1776.* London: 1961.

Keller, Charles Roy. *The Second Great Awakening in Connecticut.* New Haven: 1942.

Kelsey, Rayner Wickersham. *Friends and the Indians, 1655-1917.* Philadelphia: 1917.

Kittredge, George Lyman (ed.). *Letters of Samuel Lee and Samuel Sewall.* Cambridge, Mass.: 1912.

Latourette, Kenneth Scott. *A History of the Expansion of Christianity.* 7 vols. New York and Evanston: 1937-1945.

Lovett, Richard. *The History of the London Missionary Society, 1795-1895.* 2 vols. London: 1899.

Löwe, Wolfgang Eberhard. *The First American Foreign Missionaries: "The Students," 1810-1820.* Unpublished doctoral dissertation submitted to Brown University, 1962. Ann Arbor: University Microfilms, Inc., 1962.

Maclean, Donald. "Scottish Calvinism and Foreign Missions." *Records of the Scottish Church History Society,* VI, 1938, 4-12.

Manuel, Frank E. *Isaac Newton, Historian.* Cambridge, Mass.: 1963.

——. *A Portrait of Isaac Newton.* Cambridge, Mass.: 1968.

McLachlan, H. (ed.). *Sir Isaac Newton: Theological Manuscripts.* Liverpool: 1950.

Mechie, Stewart. "The Marrow Controversy Reviewed." *The Evangelical Quarterly,* XXII, 1950, 20-31.

Miller, Perry. *Errand into the Wilderness.* Cambridge, Mass.: 1956.

Moorman, John R. H. *A History of the Church in England.* London: 1953.

Morris, J. W. *Memoirs of the Life and Writings of the Rev. Andrew Fuller.* London: 1816.

Müller, E. F. Karl. *Die Bekenntnisschriften der reformierten Kirche.* Leipzig: 1903.

Mullinger, James B. *The University of Cambridge.* 3 vols. Cambridge: 1873, 1884, 1911.

Murdock, Kenneth Ballard. *Increase Mather: The Foremost American Puritan.* Cambridge, Mass.: 1925.

Newton, John A. "Methodism and the Puritans." Eighteenth lecture of the Friends of Dr. Williams's Library. London: 1964.

Niebuhr, H. Richard. *The Kingdom of God in America.* Hamden, Conn.: 1956.

Nuttall, Geoffrey. *The Holy Spirit in Puritan Faith and Experience.* Oxford: 1946.

——. "Northamptonshire and *The Modern Question.*" *The Journal of Theological Studies,* New Series, XVI, 1965, 101-123.

——. "The Significance of Trevecca College, 1768-91." Cheshunt College,

Cambridge Bicentenary Lecture delivered at Westminster and Cheshunt Colleges, 18 May 1968. London: 1969.

——. *Visible Saints*. Oxford: 1957.

Orchard, Stephen C. *English Evangelical Eschatology, 1790-1850*. Unpublished doctoral dissertation submitted to Trinity College, Cambridge, 1968. Manuscript.

The Oxford Dictionary of the Christian Church. F. L. Cross (ed.). London: 1958.

Pauck, Wilhelm. *Das Reich Gottes auf Erden*. Berlin and Leipzig: 1928.

Paul, Robert S. *The Lord Protector*. London: 1955.

Payne, E. A. "Doddridge and the Missionary Enterprise." *Philip Doddridge*. Geoffrey F. Nuttall (ed.). London: 1951.

——. "The Evangelical Revival and the Beginnings of the Modern Missionary Movement." *The Congregational Quarterly*, XXI, 1943, 223-236.

Pennington, John. "Church Principles in the Early Years of the Church Missionary Society: The Problem of the 'German' Missionaries." *The Journal of Theological Studies*, New Series, XX, 1969, 523-532.

Pollard, Arthur and Michael Hennell (eds.). *Charles Simeon (1759-1836)*. London: 1959.

Powicke, F. J. (ed.). *Some Unpublished Correspondence of the Reverend Richard Baxter and the Reverend John Eliot, the Apostle of the American Indians, 1656-1682*. Manchester: 1931.

Psalter Hymnal. Centennial edition. Grand Rapids: 1959.

Die Religion in Geschichte und Gegenwart. H. F. von Campenhausen *et al.* (eds.). 7 vols. 3rd revised edition. Tübingen: 1957-1965.

Rogers, P. G. *The Fifth Monarchy Men*. London: 1966.

——. *The Sixth Trumpeter*. London: 1963.

Rooy, Sidney H. *The Theology of Missions in the Puritan Tradition*. Delft: 1965.

Sanford, Charles L. *The Quest for Paradise*. Urbana, Ill.: 1961.

Schaff, Philip. *The Creeds of Christendom*. vol. 3. 3rd rev. ed. New York: 1877.

Schmidt, Martin. "Eigenart und Bedeutung der Eschatologie im englischen Puritanismus." *Theologia Viatorum*, IV, 1952, 205-266.

——. "Das hallische Waisenhaus und England im 18. Jahrhundert." *Theologische Zeitschrift*, VII, 1951, 38-55.

——. *John Wesley*. 2 vols. Zurich and Frankfurt: 1953 and 1966.

——. "Der Missionsgedanke des jungen Wesley auf dem Hintergrunde seines Zeitalters." *Theologia Viatorum*, I, 1949, 80-97.

Schoeps, Hans Joachim. *Philosemitismus im Barock*. Tübingen: 1952.

Smith, H. Shelton, Robert T. Handy, and Lefferts A. Loetscher. *American Christianity*. 2 vols. New York: 1960 and 1963.

Staehelin, Ernst. *Die Verkundigung der Reiches Gottes in der Kirche Jesu Christi*. 7 vols. Basel: 1951-1964.

Stauffer, Vernon. *New England and the Bavarian Illuminati*. New York: 1918.

Sweet, William Warren. *The Story of Religion in America*. Revised and enlarged edition. New York: 1950.

Thompson, Bard. *Liturgies of the Western Church*. Cleveland and New York: 1961.

Toon, Peter. "Puritan Eschatology: 1600 to 1648." *The Manifold Grace of God*, papers read at the Puritan and Reformed Studies Conference, 1968. [London: 1969].

Turnbull, G. H. *Hartlib, Dury and Comenius*. London: 1947.

Van den Berg, Johannes. *Constrained by Jesus' Love*. Kampen: 1956.

——. *Joden en Christenen in Nederland Gedurende de Zeventiende Eeuw*. Kampen: 1969.

Van Genderen, Jan. *Herman Witsius*. 's-Gravenhage: 1953.

Van Halsema, Dick Lucas. *Samuel Hopkins: New England Calvinist*. Unpublished doctoral dissertation submitted to Union Theological Seminary, 1956. Ann Arbor: University Microfilms, Inc., 1956.

Vaughan, Alden T. *New England Frontier, Puritans and Indians, 1620-1675*. Boston: 1965.

Visser, A. J. *Calvijn en de Joden*. 's-Gravenhage: [n.d.].

Walker, Williston. *A History of the Christian Church*. Revised edition. New York: 1959.

Walsh, John. "Origins of the Evangelical Revival." *Essays in Modern English Church History*. G. V. Bennett and J. D. Walsh (eds.). London: 1966.

Warren, Max. *The Truth of Vision*. London and Edinburgh: 1948.

Wellwood, Henry M. *Account of the Life and Writings of John Erskine, D.D.* Edinburgh: 1818.

Wilson, John F. "A Glimpse of Syons Glory." *Church History*, XXXI, 1962, 66-73.

Winslow, Ola Elizabeth. *Jonathan Edwards, 1703-1758*. New York: 1941.

——. *Samuel Sewall of Boston*. New York: 1964.

Wolf, Lucien. *Menasseh Ben Israel's Mission to Oliver Cromwell*. London: 1901.

Wright, Louis B. *Religion and Empire*. Chapel Hill: 1943.

Zwemer, Samuel. "Calvinism and the Missionary Enterprise." *Theology Today*, VII, 1950, 206-216.

Index of Principal Names

CPSIA information can be obtained at www.ICGtesting.com
Printed in the USA
BVOW061611220911

271798BV00003B/1-114/A